Remember Him at the Altar

Bloxham School and the Great War

Matthew Dixon & Simon Batten

Helion & Company Limited

Helion & Company Limited
Unit 8 Amherst Business Centre
Budbrooke Road
Warwick
CV34 5WE
England
Tel. 01926 499 619
Email: info@helion.co.uk
Website: www.helion.co.uk
Twitter: @helionbooks
Visit our blog at blog.helion.co.uk

Published by Helion & Company 2022
Designed and typeset by Mary Woolley (www.battlefield-design.co.uk)
Cover designed by Paul Hewitt, Battlefield Design (www.battlefield-design.co.uk)

Text © Matthew Dixon & Simon Batten 2022
Images © Bloxham School Archives 2022

ISBN 978-1-915113-64-1

British Library Cataloguing-in-Publication Data.
A catalogue record for this book is available from the British Library.

For details of other military history titles published by Helion & Company Limited contact the
above address or visit our website: http://www.helion.co.uk.

We always welcome receiving book proposals from prospective authors.

Contents

List of Illustrations

In colour section

List of Abbreviations

ABA	Amateur Boxing Association
ANZAC	Australian and New Zealand Army Corps
BA	Bachelor of Arts
BEF	British Expeditionary Force
BGRA	Brigadier General, Royal Artillery
BSAP	British South Africa Police
CB	Companion of the Order of the Bath
CCF	Combined Cadet Force
CCS	Casualty Clearing Station
CEF	Canadian Expeditionary Force
CIGS	Chief of the Imperial General Staff
CMG	Companion of the Order of Saint Michael and Saint George
CO	Commanding Officer
CWGC	Commonwealth War Graves Commission
DAAG	Deputy Assistant Adjutant General
DCM	Distinguished Conduct Medal
DSO	Distinguished Service Order
HMAT	His Majesty's Australian Transport
HMML	His Majesty's Motor Launch
HMS	His Majesty's Ship
JP	Justice of the Peace
KAR	King's African Rifles
LI	Light Infantry
MA	Master of Arts
MBE	Member of the British Empire
MC	Military Cross
MCC	Marylebone Cricket Club
MCS	Magdalen College School, Oxford
MGC	Machine Gun Corps
MID	Mention in Despatches
MM	Military Medal
MO	Medical Officer
MVO	Member of the Royal Victorian Order
NCO	Non-Commissioned Officer
OB	Old Bloxhamist

OBLI	Oxfordshire and Buckinghamshire Light Infantry
OC	Officer Commanding
OE	Old Etonian
OTC	Officers Training Corps
POW	Prisoner of War
QSA	Queen's South Africa Medal
RAF	Royal Air Force
RAMC	Royal Army Medical Corps
RF	Royal Fusiliers
RFA	Royal Field Artillery
RFC	Royal Flying Corps
RGA	Royal Garrison Artillery
RHA	Royal Horse Artillery
RIC	Royal Irish Constabulary
RIR	Royal Irish Rifles
RNVR	Royal Naval Volunteer Reserve
SAI	South African Infantry
SMS	Seiner Majestät Schiff (His Majesty's Ship)
SS	Steam Ship (screw steamer)
VC	Victoria Cross
WO	War Office

Foreword

General Sir Adrian Bradshaw KCB OBE was a pupil at Bloxham School between 1970 and 1976. He served as Commander UK Land Forces between 2013-14 and as NATO's Deputy Supreme Allied Commander Europe from 2014-17. He is Governor of the Royal Hospital Chelsea and Chairman of BLESMA – the charity for limbless ex-Service members. He is a Senior Associate Fellow of RUSI and he holds a commission as a pilot in the RAF Reserve. He has degrees in Agriculture, Defence Studies and International Relations, and has been a Visiting Defence Fellow at Balliol College, Oxford.

This book presents us with the stories, similar to others which could be told of young people from across the length and breadth of the kingdom who made the ultimate sacrifice, having joined up to do their duty to King and Country during the Great War. The book tells, in particular, of the service given by the graduates of just one of the many schools around the nation which imbued in their students the importance of working for the good of one's fellows and for the community at large, values which are in danger of being undermined by the modern obsession with 'self'. Such values have, however, once again proven their importance during the recent COVID pandemic, which hit us about a century after the great Spanish Flu' pandemic that swept across much of the globe in the aftermath of the First World War, the centenary of which was the stimulus for writing this book. The recent commemorations of the 1914-18 War and the COVID crisis over the last year or so have reminded us of the ever-present danger we face from devastating phenomena such as disease and war, the avoidance of which should be amongst our highest priorities.

Those whose wonderfully researched and moving stories are told in the pages ahead are appropriately commemorated in the All Saints Chapel at Bloxham School and are also remembered on the memorials that stand amongst the long-since peaceful and pastoral battlefields of the Great War. Many are buried alongside their fellows in carefully tended and beautifully evocative war cemeteries across the Western Front and further afield. As the young people of this generation file past those graves and memorials one hopes they will think of the service and sacrifice of their predecessors, whose lives were so cruelly cut short in the furtherance of a cause which most, if not all of those remembered in this book, would have believed fervently to be for the greater good. No doubt their adversaries felt the same way. Today's generation must work to strengthen the bonds of peace and friendship that link us with our former foes. They should also consider the importance, nevertheless, of maintaining the dedication and aptitude for Service fostered in schools such as Bloxham, which will lead some who are thus inclined to join our nation's Armed Forces to work for stability and peace in a volatile world. By sustaining strong, well trained and capable Armed Forces they will also deter those who might risk the disaster of war by violating the security of nations such as ours which value democracy, freedom and the rule of law.

I congratulate the authors for their painstaking research and for the fascinating stories they have discovered of individual lives and service, and for the insights they give to the reader of the social history of an age long past, the lessons of which nonetheless remain enormously relevant today.

General Sir Adrian Bradshaw KCB OBE

Acknowledgements

The authors' primary debt is to Duncan Rogers of Helion & Company, who suggested the project in the first place and gave it his full support. They would like to express their profound gratitude to General Sir Adrian Bradshaw for agreeing to write the Foreword to the book; we were very fortunate to have a contribution from someone so uniquely qualified for the task. Andrew Whiffin once again did an exemplary job as proof-reader, and Toby Clark provided invaluable assistance in pointing out some inconsistency in army terminology in early drafts. To both, we are very grateful. Dr Michael LoCicero and Victoria Powell at Helion provided excellent support at the editing and production stage. We are grateful to Paul Hewitt for his work on the design of the book.

One of the pleasures of writing this book was making contact with several of the families of the Old Bloxhamists who died in the Great War, and we would like to place on record our thanks and appreciation to them, in particular Helen Brooks (Basil Brooks), Joy Auld (Harry Ayres), Elaine Cottrell and Steph Lynch (Hilary Pullen Burry), Dorothy Hemmings (John Simons), Chris Jackson and Wendy McVittie (Edward Board).

Simon Batten would like to express his thanks to the school archivists who have assisted his research especially John Hamblin (Lancing), Rebecca Rossef (MCS Oxford), Chris Nathan (St Edward's, Oxford), Charles Knighton (Clifton), Sally Todd (St John's, Leatherhead), Felicity Kilpatrick and Glen Horridge (Christ College, Brecon), Robyn Gruijters (Michaelhouse, KwaZulu Natal), Terry Rogers (Marlborough), Robin Brooke Smith (Shrewsbury) and to the following historians: Neil Pudney, David Walsh, Sir Anthony Seldon, Barry Blades, Paula Kitching, Kathryn White, Spencer Jones, Conor Reeves, John Lewis Stempel, Jim Smithson and Stephen Barker. Tim Halstead was an especially valuable source of ideas and encouragement, and I benefited from his research and expertise on school OTCs. Dr Emily Mayhew of Imperial College, London provided invaluable insights on the treatment of casualties. I am grateful to the staff and pupils of Bloxham School, especially to Headmasters Mark Allbrook and Paul Sanderson for their support, and to Michael Price, Duncan Weaver, Dan Jordan and Roger Stein in particular. My departmental colleagues Robert Hudson and David Bowden were always ready to discuss the project and offer ideas, while it is true to say that the archival foundations for much of this work was laid by the efforts of the late Shaw McCloghry and Peter Barwell. Many Old Bloxhamists assisted us with their memories of remembrance at the school. Keith Janes provided valuable information from the perspective of the village of Bloxham.

The following were of particular assistance in writing the individual biographies: Elaine Colwell (Pullen Burry), Stephen Cooper (Wilkins), Simon Harley (Shorland), Linda Hutton (Guest), Gareth Davies (Robinson), Rachael Muir and Hannah Cleal of the Bank of England Archive (Stevens), Alexandra Churchill (Nixon), Stephen Haynes (Board), David Bebington

(Thomas), John Catton (Hill), Timothy Dickens (Bidlake), Robin Marriott (Simons), Alistair Cook (Marshall), Emily Mayhew (Sawyer), Veronique Eckstein (Roberts).

Many people have helped Matt Dixon since the first Bloxham School Roll of Honour website was produced almost 20 years ago and have also provided immeasurable support for the writing of this book.

Matt would particularly like to thank the following for their contributions, Andrew Radgick (Carandini-Wilson), Andy Pay (Davy MC – an incredible mine of information for all things Rifle Brigade), Dorothy Hemmings (Simons), Aurel Sercu (Horner and Clement Smith). There are many members of the Great War community who have been so kind sharing their knowledge freely and willingly, especially Paul Reed, Chris Baker, Peter Barton, Taff Gillingham, Professor Peter Doyle, Simon Verdegem, Andy Lock, Will O'Brien, and Michael Nugent. Particular thanks must go to Jeremy Banning, whose enthusiasm and willingness to share documents, especially hard to come by trench maps has been incredibly useful.

Throughout my travels I have met many memorable people, all of whom have shown great kindness and hospitality, most notably Eric and Oslem Goosens at the fabulous Gallipoli Houses in Eceabat, Martine Warlope, François and Thérese Grossin, and the Cardoen-Descamps family at Varlet Farm near Ypres.

I am especially indebted to 'Sarah' from the National Archives of Zimbabwe for her assistance in providing information on Ralph Grenfell Hill, at great personal risk – both authors hope you stay safe. Finally, thanks to 'JB' a serving member of the UK armed forces who braved a gun battle and an IED explosion to take the pictures of the Basra Memorial in Iraq.

Thanks also to Michael Green, Simon Speed, Tom Mawby, Adam Clarke, Mark Hobbs and the rest of the magnificent Jolly Boys who make trips to the Western Front such fun.

My father Edward, (also an Old Bloxhamist) took me to my first CWGC cemetery some 35 odd years ago and planted a seed of interest in me that still lives on today. We have travelled thousands of miles together and visited hundreds of cemeteries. A finer travelling companion I could never wish for.

My final and most heartfelt thanks go to my long-suffering and supportive wife Kirsty. On many occasions she has held the fort (and the children) to allow me to drive to the battlefields for days at a time. She has remained in good humour (mostly) as more bookshelves needed to be built to accommodate the ever-expanding Great War book collection and the living room floor disappeared under piles of paper and research. She's travelled France and Belgium and walked in the rain with me in search of 'just one more picture I promise', but above all, she has welcomed the ghosts of the past into our home, and for that I will be eternally grateful.

Introduction

On 22 July 1916 Lieutenant Arthur Stevens of the 9th Battalion, Royal Fusiliers, sat down to compose a letter to the chaplain of his old school, All Saints' School, in the village of Bloxham in Oxfordshire, informing him of the death of Gordon Peecock, an officer in the same battalion as well as a contemporary at Bloxham. Stevens had a favour to ask of the Rev. Hugh Willimott: 'As his closest friend out here, I would like to ask you to remember him at the altar.' Peecock was killed by machine gunfire coming from Prussian Guard positions to the north of Ovillers on 7 July, a week into the Battle of the Somme. By the time the school received Stevens' letter the summer holidays had begun, and so it was not until the first Saturday of term in September that Gordon Peecock's name was remembered in the school chapel, and by this time Arthur Stevens too was dead, killed in early August at Pozières, a few miles away from the spot where Gordon was killed. Arthur Stevens was 19 years of age when he died, Gordon Peecock 22.

Taking one small boarding school in rural Oxfordshire as its subject, this book tells the story of the 80 Bloxhamists who died in the Great War, tracing their lives from school to the grave, but it also examines the experiences of those who served and survived and looks at the way in which the lives of those at home were affected by the war. The authors take the story up to the present day to study the way in which the remembrance of those who fell has changed over the years, and what these changes tell us about how we view the war. The book is based on many years of research by the authors, including retracing the footsteps of the men and, in some cases, working with their relatives in order to tell the stories of the 80.

Matthew Dixon writes:

The Great War has been a part of my life for as long as I can remember. My father, also an Old Bloxhamist, has a great interest in the First World War and I remember spending many hours as a small boy, leafing through his huge collection of books on the subject. Rose Coombs' classic *Before Endeavours Fade* kept me captivated with its black and white pictures of war cemeteries and veterans. I remember vividly my disappointment when I couldn't find a town called 'Somme' on a map of France, not knowing of course that it was a river, not a place.

My father shared with me stories of a Great Uncle who served in the 9th Lancers and was wounded in a cavalry charge near Mons in August 1914. Great Uncle William died of the wounds he received in this charge, and he lies buried in a war cemetery in Northern France. It was always a massively exciting moment each 11 November remembrance when I was allowed to hold his medals, not really understanding what they signified, but understanding that they clearly represented something to be very proud of.

One summer, driving back from a holiday in the Alps, my father's usual exemplary timing was awry and we arrived near the Channel coast with time to spare. He swung the car off the motorway and said he would show me something related to the Great War, in order that we might fill the hour we had to kill. I remember clearly pulling up outside Canadian Cemetery Number 2, lying amongst trees at the bottom of Vimy Ridge. It was my first ever visit to a Commonwealth War Graves cemetery, and it took my breath away. The immaculately tended green lawns, laid with beautiful flowers, their bright colours in stark contrast to the white headstones of Portland stone, stretching as far as the eye could see in perfectly straight lines. I walked the length of each row, pausing to read the names of the dead, struck by how young many of them were. It was my first taste of the tangible history of the Great War, and it sparked an interest in me which has remained ever since. That first cemetery, more years ago than I care to remember, is engraved in my memory. Each school holiday my father and I would spend at least one day on the battlefields visiting the cemeteries of the Western Front. I was clearly hooked from a fairly early age!

As often happens, I went to university and discovered other interests, but whilst momentarily diminished my passion for the Great War remained. In 2003, I had the misfortune to break my ankle at work, and whilst recovering with a leg in plaster at home, I decided that I would use the time wisely, and would set myself two challenges. Firstly, I would learn how to use a computer properly and secondly I would teach myself to type. I succeeded in both of these aims and began to discover the wonders of the World Wide Web.

Searching for Great War related content, I began looking at school websites relating to their war dead. I found many sites, ranging greatly in quality. Some contained little more than a list of names of the dead, others contained pictures, and vast reams of information about the men, their lives and the actions that they were killed in. This naturally set me wondering about the war dead from Bloxham School. I suspected that there must have been some, and I wondered whether anyone had ever researched the men. I am ashamed to admit that in my five years at Bloxham I barely passed more than a cursory glance at the War Memorial in the school chapel and had no clue that the main gate into the Quad was in fact also a commemorative monument related to the Great War.

I reached out initially to the secretary of the Old Bloxhamist Society, the indomitable and now sadly departed Shaw McCloghry, or 'Major Mac' as he was universally known, and he informed me that there was indeed a list of the names of the dead, and indeed there was also a collection of portrait pictures of some of the men. I learned that sadly one of the frames had been destroyed in a fire and the others had subsequently, and thankfully (!) been rescued from a skip!

I attended an Old Bloxhamist lunch at the school and duly received the information, several typed sheets of names and some basic biographical information about each man. It was clear that no one had to that point ever conducted a really in-depth research project into the men from Bloxham School who died in the Great War.

The first step in this project was to identify the final resting place of the men, as well as trying to discover more about them, their lives and their families. The initial list contained 76 names, equating to a casualty ratio of approximately 20 percent of the men from the school who actually served. This figure is remarkably consistent with other schools of a similar size to Bloxham. They also came from a huge variety of backgrounds and locations. There were some who were career soldiers having served in India and the South African War, others who left school to join up. Many were members of the militia or reserves and like so many young men who had been part of the Officer Training Corps of their respective schools, they used this experience to obtain their commissions as officers. Between them, the Bloxhamists held every rank in the services from Private through to Brigadier General.

I duly searched each name on the database of the Commonwealth War Graves Commission and plotted the location of each grave on a map. The span of pins on my map stretched from Wales as far east as Iraq and south as far as Tanzania. When considering whether it would be possible to visit the sites and obtain pictures of their headstones or their names on Memorials, my wife suggested that my plans for trying to get to Basra might need to be readdressed, and with hindsight, she was probably right.

I was struck first of all by how many of the men had headstones as opposed to being just names engraved on memorials. It is a sad testament to the power of both artillery and machine guns in the Great War that so many men's bodies were never found on the battlefield, and they are commemorated simply as 'missing' on one of the dozens of memorials that lie across the length and breadth of Europe. In the Belgian city of Ieper, or Ypres as it is more commonly known, stands the magnificent Menin Gate Memorial. Its walls carry the names of 54,000 men who died in the Ypres Salient up to 16 August 1917. Just nine miles up the road from Ypres is the small village whose name has become synonymous with the horrors of war – Passchendaele. The Tyne Cot Memorial, which stands on the top of Passchendaele Ridge contains over 11,000 headstones and a memorial wall containing a further 34,000 names of men who died in the Salient whose bodies were never found. Bloxhamists are commemorated on both these memorials.

Having plotted the locations and started the first of many spreadsheets to record my data, I duly headed off to Belgium one weekend and visited my first Old Bloxhamist, Lt Archibald Horner who lies in the Menin Road Cemetery near Ypres. When I visited, Belgium had been enduring an almost unprecedented heat wave. Of course, on the day I went, the heavens opened and I got duly soaked in almost Biblical rain. I photographed his headstone from under an umbrella and emptied the rain water from my shoes before I got back in the car. Horner, being the first man I 'visited' will always hold a special place to me amongst the Old Bloxhamists.

In time, research began in earnest. In the early days, the resources available on the Internet were not what they are today, and I became extremely well acquainted with the inside of the National Archives in Kew. This is a wonderful facility and holds masses of records of interest to the genealogist and military historian alike. In the early days of this project, very few of the records were digitised and the system of filing was, to put it mildly, complicated. Searching for a service record was a tortuous process, involving microfiche records, paper lists and files. Only after these steps were completed did I sometimes discover that in fact the records didn't exist at all. It's a sad loss to the researcher that so many of the records held by the National Archives were destroyed in a fire following a bombing raid in the Blitz.

Despite the trials and tribulations, I was extremely fortunate just how many of the men's service papers still remained intact. It's an extremely special moment to hold in your hand a piece of paper that has the actual signature of a man you have been researching for so many years. Even now, it makes the hair on the back of my neck stand up. These documents vary enormously in quantity and quality. Some files contain little more than a few pages of meaningless Army forms, others contain vast quantities of information about the men concerned. Through studying these documents, I learnt a great deal about some of the men, their service and what they went through. It was through studying these papers that I learnt of the anguish suffered by Alick Sawyer's mother, who, being hamstrung by Army bureaucracy was unable to reach her dying son's bedside before he died. I read the telegram sent to Phillip Davy's mother informing her of his death, which arrived on 11 November 1918, as the bells were ringing out to proclaim the Armistice. Her son had survived four years of war only to be killed seven days before the war ended. Questions were raised about the age of some of the men, one father complaining that his son was underage and should never have been allowed to go and fight. I read some truly horrific reports of injuries suffered; those of Alan Cowan and Wilfred Bury in particular make truly harrowing reading.

The majority of the men who served were determined and hardworking officers and men, however not all who served passed through the War unblemished. Charles Hammill was as far removed from the stereotype of the English public school boy as it is possible to be. His masterplan to avoid the war by spending most of it in military custody sadly didn't come to fruition and he died on the battlefield in 1918.

As the pen portraits of the men got bigger, in 2010 I produced my first website <www. bloxhamschoolwardead.com> with some of the information that I had discovered to that date. If the website had been a school report it would probably have read 'OK but could do better', and so in 2015, having twelve years of research I produced a new and updated website, of which I am very proud. I would like to think that if any armchair historians with broken legs came across it, they would like what they see.

One of the things I am most grateful for throughout this project is the great friendship I have built up with Simon. This book is very much a joint effort and it was indeed Simon's suggestion that we take the content of the website and look at the possibility of transforming it into a book. This joint effort has produced some extremely detailed information about some of the men. I have mainly concentrated on the military side of their lives, while Simon has focussed his efforts on the family history and their time at the school. We have to date, usually been in agreement about the research that has been done, and I am extremely grateful to Simon for his historian's eye for detail, and his dedication in checking facts. His access to the school archives has been utterly invaluable and has added a huge dimension of extra information about the men and their time at the school. Our mutual interest in military history and red wine has led to some very enjoyable evenings spent on the battlefields!

When this project first started, there were 76 names on the school war memorial, and as this book goes to print, the number now stands at 80. Through his painstaking research, Simon discovered the missing Old Bloxhamists Harry Ayres, Hilary Pullen Burry and John Simons, and along the way my chance discovery in the Australian National Archives of a reference to 'Bloxham College' led to John Carandini Wilson's name being added on to the memorial in the Chapel. There have been some false starts and wrong turns along the way, and despite some 15 years of research, there are some big gaps in our knowledge about some of the men. Missing service papers and war dairies mean that sadly some of their stories may never be fully told.

Continued research has meant that now, somewhat miraculously we have pictures of all 80 of the men who died, and therefore the lost frame has effectively been replaced. I had a nine-year quest to find a picture of James Clement Smith, who served with the Royal Fusiliers – considering there were 47 battalions of Royal Fusiliers and over 2000 Smiths who died, to track down one picture was a feat of which I am extremely proud! The advent of digitalisation and many trips to the National Newspaper Archives in Colindale enabled me to find one picture of him measuring an inch across in a copy of the Illustrated London News. The marvellous picture of Reginald Harris came from the South Devon Fisherman's Benevolent Fund and my interactions with some living relatives of the men also produced some wonderful treasures, such as the picture of Alick Sawyer in uniform in his sister's garden. Compared to the fresh-faced handsome man in the picture held by the school, the strain of six months in the trenches is clear to see.

I have travelled many miles in search of pictures of the headstones and memorials to the dead and these trips have provided some very happy and very special memories for me. A special highlight was visiting Gallipoli, a truly beautiful landscape populated by some of the nicest and most generous people you could wish to meet. I spent a lovely hour my back against an olive tree, watching a Turkish war ship turning lazy figures of eight in the sea off Anzac Cove, whilst enjoying the sun and a large bucket of fresh olives. The sea of wild flowers near Suvla Bay was one of the most beautiful things I have ever seen. At the opposite end of the spectrum I remember the kindness of a Commonwealth War Graves gardener who made me a cup of tea in his hut on a bitterly cold day, where the snow lay thick in Marissel, France. I had my sandwiches stolen by a ginger cat who hides in a cemetery near Zonnebeke; when I drove back past the cemetery an hour later, a couple of Australians had been robbed by him as well –he's a cat clearly onto a good thing. I was shown the entrance to a British dugout unearthed by some workmen near Fromelles and had the privilege of laying a wreath under the Menin Gate in memory of all the Bloxhamists who died.

As the centenary of the end of the Great War is upon us and we come to the end of four years of commemoration, both Simon and I see this book as the culmination of the 15-year journey we have been on through the lives of 80 brave, mostly young men, from All Saints' School, who paid the ultimate sacrifice in the name of duty. As the present is rapidly elbowing the past out of the way, it is even more important that we remember the sacrifices made by a generation of brave young men a century ago. I hope very much that this book might encourage a future generation of young people at Bloxham to hold high the torch in remembrance of the ghosts of the past, whose sacrifice is our legacy. *Justorum semita lux splendens*

Matthew Dixon & Simon Batten

***

Outside the field of memoirs, authors are generally encouraged not to refer to themselves in their text, but in this case the process of research and discovery is so much a part of the story that we felt this would appear pointless and contrived. Where one of the authors is referred to in the biographies of the 80, he is denoted by his initials, MD (Matt Dixon) or SB (Simon Batten).

1

Bloxham School in 1914

At the outbreak of war in August 1914 Bloxham School (officially All Saints' School, Bloxham) was 54 years old. It had been founded in 1860 by Philip Reginald Egerton, a 27-year-old clergyman educated at Winchester and New College, Oxford, who sought to provide a Christian education for the sons of the middle classes along similar lines to the Rev. Nathaniel Woodard, who had set up a network of schools, including Lancing, Ellesmere and Worksop, with a distinctive Anglo-Catholic flavour. Having opened the school with just one pupil on 30 January 1860, Egerton had seen it grow to 180 pupils by the time he handed over the headmastership to his successor and former star pupil Frederick Boissier in 1886.

Thereafter the school encountered challenging times, as numbers went into steep decline for a number of reasons. The first of these was a series of epidemics, chiefly scarlet fever, influenza and typhoid fever, which resulted in deaths of pupils (at least eight between 1886 and 1914) and a loss of parental confidence in the school's standards of hygiene, above all the water supply, derived from a well on the main field. A second issue, as Boissier admitted to his school council, was that there was evidence that the school's emphasis on Chapel, noteworthy even by the standards of the day, especially its local reputation for High Church practices, was putting people off in an area with a long-established anti-Catholic reputation (even now Banbury's football team is called the Puritans). Egerton, who remained influential even after his departure from Bloxham in 1891, vainly insisted that 'I venture to repudiate one reason given me for the gradual falling off of numbers – the 'sectarian' character of All Saints' School.'

It is surely indicative of Bloxham's religious tenor that fifteen Old Bloxhamists would serve as chaplains in the war, a very high number for such a small school, and a rate comparable only with Stonyhurst, the Jesuit school with which Anglo-Catholic Bloxham had much in common. It is also highly significant that twelve of the 80, 15% of the total, were the sons of clergymen (analysis of the pre-war British Army suggests that about 10% of its regular officers had fathers who were clergymen).

Even more serious than the religious question were the twin threats posed by an agricultural depression which was starting to hit the farmers and local businessmen on whom the school depended, and competition both from the new state-funded board schools set up after the 1870 Education Act and the reformed grammar schools. Several public schools in the region, for example Bradfield and St Edward's, Oxford, suffered similar difficulties at this time, but in Bloxham's case the results were financially catastrophic, with numbers declining from 180 when Boissier took over to 140 in 1889 and 125 in 1890. By the time Boissier resigned in 1898, numbers had fallen to just 62. The only solution was the takeover of the school by the Woodard Corporation, which stood for a similar brand of High Church Anglicanism, and the installation of a new Headmaster with no connection with Egerton.

Boissier's replacement was chosen for Bloxham by the Woodard Corporation. Looking for a dynamic figure to transform the school's fortunes, they found him in the shape of the Rev. George Herbert Ward, a mathematician and scholar of Hertford College, Oxford, who had been an assistant master at St Paul's for eleven years before his arrival in Bloxham at the age of 37 with a young family. His High Church credentials won him Egerton's support just as surely as his annual speeches at the Old Bloxhamists' London dinners succeeded in allaying the suspicions of those old boys who viewed the new regime with trepidation.

The Corporation's priorities were to modernise the buildings, many now starting to show their age, and to increase the numbers in the school. Considerable sums were spent on advertising the school, and numbers did increase, to 104 by 1907, though they were down again to 70 seven years later. Ward was a determined man – his strength of character shines out from his photograph – and Bloxham's first headmaster with experience of other schools. His response to the conundrum of raising academic standards at the same time as increasing numbers was multi-faceted; the methods adopted included changing the school timetable (introducing early morning school at 7:00 a.m.), cutting the number of half-holidays from three to two and introducing a system of report cards, by which each pupil's progress was assessed at the end of every lesson, the Headmaster examining each card at the end of the week. By 1913 Bloxham's examination results were better than any other Woodard school save Lancing and there were more Bloxhamists at the universities than ever before.

Nevertheless, Bloxham could not yet be counted as a Public School by any of the criteria then in common usage. Its size, especially that of its sixth form, the strength (or otherwise) of its fixture list and above all the fact that its Headmaster was not a member of the Headmasters' Conference all disqualified it. Such distinctions would have been lost on most contemporaries, but to those within the charmed circle of the public school world they would have been very apparent. However, changes were afoot. Ward was keen to see his school equipped with the facilities expected of a public school, and he immediately started a building fund for a gymnasium with flanking fives courts and swimming baths. He reflected current thinking when he stated that 'Every year, educationalists are becoming more and more alive to the importance of physical training, and to the fact that it is only second to mental and moral training in the education of boys.' The gym was opened in 1903, and a gym instructor, Colour Sergeant William Grinter, a Boer War veteran, was appointed on a generous annual salary of £78. The village school was given use of the gym two evenings a week.

The fives courts were added in 1909, but the swimming pool took a lot longer; the editor of *The Bloxhamist* for 1911 declared 'How we have longed for that swimming bath this term! How delightful it would have been to adjourn from cricket or tennis to its cool waters instead of a walk along a dusty road, followed by immersion in watery mud..... perhaps by next year something may be done.' In the event, the school would be forced to use the murky waters of Wykham Mill until 1926, when an open-air swimming bath was finally opened. Ward was determined to widen the school's horizons; it is significant that Bloxham entered the Public Schools Gym competition for the first time in 1904 and the Public Schools Boxing competition five years later. Standards in football were rising, with the goalkeeper Frederick Horner instrumental in the successful 1900 team; he would go on to play for Watford FC before dying at the age of 29 in

Argentina. The outstanding sportsman of the time was the cricketer Hugh Tordiffe, who broke all records by amassing 1,157 runs in one season (1901), including three centuries; his 181 not out against Magdalen College School, Oxford, still a 1st XI record for a school match, helped Bloxham to a victory by the massive margin of 269 runs.

As well as its diet of sport, chapel and the classics, another characteristic which Bloxham shared with bigger and more prestigious schools was its commitment to Britain's imperial mission. Large numbers of Bloxhamists went out to populate Britain's burgeoning Empire, with Canada being the most frequent destination, especially for those with farming connections. The pages of *The Bloxhamist* were filled with news of Old Boys occupying military and administrative roles in the Empire. To take a few examples, Eustace Maude, who as Viscount Hawarden was a rare instance of an aristocratic Old Bloxhamist, served as Governor of Bahr al Ghazal Province in the Sudan, a region the size of Great Britain. As Commissioner of the British Red Cross in Egypt, Palestine and Syria, Dr Alexander Granville ('Granville Pasha') did important work for the sick and wounded in the Middle East and later acted as President of the International Quarantine Board as well as representing the Egyptian government at the League of Nations. Abdy Fellowes, after seeing action in the Zulu War, served the administration of the Nizam of Hyderabad for many years, latterly as a Plague Commissioner, while Frederick Urquhart joined the Queensland Native Mounted Police, earning a bloody reputation for the brutality of his dealings with the indigenous Kalkadoon (properly Kalkatungu) tribe. Urquhart's actions serve as a valuable reminder of the impact of British rule on inhabitants of its empire, and the ambiguous nature of its legacy. Large numbers of Old Bloxhamists served as missionaries and priests throughout the Empire, for example George Hand, who became Bishop of Antigua, and John Tsan Baw, who returned to Burma after a successful academic career in England to become the first Burmese Christian priest.

The clearest statement of the school's role in preparing pupils for an imperial mission came in a speech given by Lieutenant General Neville Lyttelton in July 1901, on the occasion of the laying of the foundation stone for the new gymnasium. While on leave from South Africa, where he commanded a division in the Boer War, the future CIGS told his audience on Founder's Day:

The public schools of England had contributed their full quota of those who responded to their country's call in the recent emergency. When England called upon its young men for help, how well the schools took their part in responding to that call. Five Bloxham boys had laid down their lives in their country's service, which made a pathetic side to their festivities that day.

1910 saw the school's Jubilee, the celebrations including a thanksgiving service in the parish church, a two-day cricket match and a lunch followed by speeches from the great and the good, who included the Bishops of Chichester and Reading, the Warden of Keble College and the Provost of Lancing, the first of the Woodard Schools. Egerton, the Founder, was too ill to attend the celebrations, though his daughter Ellen Hinde and his brother Hubert were present. He died at the family home, Vale Mascal in Kent, on 28 April 1911 at the age of 79. His last years had been overshadowed by his own ill health and that of his wife, who died in 1907, but he had lived long enough to see the jubilee of the school he had founded. A link with the Egerton family was maintained by the presence of his daughter, Ellen Hinde, who lived locally and for many years presented a Banbury Cake to each boy on 14 July in her father's memory.

As well as Ward, the two key figures in the school at the outbreak of war were Charles Wilson, the school's first boarder in 1860 and still there as Bursar 54 years later, and Hugh Willimott, the chaplain. Willimott, appointed in 1904, was a crucial figure in developing the school chapel in an Anglo-Catholic direction with an even greater stress on ceremonial than his predecessors. He organised the 1910 Jubilee and edited *The Bloxhamist* for many years, and he was also instrumental in reviving the dormant Old Bloxhamist Society. Thanks to Willimott and an energetic new committee, fixtures in football and cricket against the school were restarted.

Life at Bloxham in the early years of the twentieth century was spartan. Colonel Lancelot Roberts, a pupil between 1903 and 1907, recalled in 1984 that 'It was a hard, tough school and devoid of any creature comforts. The discipline was very, very severe indeed.' Conditions in the dormitories were austere and the food meagre by modern standards. On a return visit in 2009, the school's oldest Old Boy, Commander Anthony Lyle, described the food in 1920 as 'very bad'. Memories of the school menu were still vivid for Lancelot Roberts when he recorded his recollections eighty years later.

The main meal of the day was at midday: 'the whole four years I was at Bloxham (1903-1907) it never changed once....Monday was Monday hash...Tuesday was roast mutton....Wednesday pie was the remains of the cold mutton made into a pie.... Thursday roast beef....Friday, oh dear! It was the cold beef salted – hard, tough and very salty.' In the evenings boys could look forward to 'bread and scrape' for their supper at six o'clock. Roberts recalled that 'we called it bread and scrape because they put some marge on a piece of bread and scraped it off again leaving a faint film of grease on the bread'. The food was served 'by village boys dressed in little blue and white striped coats under the guidance of a chap called Jumbo who had only one arm. How he lost his arm none of us were (sic) able to discover.' This was Fred Mallett, who Boissier recorded in his log for 1 October 1896 as 'having caught his arm in the gas engine while dusting it in motion and it was so badly crushed that it was necessary to amputate it at once below the elbow. The operation was carried out by the school doctor in the school hospital.' Fred Mallett would go on to work for the school for another sixty years after his accident, eventually retiring in 1955 after stalwart service in the dining hall. Generations of Bloxham boys recalled his extraordinary dexterity flicking letters from home across the breakfast table.

The single most important development of Ward's time as Headmaster was the creation of the Officers Training Corps (OTC) in November 1910 under the command of the new science master Arthur Child. After Britain's dismal performance in the Boer War (in which 47 Bloxhamists served, five losing their lives), there was much soul-searching among politicians and the press and growing pressure for the public schools to prepare their pupils for military leadership; this only increased as great power rivalries intensified in the lead-up to the Great War. A total of 39 schools already boasted a Volunteer Corps by the time the Boer War broke out, and another 71 schools started them between then and the formation of the OTC in 1908. Bloxham was one of a further 46 to introduce a cadet corps by the outbreak of war, including Oakham and Manchester Grammar School in the same year. Approval was received from the War Office in October 1910, and the Bloxham OTC paraded for the first time on 19 December 1910.

Beginning with 22 boys, there was a slow start, with *The Bloxhamist* expressing concern that 'the number of recruits is not as great as was hoped for', due mainly to concern over the entrance fee of two pounds, which covered all uniform and equipment, in addition to a subscription of five shillings a term. In addition, several boys were slow to obtain written permission from home. However, by 1914 more than half the school's pupils were enrolled and the corps' activities were, as at other schools, an increasingly dominant part of Bloxham school life. Thursday afternoons were given up to the corps' activities, including Grinter's drill classes, range shooting, bugling and semaphore signalling, while the rest of the school went on a run (the 'grind', all six miles of it). Sixteen cadets attended the 1911 Coronation Royal Review at Windsor, while the annual camp at Tidworth (1911 and 1914), Bordon (1912) or Rugeley (1913) and field days and exercises with other schools became highpoints of the school year for many Bloxhamists. These field days would reach their peak in 1923, when over a thousand cadets were involved, with Cheltenham and Bloxham defending Hobb Hill, which overlooks the village, against an attack from the forces of Rugby and Radley. The prestige of the school, still a 'private school' very conscious of its small size and lack of social distinction, was enhanced by the contacts made with other schools by boys attending OTC camps.

At the end of the summer term in 1914, the OTC numbered 53 cadets in two sections, one commanded by Sergeant Philip Higgs and the other by Sergeant Kingsley Fradd. There were two officers, Captain Arthur Child and Lieutenant Charles Allan, assisted by Colour Sergeant Grinter. The War Office inspection of 2 July 1914 adjudged it to be 'a small but efficient contingent' which 'reflected great credit on the officers and cadets'. The corps 'is popular in the school and all ranks appeared to be very keen.' The OTC had swiftly become a central feature of a school with little previous military tradition.

The values inculcated at Bloxham were thought to be important in enabling a young man to take command of large bodies of men, many of them much older than him. For example, 19-year-old Arthur Stevens had received valuable leadership training at Bloxham as School Captain and as a Sergeant in the OTC, though it is worth remembering that as a Captain in the 9th Royal Fusiliers Stevens would have commanded a company of about 200 men, considerably more than the number of pupils at Bloxham during his time at school. For 18-year-old 2nd Lieutenant Kingsley Fradd, leading a platoon of 50 men of the 2nd London Regiment into action on the first day of the Battle of the Somme may have been a far cry from commanding a section of 26 of his schoolmates in the Bloxham Corps, but there can be no doubt that on a national scale the OTC played a vital part in building the junior officer corps of Britain's hastily improvised citizen army.

The First World War happened just at the point when Bloxham was undergoing a transformation into a recognisable 'public school'. In this process the new gymnasium and fives courts were important developments, to be followed by the introduction of a house system (1916), the adoption of rugby football (1920) and the growth in the size of the Sixth Form, finally culminating in the election of the Headmaster to the Headmaster's Conference in 1929, confirmation that Bloxham was now to be considered a 'public school'.

On 1 July 1914, three days after the assassination of the Archduke Franz Ferdinand in faraway Sarajevo, the school's Camera Club paid a visit on a balmy summer afternoon to the Old Prebendal House, Ellen Hinde's rambling mansion in the village of Shipton-under-Wychwood, and a poignant photograph taken by the Headmaster that day records an idyllic tea party in her garden. None of those photographed could have suspected the part unfolding events in the Balkans would shortly play in their lives. By the time term ended, the escalation to war was well under way, and although the school's OTC set off for their annual camp at Tidworth as usual on 28 July, cadets were warned on Monday 3 August, the day that Germany invaded France, to prepare for departure the next day, and the camp was duly cut short on Tuesday 4 August. The Bloxham cadets returned to school to be picked up by their parents, and by the end of the day, Britain was at war with Germany.

2

Bloxham School in Wartime

Bloxham School reassembled in September 1914 to discover that several of the senior pupils had chosen to join up rather than return to school, as had two of the masters, Mr Pastfield and Mr Hunt. *The Bloxhamist* for the following October recorded the names of 64 Old Bloxhamists serving in the Army and a further eight in the Navy, a combination of career soldiers and those who had volunteered since August. By the time the Michaelmas Term started, the BEF had already suffered heavy losses at Mons and Le Cateau, and it was clear that this would not be a short war, certainly not one that would be 'over by Christmas'.

The number of Bloxhamists in the regular army before the outbreak of war was not large. The school had little military tradition; a census of parental occupations in 1870 revealed that of 164 pupils at the school, only 4 fathers were military men, compared with 50 farmers, 42 in business, 21 clergymen, 10 lawyers, 7 doctors and 30 miscellaneous professionals. Nor did it possess an army class, as at schools like Wellington, Clifton or Cheltenham, to prepare pupils for entry into either of the military academies, Sandhurst or Woolwich. This was remarked on in a speech by Colonel Bruce Skinner at the 1913 Old Bloxhamist dinner at the Trocadero Restaurant in Piccadilly, when he 'regretted that he had been unable to send his own sons to the school, owing to the fact that no army class existed there, and he hoped that the time would come when provision would be made for boys desirous of entering the army and navy.' The Headmaster responded by saying that 'such a class could be provided if there were any demand for it', but that during all the fifteen years he had been at Bloxham he could only recollect one boy who had gone into the army (though Ward's memory was clearly faulty, as there were several such examples). Skinner would go on to become one of five Bloxhamist generals of the Great War, and the most senior of them (the others were all brigadier generals). As Major General Bruce Morland Skinner CB, CMG, MVO, he served as Commandant of the Royal Army Medical College and later as Director of Medical Services of Fifth Army and was mentioned in despatches on five occasions.

Bloxhamists volunteered in similar numbers, and for similar reasons, to those from other schools, a mixture of motives which included patriotism, peer pressure and an urge to be of service. A sense of duty weighed heavily with Bloxhamists who had been exposed over the course of their school career to ideas of duty, service and leadership, whether in lessons, debates and addresses on Speech Day or more generally by the ethos inculcated in games and chapel, both prominent elements in the life of the school. This was especially the case for those who had been members of the OTC. One cadet, P.E. Read, recorded his impressions of 'a lecture given by some big man' on OTC camp in August 1911: 'The lecturer ended by saying that England might at any time be attacked, and that as we had gained our territory by war, so we should either lose it altogether or else make it vaster and stronger than before.'

Edward Bliss, a pupil between 1904 and 1906 who had joined the Queen's Own Oxfordshire Hussars, was probably typical in his views, expressed in a letter from the trenches written in February 1915: 'It is very different being out here from being at Bloxham, but I mean to do my duty to my Country and School.'

In this respect, Bloxham was firmly in the mainstream of the public school experience. An address by the Headmaster of Malvern College on Speech Day, July 1915 – by which time that school had lost seventy Old Boys, all officers – advanced the opinion that their sacrifice had vindicated the English public school system: 'This has been a subalterns' war and the heaviest losses have fallen upon young officers between the ages of twenty and twenty-five.' Those seventy lives, he went on, 'stand I think, for all the best that we can teach here; and their lives have not been wasted if they have taught the world that at our English public schools we learn the lesson of discipline and service.'

At Bloxham as elsewhere, these lessons were the product of decades of inculcation. Lord Jersey, speaking on the school's Speech Day in 1898, was certainly representative of visiting speakers in stressing the importance of moral factors: 'He would impress upon them most strongly … the advantage of character. It was of the utmost importance to every boy at school and also when he left school that he should have character. … Character would carry them through many difficulties and trials.' Writing after the war, Admiral the Earl Jellicoe agreed with this view: 'It is the character training which plays so important a part in the Public School life which develops leadership both in peace and war.' The final verse of the school song, written in 1893 (music by W. E. Thomas, lyrics by J. H. T. Goodwin) conflated war, sport, Empire and religion in a manner characteristic of the period:

> *We too a roll of honour boast, we too can wield the willow,*
> *And some our country's battles fight, some face the restless billow,*
> *Some bear to far colonial shores a heart that nought can sever,*
> *And still ascends and never ends their cry 'All Saints Forever'.*

With the war only a few months old, and the school unsettled due to pupils and staff departing to join the colours, there can scarcely have been a worse time for Bloxham to lose its Headmaster. It was announced that the Rev. Ward had been offered the parish of Hillgay in Norfolk, an offer he accepted without hesitation. He and his wife were at sea when war was declared, having just sailed from Liverpool for Canada, where they witnessed the sight of 4,000 troops marching through Winnipeg en route to the war in Europe. Ward returned for the start of the Michaelmas Term but left at Christmas. *The Bloxhamist* gloomily observed that 'Changes are not pleasant; at any rate, prospective changes are not.' The new Headmaster was the Rev. Roy Grier, himself a member of the Woodard family, having been educated at Denstone before reading history at Oxford. Within five years of starting his teaching career at another Woodard school, Worksop, he had been appointed its Headmaster at the age of 28. There he had earned himself a reputation as a building headmaster under whom the school had thrived and coming to Bloxham as a 37-year-old he was expected to do the same for his new school. As it was, his headmastership was to be brief and almost entirely overshadowed by the war, but one of his pupils, Rex Bateman, could recall him vividly over fifty years later – 'above medium height, dark hair greying at the temples, a strong face and, in my opinion, good looking and impressive, he certainly had a presence'.

Grier's most significant achievement, and the one with the most long-term significance, was the introduction in 1916 of a house system in order to develop the 'public school spirit' in place of the seven dormitories which had traditionally contested internal fixtures. The original building became Wilberforce, named after the bishop who had opened it in 1855, with episcopal purple as its house colour, while the 1864 wing was named after its former occupant Crake (Chaplain 1865-78), with clerical scarlet. The old farmhouse and headmaster's house, already known as Head's, was later renamed Wilson in honour of Charles Wilson, with gold as its colour.

The first Bloxhamist to be killed in action, in December 1914, was a master, James Pastfield, and his name would have been read out at the altar in chapel at the service of Holy Communion held every Wednesday at 7:00 a.m, a custom which went on throughout the war. The numbers thus remembered began to mount in 1915, and a melancholy succession of obituary notices filled the pages of *The Bloxhamist*, most of them recording the loss of young men well known to current pupils as well as the staff. This reached its peak in 1916 with the Battle of the Somme. The July 1916 number contained obituaries for eight Old Bloxhamists, including two killed at Jutland and the first casualties of the Battle of the Somme, as well as Brigadier General Wilfred Ellershaw. The next edition, for October 1916, carried news of the loss of a further 11 former pupils, as the toll on the Somme continued to mount.

The school magazine also kept its readers up to date with enlistments, promotions and decorations as well as news from Old Boys serving all around the world, often recounting their experiences or stories of bumping into fellow Old Bloxhamists in unexpected places, be it Sudan, Gallipoli or Ypres. The magazine provided a regular diet of letters sent from the front. These included letters sent to the chaplain or Charles Wilson as well as ones to families which were then forwarded to the editor. Many of these letters did not shy away from describing the grim reality of modern war. Ellershaw, then a Major commanding a battery at the Battle of the Marne (September 1914), wrote that 'I am writing this in the middle of a terrific battle, it has been awful slaughter ... I cannot tell you the awful sight it was up there when I had been shelling their trenches. It looked as if they were still all there, but no living.' A letter from another artilleryman, Lieutenant Walter Ward, son of the recently departed headmaster, is extraordinarily graphic in its description of the Battle of Aubers (9 May 1915), especially considering that it could have been read by every pupil in the school and relatives of some of those involved, including the family of Robert Cunliffe who died in the battle:

> Directly they were past our trenches I began to see casualties, about every yard or two a man would fall forward flat and I saw some sitting up who were wounded. After they had gone about 50 yards to the right they came to a hedge running at right angles to the trenches which had obviously been barb-wired and they were held up for a minute and machine guns must have opened on them as they began to fall all over the place, one on top of the other, but they soon got through and went on and I lost sight of them ... The next day I counted over 50 bodies in front of the hedge within 200 yards of me. The end of it all was that our infantry advanced right up to F_____ s but got terribly cut up by the machine guns the whole way, some battalions being absolutely wiped out. One rather horrible thing was that there were very few wounded brought in, as they all

fell behind the line which the Germans hold now, so Heaven knows what has become of them. Our casualties in this part must be well over 6,000.

As well as writing letters, many Old Bloxhamists on leave chose to use some of their precious time at home to visit the school, and there can be little doubt that the pupils would have been under few illusions about the realities of trench warfare. The notion that young men joined up ignorant of the conditions they would face out at the front, if it was ever true, was certainly not by the end of 1914. Ward's notably frank letter confirms that censorship was nowhere near as widespread, and the public not so uninformed, as is usually thought to be the case. *The Bloxhamist* also played an important role in keeping nostalgic Old Boys connected with the familiar routine of school life, whether they were serving in the trenches of Flanders or the deserts of the Middle East. Warwick Pearse, aboard the dreadnought battleship HMS *Marlborough*, wrote that 'I have had no news of Bloxham for some time and am looking forward to this term's number of *The Bloxhamist*', whilst Edward Bliss wrote, 'I very often think of you all at school and wonder how you are getting on.'

Apart from news from the war, the pages of the school magazine were mainly taken up with sport, which continued to play an important part in school life. The number of football matches was in decline, a development which was already under way before the war, eventually leading the school to switch to rugby football after 1920. Cricket, however, continued to dominate the summer term, with Abingdon, Warwick and Magdalen College School, Oxford the main opponents as before. On 1 July 1916, the first day of the Battle of the Somme, a Saturday, the school's 1st XI was playing the village, and a week later, the XI dismissed Warwick School for 47 in reply to the home team's 127, with the captain, Douglas Cain, top scoring with 43 and taking 5 for 17.

Cain was obviously a remarkable young man, having also been Head of School and Captain of Football, Gymnastics, Running, Swimming and Fives, even though he was known as 'Pennyweight' because of his small stature. It is interesting to note his eagerness to leave school and join up as soon as he could, departing from Bloxham at Christmas 1916 rather than waiting for the end of the school year. Days after scoring the winning goal for Wilson against Wilberforce in the inaugural House Football final he joined the Royal Flying Corps, and by July 1917 he was out in France (half of the 1916 1st XI served as pilots before the war ended). Two months later, he found himself in a dogfight with four German planes, his machine breaking up in the air. He fell 1000 feet onto a hangar, somehow escaping with his life; *The Bloxhamist* observed that 'his own pluck prevented the doctors giving him up.' He was discharged from hospital in August 1918 and returned to Bloxham to help out as a teacher. One of Cain's pupils who commented that 'thereafter, he limped badly', was seemingly unaware that he had had one foot amputated, though this did not stop him from playing in Old Bloxhamist cricket fixtures.

The OTC continued to play a central role in school life, and this was enhanced as the war went on. Numbers rose from 59 cadets in two sections in 1914 to 83 three years later. Starting in November 1915, the corps was mobilised on Sundays to help packing and loading ordnance stores at Didcot, an important railway junction. Forty NCOs and cadets would march to Banbury Station every Sunday after Chapel to catch the train to Didcot, getting back to Bloxham at about 8:00 p.m. *The Church Times* commented on the incongruous sight of uniformed preacher and schoolboys singing plainsong in chapel before marching to Banbury station to head to the depot 'to do their bit'.

Captain Child remained in command of the OTC until July 1915, when he left to serve with the London Regiment on the Western Front, where he won the Military Cross. His deputy Lieutenant Allen left at the same time to join the Royal Berkshire Regiment, while Sergeant Grinter was taken by the War Office to serve in a camp of instruction for officers. Lloyd Jacob was appointed to replace Child in November 1915 and was soon joined by L.E. Smith to take command. Like Grier, Smith came from Worksop, where he ran the OTC and games. After the departure of Child and Grinter, more of the work fell on the shoulders of senior pupils such as Douglas Cain, who as Captain of Gymnastics took over running the Gym.

A regular diet of parades, exercises and shooting and signalling was followed. From September 1915 the OTC could boast a band of bugles and drums. Charles Wilson donated a third side drum and the Tuck Shop a big drum the following year, to provide a full band. Every cadet had to learn Morse signalling (semaphore was abandoned in July 1916) or be in the band. Some idea of the seriousness with which OTC operations were taken in war time can be gleaned from the route march undertaken in late July 1917, which began on the afternoon of Monday 23 July and covered seventy miles of road, taking in Chipping Norton, Burford, Witney and Woodstock, arriving back in Bloxham at 6:30 a.m. on Saturday 28 July before the cadets dispersed in civilian garb for the summer holidays. The Chaplain, Hugh Willimott, accompanied the marchers as head of the commissariat and arranged prayers and meals, the supplies being transported in a van which accompanied the corps on its way.

As the war dragged on, pupils continued to be touched by loss. Many of the boys had fathers or older brothers serving, and most families were affected in some way. Eight members of the Boissier family served during the war, and three pairs of brothers (Smith, Robertson and Rylands) were killed. Of the five Bowler brothers, the three oldest served. All three survived, Leslie winning the Military Cross and Bar, Geoffrey losing a leg at Gallipoli and Frank piloting a fighter plane, but, in a hideous irony, the two youngest boys, Cyril and Jack, both pupils at the school and so supposed safe at home, were drowned in the river Cherwell near Deddington in September 1917.

As well as the deaths of Old Bloxhamists, members of the school community were directly touched by other losses. The nephew of the school's first Headmaster, Philip Reginald Egerton, and the youngest son of the second, Frederick Boissier, were both killed on the Western Front, and Captain Child's brother was lost aboard HMS *Monmouth* at the Battle of Coronel in November 1914. Another family touched by loss was that of the school's former Drill Sergeant John Billington, who served as an Army Scripture Reader in France. His daughter Sarah joined Queen Mary's Auxiliary Army Corps, the women's unit of the British Army, which was set up by the Adjutant-General, Sir Neville Macready, in July 1917 to replace male soldiers in offices, canteens, stores and army bases. Ultimately some 57,000 women served in the Corps, and 84 of them died before the time the war ended, including Sarah Billington, who died in the influenza pandemic in the last year of the war.

Whatever the effect of these losses was on their loved ones, harder still to gauge is the war's impact on the everyday life of the school and its pupils. Younger and more active masters left to join up, leaving older men who did not always find it easy to control their pupils and ex-officers invalided out of the army, often with severe psychological trauma. Many senior pupils also left sooner than they would otherwise have done. Gerald Gray, a pupil between 1916 and 1924, later recalled that 'the Staff were a bit on the sketchy side', meaning that 'too much power inevitably descended on the Prefects' room and discipline was pretty tough.' The quality of the food, notorious even before the war, deteriorated further, with a severe shortage of fruit and vegetables. Gerald Gray claimed that 'we had to rely on our tuck boxes, otherwise I think we would have probably starved to death. There was a war on and things were difficult for everyone.'

While food rationing was not the prominent feature of British society during the First World War that it would be in the Second, the country did suffer from severe food shortages and price rises as the Germans' introduction of unrestricted submarine warfare in 1917 started to bite. By early 1918, ration cards had been distributed and shop owners were asked to send details of tea, butter and margarine stocks to the Food Control Committee. Ellen Hinde, the daughter of the school's Founder, was charged with hoarding 122 lb. of tea in January 1918 and fined £50 for breaking the Food Hoarding Order. Although the case was dismissed on appeal, it must have been a shattering blow for a respectable lady of local standing to be prosecuted in a high-profile case which turned on whether tea could be classed as a food – the Court of Appeal decided that it could not.

It would be heart-warming to record that when the war ended on 11 November the school was swept up in a paroxysm of jubilation as the country celebrated, as it had at the end of the Boer War in 1901. This was certainly the case at other schools, for example Uppingham, where news of the armistice was greeted with a brief service of thanksgiving, the singing of the National Anthem on the green and an impromptu concert in the evening. News reached the village of Bloxham shortly after midday. Flags were hoisted, bells rang out and everyone downed tools and took a holiday. Fireworks were let off in the evening, and it seems that things got out of hand, as the police raided the White Lion and charged the landlady, Mrs Bennett, and the eight villagers present with drinking after hours. The magistrates dismissed the charges on the basis that the beer had been bought before closing time, ten o'clock.

At the school, however, there were no celebrations, as there were no pupils in residence. Spanish Influenza had struck just before half term and the Headmaster had announced the ending of term early on 3 November, shortly after the annual All Saints' Day, the school's Patronal Festival. The next edition of *The Bloxhamist*, now published only biannually rather than the eight issues a year before the war, did not appear until July 1919 and was markedly downbeat in tone, with little reference to victory. This was partly because of the continuing impact of influenza as well as an outbreak of mumps, which meant that only four football matches were played all season and exams and schoolwork were badly disrupted, but also because of the news of the unexpected departure of the Headmaster. Grier had been offered the headmastership of his old school, Denstone, and felt unable to refuse. His four years at Bloxham contained enough clues to suggest that he could have become one of the school's great headmasters in time.

The school did its best to return to normal as quickly as possible after the cessation of hostilities. At the start of June, the Old Bloxhamists' cricketers came to play the school for the first time since 1914. *The Bloxhamist* reported that 'the weather could not have been better, and it was quite like old times again.' The Old Boys side contained three brothers of Arthur Whiting, killed in the war the previous August.

It should, of course, be remembered that the end of the war did not mean the end of the fighting or dying. Two of those on the school war memorial, David Abbott and Eustace Cree, died after the Armistice, and Bloxham continued to be touched by losses from the war for some time to come. Fighting continued throughout 1919 in Eastern Europe, the Caucasus and the Middle East, and a sizeable force of British troops had been sent to Archangel in Northern Russia to intervene in the Russian Civil War. Gwynne Jacob, younger brother of the commander of the school's OTC, was killed fighting the Bolsheviks in Northern Russia in August 1919 and is commemorated on the village war memorial. He also had another brother, Owen, at Bloxham School at the time of his death, as well as his mother Annie, who ran Merton Cottage as the school's junior boarding house, so his loss must have impacted heavily on the school community.

It is also important to emphasise that the end of the war did not mean an end to the suffering of those who had fought, most of whom survived. Many had suffered traumatic and life-changing wounds, and many had suffered psychological trauma which might never heal. There is a tendency among those studying the Great War to focus solely on those who perished in the war and to forget both those who served and survived, and those who stayed behind. Some of the entries in the school's Roll of Honour hint at the lasting impact, such as Captain Beauchamp Friend ('wounded twice, gassed, shell shock') and Captain Carl Dieterle ('left leg off, right leg badly wounded, severe body wounds'). Dieterle, whose father came from Württemberg and taught German at the school between 1879 and 1883, is listed on the war memorial of his local church in Chiswick, suggesting that his death at the age of 49 in 1933 was connected with his wounds. When Henry Mello, who served with the Canadian forces, died in October 1930, *The Bloxhamist* stated unequivocally that 'he was so badly gassed that he never got over it and died at Bristol from the effects which had caused him to suffer greatly from asthma.'

The case of Beauchamp Friend reveals the complexity behind the bald facts in the Roll of Honour and serves as a warning against endowing all those who served with heroic status. Friend informed his old school that he had been awarded the Military Cross and was further mentioned in despatches. He had been badly gassed in November 1915, had been wounded twice and 'also suffered much from shell shock'. He also wrote that at Loos in October 1915 he had spent ten days fully equipped without taking anything off to wash, shave or sleep. In one trench 'they were up to their knees in dead and wounded.' However, there is no record of the Military Cross or the mention in despatches in official records, and his wounds – one 'about the size of a threepenny bit' and the other to his left thigh 'about the size of a sixpence' according to his medical file – were deemed by the War Office to be insufficiently severe to merit a wound gratuity. What the Roll of Honour does not reveal is that Beauchamp Friend was court martialled on two occasions and found guilty of one charge of absence without leave and three charges regarding dishonoured cheques, and he was dismissed from His Majesty's Service on 7 October 1918. A Mrs Hunt of Sidcup, whose daughter was Friend's fiancée, was warned by an officer that Friend was 'utterly bad and was cashiered out of the West Kents for overstaying his leave and monetary matters.' The engagement was broken off, and Friend made a new life as an engineer in Cape Town, where he died in 1946.

The ending of the war also brought the return of Old Bloxhamist prisoners of war, including St. John Maitland Young, taken prisoner at Messines in November 1914, and Second Lieutenant Edgar Lingard Green of the 2nd Bedfordshire Regiment, one of thousands of British troops captured in March 1918 at the outset of the German spring offensive. His captivity was relatively brief, while Young was incarcerated for over four years in Gustrow in Mecklenburg, where conditions were notoriously bad. Another to return was Private Horace Bowen of the 1st King Edward's Horse, who was taken prisoner at Vieille-Chapelle on 11 April 1918 at the start of the Battle of the Lys, the second stage of the Ludendorff offensive. Horace managed to escape from his captors in Brussels on 1 November and was still at large when the fighting ceased ten days later.

Not every Old Bloxhamist contribution to the war effort was made on the battlefield. F.O. Fisher was reported in *The Bloxhamist* to have been 'engaged in tracking the espionage practised by Bolo Pasha and others'; Bolo Pasha was a French financier accused of being a German agent and executed by firing squad in April 1918. Henry Tonks served as an official war artist and produced a remarkable set of watercolours illustrating the ground-breaking plastic surgery carried out by Dr Harold Gillies at the Queen's Hospital, Sidcup. Tonks was a professor at the Slade School of Art who was the teacher of an outstanding generation of young British artists which included Augustus John, Paul Nash, Stanley Spencer and Christopher Nevinson. Stephen Reynolds, who made his name as a writer and social reformer, also made an important contribution as Inspector of Fisheries for the South-West, persuading the War Office not to conscript fishermen, thereby avoiding damage to fishing fleets. Reynolds seemed set to play an important role in post-war politics but died during the influenza pandemic in February 1919.

3

The 80 – Biographies of the Fallen

1914

On 28 June 1914, the heir to the throne of the Austro-Hungarian empire, the Archduke Franz Ferdinand and his wife Sophia were visiting the Bosnian capital of Sarajevo. As they toured the city, their driver took a wrong turn and was forced to turn the open top car around. As he did so, a 19-year-old Bosnian-Serb anarchist named Gavrilo Princip stepped out from the pavement and pulled a pistol from his jacket pocket. He fired and killed both the Archduke and his wife.

While Princip was quickly arrested, the assassination of the heir to the Habsburg dynasty created a series of political, military, and diplomatic miscalculations that propelled the nations of Europe towards war. Europe at this time was connected by a complex series of treaties and alliances between the various nations, all created on the assumption that at some point the nations of Europe would be at war with each other. Everyone knew that war was inevitable, it was a case of when and not if.

Austria-Hungary, the affronted victim of Serb terrorism, threatened military action, primarily in retribution for the assassination, but also to flex its metaphorical muscles in the face of support for Serbian nationalism, which it viewed as a major threat to its supremacy in the Balkans. Austria-Hungary, however, was wary of the potential involvement of Russia, Serbia's strongest ally in any future conflict, and sought reassurance from Germany that it would support her if war broke out. Germany pledged her allegiance but urged Austria to act quickly while public opinion was still on their side following the assassination.

Germany's leaders had long been suspicious of Russian economic and political power and was concerned that Russia's growing economy might represent a threat to them. Many believed that war was inevitable, and from a German perspective, the sooner the better.

The Russians, watching with growing concern the delicate situation between Austria-Hungary and Serbia, decided that they would support Serbia in the event of war and in consequence ordered a partial mobilisation of its forces. Russia believed that the Austrian threats against Serbia were part of a German-orchestrated plan against St Petersburg, and therefore needed to show strength on behalf of its ally Serbia. The build-up of Russian forces on its border caused huge concern in Berlin.

The planning for war had been in place for many years, and the Germans calculated that Russia's ally France would be militarily able to go to war far quicker than Russia. Consequently, any German war against Russia would involve knocking out France in the West before heading East to take on the Russians. The French also suspected that Germany would at some point attack, mainly in the hotly disputed areas of Alsace and Lorraine, which had changed hands in 1871. In preparation for a German offensive the French had fortified their borders with a series of forts and heavily defended positions all facing Germany. The German plan devised by Count Alfred von Schlieffen recognised that attacking France over the frontier would be suicidal, and so the attack was based on circumventing the French defences via neutral Belgium and Luxembourg. Once the French had been defeated in a matter of weeks, the Germans could head East to attack Russia. In response to German sabre-rattling, the French also commenced a mobilisation of their forces, which in turn increased German anxiety.

Far from acting quickly, Austria deliberated for several weeks, before handing Serbia an ultimatum on the morning of 23 July. The ultimatum so obtuse in its terms was rejected by the Serbian government on 25 July. This rejection led to Austria declaring war and the blue touch paper had been lit.

Britain had agreed in 1839 that in the event of war it would defend Belgian neutrality, and part of the success of the Schlieffen Plan depended on Britain not acting in support of Belgium. Britain, while an ally of both France and Russia, was initially reluctant to get involved in a European war, but by late July it reaffirmed that it would continue to support Belgium and by early August was mobilising its forces for war.

The British maintained a small but well-trained army at that time, which had spent the previous decades fighting colonial wars. Numbering only 600,000 men the British Expeditionary Force (or BEF) as it was known, was small but made up of well-trained regular troops and countless reservists, all trained to an equally high standard.

On the morning of 1 August 1914, over 1.2 million German soldiers began their march to the West into Luxembourg, which prompted a French declaration of war on 3 August, followed by a British declaration the next day.

The British government dispatched the BEF to France, under the command of Field Marshal Sir John French, with mobilisation beginning on 9 August. On arrival in France the BEF were sent to southern Belgium to support the French in trying to stem the German advance. The French army had been fighting against the Germans since 7 August in what became known as The Battle of the Frontiers, and had suffered appalling casualties, with almost 300,000 French soldiers being killed, wounded or missing in the first month of fighting. On 22 August, the French had over 27,000 soldiers killed in a total of 60,000 casualties, the highest single day's loss of life suffered by the Allies in the Great War.

Many of the career soldier Bloxhamists would have been part of the BEF at this time. The BEF first went into action against the Germans near Mons on 23 August 1914, but despite great heroism, the sheer volume of German soldiers meant that the BEF was swamped and in danger of being encircled by the Germans, and so was soon in full retreat. The speed of the retreat took the Germans by complete surprise and allowed the BEF five days of marching away from the Germans, who followed. The British and French came together on the banks of the River Marne, where a defensive action was fought which slowed the German advance once again. A further retreat to the River Aisne saw the development of what we would recognise as trench warfare, as the British and French prepared to block a German advance into Paris. The Allies held the high ground to the south of the Aisne, the Germans the high ground to the north. The terrain made attacking impossible in a frontal direction, and so each side began to dig in opposite each other. Each side attempted to gain the upper hand by outflanking the enemy's trenches in what became known as the "race to the sea". Whoever gained control of the Channel ports would have a significant advantage in terms of supplies. As the line spread north, the trenches spread across the pancake-flat fields of Artois and into Belgium, and to the south into the rolling hills of Champagne and down to the Vosges mountains. In Belgium, the small city of Ypres (or Wipers as it was known to the British) was defended heavily, and the fighting saw the German and British lines form a bulge known as a 'salient' around the city. By the end of November, the 450-mile-long line of trenches known as the Western Front had been dug, stretching from Nieuwpoort on the Belgian coast to Pfetterhaus on the Swiss Border, and the armies of Europe would remain largely immobile in these trenches for the next four years.

By the time 1914 drew to a close, the BEF had lost almost 90,000 men, and most crucially many of its officers and experienced NCOs, and the cold, bitter winter gave it time to recuperate and face the challenges that 1915 might bring.

Second Lieutenant James Thomas Robinson Pastfield
5th Battalion, Middlesex Regiment, attd. 1st Northamptonshire Regiment
Master at Bloxham School 1913-1914
Killed in action 21 December 1914, aged 23
Commemorated on the Le Touret Memorial to the Missing, France
Panel 31

The first Bloxhamist to perish in the Great War was not a former pupil but a member of the teaching staff, the Classics Master James Pastfield.

James Thomas Robinson Pastfield was born on 18 December 1891, the third of ten children born to John Robinson Pastfield and Elizabeth Olive Pastfield. His father was a Superintendent in an insurance agency, and in the 1911 census the family was shown as residing at Olivedale, 286, Princes Road South, Exeter. James was at this time studying at university. His older brother John was a student of theology, and his older sister Gladys resided at home. He had three younger siblings, Olive, Catherine and David, all of whom were at school. His other siblings are not mentioned on this particular census, but there was also a younger brother Joseph, known by the family as Victor.

Having completed his education at Exeter School, James then progressed to Keble College, Oxford where he played football for the college and graduated in 1913 with a degree in Classics. He lived at 25, Farndon Road in Oxford. Keble College had an active Officers

Training Corps and we know that James was a member of this. The OTC was known at the University as 'the Bughunters', as the recruits spent many hours in Christ Church Meadow, performing endless rifle drills with nothing to shoot at apart from bugs and butterflies. A total of 996 men from Keble served during the Great War, with a remarkable 202 of them serving as military chaplains.

After Keble, James took a post as Classics Master at Bloxham School, an ideal position for a keen young sportsman. At this time, masters were still allowed to play for the school in matches against clubs and village sides, though not against other schools, and team photographs from his brief time at Bloxham show James and his young colleague John Nuthall alongside the football and cricket sides they coached, as well as the XI for hockey, which the school had only taken up a few years before. Between them the two young masters greatly strengthened the school teams; when the football XI beat Exeter College, Oxford 4-0 in November 1913, *The Bloxhamist* admitted that 'the assistance of two masters.....made an immense difference to the team, especially forward. Mr. Nuthall was a great success at centre-forward, and Mr. Pastfield showed a fine turn of speed until he was unfortunate enough to put his knee out.'

James also assisted the school OTC with its shooting, and it can have come as no surprise to anyone at Bloxham when, at the outbreak of war in August 1914, he took the decision to join up and not to return to Bloxham for a second year, eventually to be followed by John Nuthall. The Headmaster returned from British Columbia at the start of the Michaelmas Term to the unwelcome discovery that he had lost two of his most valuable members of staff; as *The Bloxhamist* observed, 'Like most other schools, we have to suffer from a reduction in our staff of masters. No one has been found to take Mr. Hunt's place, and Mr. Pastfield has got a commission in the army.'

James enlisted in the Army on 13 August 1914, days after the British declaration of war, at a recruiting office in Exeter, and was commissioned as a 2nd Lieutenant into the 5th (Reserve) Battalion of the Middlesex Regiment, in the Special Reserve of Officers. James' enlistment papers, which list his address as 7 Victoria Terrace, Exeter, give his height as 5 feet 8 ½ inches and weight as 150 lb., with his vision and hearing described as 'good' and his teeth as 'fair'. Overall he was evaluated as 'fit'. His commission was recorded in the London Gazette of 21 November 1914.

We know that James paid a visit to Keble before joining up, and that he was posted to Rochester for training, but there is some confusion as to when he actually arrived in France, as we shall see.

Whenever he did arrive, James Pastfield was now in a different unit, having been transferred to the Northamptonshire Regiment, which had already lost large numbers of officers due to its heavy engagement in the first months of the war. With British casualties running at almost 90,000 men in the first three months of the war, the Army was desperately short of trained officers, and with his OTC background, James Pastfield would have been in demand.

The Northamptons' war diary for the month of October 1914 has been lost, but a later entry states that between 25 October and 14 November, the battalion was in action daily and suffered an appalling casualty rate. At roll call on 14 November the 1st Battalion was only able to parade two officers and 300 men from a nominal strength of nearly 700. Following this mauling, the Battalion rested almost a month near the small French town of Hazebrouck. During this time, officers were drafted in and it seems likely that James joined the battalion at this time, though his arrival is not recorded in the war diary.

On the morning of 21 December, the Battalion went into action once again, presumably James' first engagement. The battalion left Hazebrouck at approximately 7:00 a.m., and following a four-hour march, they stopped for rations near Le Touret. They marched a further four hours towards Rue de Bois, being guided by an officer of the 2nd Gurkhas, where they received orders to launch a night attack in company with the 1st Battalion the Loyal North Lancashire Regiment. Their objective was to retake trenches which had been lost to the Germans the previous night, about half a mile south of Rue de Bois. The diary of the Loyal North Lancs. records that information about the exact location and number of Germans was 'somewhat vague'.

At 7:00 p.m. they attacked, the Northants to the north of the village, the North Lancs to the south. The men were carrying 170 rounds of ammunition and iron rations and were ordered to leave packs behind. By this time, the night had fallen and the weather closed in, and the attack started in freezing rain. The two regiments attacked on a front of 300 yards with fixed bayonets. They immediately ran into heavy rifle fire coming from the edge of an orchard, and promptly charged the enemy. They managed in the next three hours to retake three lines of trenches and advance over 400 metres. The Germans counterattacked with bombs (grenades) and rifle fire but successive attacks were beaten off. The 1st Northants took the brunt of the onslaught to the north of the position, heading towards a road known as La Quinque Rue.

Our research leads us to believe that the orchard remains to this day and its current size and shape appear to match the description provided in the North Lancs' war diary. Five months later, another Bloxhamist, Francis Riddle, was to die in these same fields to the east of the orchard, during the opening stages of the Battle of Festubert. By 10:00 p.m., the trenches had been retaken but casualties were heavy, mainly coming from artillery fire located in woods to the east of Rue de Bois. The night remained wet and cold, and the constant artillery fire prevented packs or rations being brought up.

The following account of what happened was provided by a soldier wounded in this engagement and was passed to the school:

> We left Hazebrouck on the morning of the 21st in motor buses, and we went to La Bassée. From there we marched some three or four miles to some crossroads and we entered some fields. At about 6:00 p.m. we were ordered to take some trenches. Our Captain had been wounded and we were hesitating, looking around for officers when Lt. Pastfield and his young friend Lt. Wainwright said, 'Come on lads, we'll lead you!' They did so, and shortly after our attack Lt. Wainwright fell badly wounded. Lt. Pastfield went on and after some murderous fighting we took the trench. The Germans got into a position about 15 yards away. Lt. Pastfield was feeling faint from a wound he had received and a Lance Cpl. begged him to go back and seek attention. He refused saying he needed to find Lt. Wainwright. He went out to where Lt. Wainwright lay, and reeling from lack of blood, he staggered and presenting an easy target, a German shot him through the head.

Lt. Wainwright was in fact Second Lieutenant Geoffrey Chauner Wainwright, who died in hospital the following day from his wounds. He was an old boy of Wellington College who had left Clare College, Cambridge at the outbreak of war. He was 18 years of age when he died. The

1st Northamptons lost three officers and 60 men killed and wounded during the attack on the night of the 21st.

Whereas Wainwright lies in a grave in Le Touret Cemetery, James Pastfield's body was never found, and his name is listed on the magnificent Le Touret Memorial to the Missing close by. He is also commemorated on the memorials at Exeter School and Bloxham as well as at Keble College. Having endured one shattering blow early in the war, the Pastfields were to suffer another near its end, when James' younger brother Joseph, who was serving as a Lieutenant with the 5/13th Battalion the Middlesex Regiment, was killed in action at the age of 20 on 9 September 1918 near Lens. The two brothers are remembered on an impressive marble memorial in St Thomas', Exeter, where their parents had worshipped for the previous 27 years. The same church was the scene of a happier occasion earlier in 1918, when James' younger sister, Catherine, was married to one of his old colleagues from the Bloxham teaching staff, Charles Allen, who had also served alongside him in the school's OTC. The school's chaplain, Hugh Willimot, assisted in the ceremony. *The Bloxhamist* reassured its readers that 'by special request all the voluntaries were British or Allied music. The service concluded loyally with the National Anthem.'

When we began this research project, MD duly listed all the Old Bloxhamists on a medal finding website, more out of hope than expecting any real chance of success. After seven years there had been nothing (which wasn't surprising, given that we were searching for 80 sets of medals from the 3 million sets that were issued), when out of the blue came an email from Australia, advising that a family (unrelated to the Pastfields) were in possession of James' medals.

After some negotiation, MD purchased the medals which had been taken to Australia when the family emigrated in the 1960s. When they arrived there was a conundrum. The medals were a trio comprising the Mons Star, War Medal and Victory Medal, known affectionately as Pip, Squeak and Wilfred after a popular newspaper cartoon strip at the time. The Mons Star was awarded to men of the BEF who served in action in France and Belgium between 5 August and 22 November 1914. Service after this date entitled the bearer to the 1914/15 Star. The dates on the medals were different and the Mons Star was identified by a small rosette on the ribbon. James' medals are correctly mounted with the rosette. The families of officers were required to claim their medals from the War Office as opposed to those of other ranks whose medals were sent out automatically. James' parents duly claimed the Mons Star Trio, but a note on his medal index card indicates that their request for the Mons Star was rejected as James didn't arrive in theatre until after the qualifying date. So how did the family end up with a Mons Star trio? Did they purchase a replacement medal? Sadly, we will never know, but in 2012 the medals and a Middlesex Regiment cap badge were presented to the school by MD on permanent loan. They hang in the Egerton Library to this day.

1915

As the new year dawned, the British and the French were licking their wounds from the mauling they had received in the first five months of the war. There was resolute optimism on the part of many senior commanders that the war would soon be over; this optimism was not shared by the Secretary of State for War, Lord Kitchener, who firmly believed that the fighting would be protracted and bloody.

The BEF were very much the junior partner to the French both in terms of troop numbers and the amount of the front line held. There was much suspicion between the two armies, and in private at least, many French generals expressed their reservations about the BEF's ability. Marshal Joffre, when asked how many British officers he would like to see in France is said to have replied, 'Just one, and we will take great care to make sure that he's killed.'

The BEF found itself tragically short of men, equipment and above all artillery shells. The production of both artillery pieces and ammunition had been geared to supply the needs of Britain's pre-war colonial fighting requirements, not the industrial slaughter on the scale of the Great War. It became apparent very quickly during the early stages of trench warfare that for an infantry attack to have any chance of success, German lines would need to be subjected to accurate, intense and prolonged artillery bombardment, which naturally required huge quantities of shells.

The lack of trained soldiers was a major cause for concern. The losses of 1914 had decimated both officers and NCOs and a campaign was launched in Britain with the famous picture of Lord Kitchener pointing, his eyes following you from wherever you stand proclaiming 'Your Country Needs You!' The campaign was massively successful and in a matter of weeks almost 100,000 men had volunteered. These so called 'New Army' battalions would take months of training to be ready but provided a ready source of resupply to the armed forces. The idea was to encourage groups who lived, worked or socialised together to join up together to form what would become known as the 'Pals Battalions'. Their names reflected their backgrounds – The 13th York and Lancaster Regiment was known as the Barnsley Pals. The 16th Middlesex Regiment was known as the Footballers' Battalion, the 13th Royal Fusiliers known as the Artists Rifles and so on.

British military planning in the early stages of 1915 fell into two distinct camps – 'Easterners' and 'Westerners'. Easterners, who included in their number the ambitious First Lord of the Admirality, Winston Churchill, favoured expanding the theatre of operations into the East, by launching a campaign to knock Germany's ally Ottoman Turkey out of the war, and thus opening a vital supply route to the beleaguered Russians via the Black Sea. The favoured location was a landing on the Gallipoli peninsula. Three Old Bloxhamists were to lose their lives in the fatally flawed Gallipoli campaign which ran from March 1915 to January 1916. The men who fought at Gallipoli endured some of the worst conditions of any campaign fought during the Great War. A barren, hot and disease-ridden landscape, defended with almost fanatical idealism by a Turkish army inspirationally commanded by Mustafa Kamal, who would go on to become the founding father of modern Turkey, Ataturk.

Those on the War Council who were committed Westerners believed that the Western Front in France or Belgium held the key to success. Sir John French was a committed Westerner, who strongly believed that Ypres held the key to Allied success in the spring of 1915. In the end his hand was forced when the 8th Division was removed from the Ypres salient and was sent to Gallipoli, along with large quantities of the already short supply of artillery shells.

Russian resistance, as well as the sterling work done by the Allies in stemming the German advance in the Autumn of 1914, meant that the Germans found themselves in a position that they really didn't want to be in; fighting a war on two fronts, against the Russians in the East and the British and French in the West. It was this commitment on two fronts that led Marshal Joffre to seek to exploit this perceived numerical advantage, and he demanded the British start pulling their weight and go on the offensive. The British were in an impossible situation; they lacked men, ammunition, and equipment, but were under enormous pressure both politically and militarily to be seen to be supporting the French.

In March 1915, the British did go on the offensive for the first time in the war, when they launched an offensive against the village of Neuve Chappelle in the Artois region of France. The plan was ambitious, capture the heavily fortified village of Neuve Chapelle, continue onto the heights of the Aubers Ridge which lay some two kilometres beyond, and then see what happened. The French would attack in conjunction on the British right from the Notre Dame de Lorrette ridge, engulfing the German lines at Vimy, before sweeping across the Douai plain towards the city of Lens.

The Germans had spent the winter of 1914-15 fortifying their lines with thick belts of barbed wire and well sighted machine gun posts, as well as constructing an equally well defended second line behind and out of sight of the first line.

The battlefields of Artois today are remarkably similar to how they were in 1915, and several Old Bloxhamists were to lose their lives in the pancake-flat fields of this industrial landscape. The attack at Neuve Chapelle was called off after three days' fighting, during which period 11,000 men had been killed, wounded or missing, for little to no material gain.   The lack of artillery shells caused a national outcry and an article published in *The Times* written by Charles à Court Repington (a great personal friend of Sir John French) blamed the Government fully for the failure at Neuve Chapelle. The scandal erupted and caused the collapse of the Liberal government, with a coalition being formed in its place.

A Ministry of Munitions had been created to oversee the production of increased shells for the artillery. Unfortunately the massive supply problems produced shells of poor quality that often failed to explode properly on impact or blew up in their own guns. One Old Bloxhamist was to lose his life later in the war from the explosion of a shell within the breech of the heavy howitzer he was commanding. The Regimental Padre collected what remained of the eight-man gun crew in a single sandbag.

On 22 April at Ypres, the Germans defied the Hague Convention and launched a poison gas attack against the Allies. Thousands of Canadian and French colonial troops were killed and the Germans came very close to securing a spectacular breakthrough, but failed to seize the advantage; heroic defence by the Canadians meant that the line around Ypres held.

In May, the British offensives in Artois continued with battles at Aubers Ridge and Festubert, both of which claimed the lives of Old Bloxhamists. Of all the battles of the Great War, Aubers Ridge is surely the one that conforms most to the viewpoint that WW1 was little more than the needless slaughter of infantry in the face of murderous German machine gun fire. What was supposed to be a gentle stroll across the Artois countryside turned into an offensive that was abandoned after only 15 hours, when 11,000 soldiers were killed, wounded or missing and the line remained staunchly in German hands.

As the fighting raged on in Gallipoli, September saw the launch of yet another British offensive against the Germans in Artois, this time at the grim mining town of Loos. Despite their condemnation of the German use of chemical weapons, Loos was to be the first time that the British would use poison gas themselves. The offensive began on 25 September, and despite mixed results along the British lines, little real ground was gained and those areas where the attack was successful switched hands repeatedly over the following days and weeks. 26 September was the worst day of the war to date for the British Army, with so many men (including an Old Bloxhamist) being killed that the Germans called the battlefield 'das Liechenfeld von Loos'

(The Corpse field of Loos). By the time the offensive ground to a halt in the middle of October, over 60,000 men had become casualties and the line remained very firmly in German hands.

The Gallipoli offensive was abandoned after six months of fighting with hundreds of thousands of casualties on all sides, and Turkey remained in the war. The final troops were evacuated off the Gallipoli peninsula in November 1915, and the survivors limped home to contemplate the unmitigated disaster that the campaign had been. Indeed, the evacuation was considered by many to be the greatest success of the whole affair.

Aside from Gallipoli and the offensives on the Western Front, the British were fighting in Mesopotamia (modern day Iraq) against the Turks and in this forgotten theatre of war two Old Bloxhamists were to lose their lives. In total 13 Old Bloxhamists lost their lives during 1915, a number that was to be dwarfed in subsequent years.

Private Hilary John Pullen Burry
2nd Battalion, Wiltshire Regiment
Pupil at Bloxham School 1910-1911
Killed in action 12 March 1915, aged 20
Commemorated on the Le Touret Memorial to the Missing, France
Panel 46-47

Hilary John Pullen Burry was the son of Horace John and Alma Anna Rosa Pullen Burry, of Rectory House, Sompting in Sussex. Horace was one of ten children, and his siblings included some colourful characters; his eldest brother, Henry, was a doctor but is best known for his membership of the Golden Dawn, a secret magical order, and his friendship with Arthur Conan Doyle, who shared his interest in spiritualism, while his elder sister Bessie was a noted travel author and anthropologist. In 1904, while en route to the West Indies, she visited the White House where she met President Roosevelt. The family were known as the Pullens until 1868, when Horace's father John added his maternal name, Burry, to the family name.

When John died in 1887, the family business was taken over by Horace and his younger brother Arthur. The fertile soil around the village of Sompting had encouraged the development of market gardens and the glasshouse industry, and H. and A. Pullen-Burry Ltd was a market-gardening business which owned 600 acres of fields, nurseries and orchards in and around Sompting, where it was the largest employer. One can still see terraces of houses built for its workers at the west end of the village.

Hilary was born in Sompting on 13 January 1895 and grew up in Rectory House, a substantial home with a Georgian style frontage. According to the family history written by his cousin Tom, Hilary had his appendix removed on the kitchen table at the Rectory, and later would delight in showing the people the scar. He was nine years old when his father died at the age of 44 in 1904. Hilary's mother moved to 53 Beaconsfield Villas in nearby Brighton and Arthur took over the sole running of the business. In 1913 he perfected a system of movable greenhouses with heating, ventilating, and watering systems combined.

Hilary attended the local Board School before being sent away to be a pupil at Bloxham between September 1910 and December 1911. He was confirmed at school by the Bishop of Oxford in April 1911 and was a chapel server. Our photograph of him comes from a group of chapel servers taken in July 1911; five of the 14 boys would not return from the war. He is recorded as having played football at school and having been in Form III. Otherwise, he left little trace in his short time at Bloxham before leaving at the age of 16.

When war broke out in August 1914, Hilary volunteered in Westminster along with his cousin Cyril, Arthur's son. Cyril, known in the family as 'Squib', sang in the choir of St Paul's Cathedral, and his name is one of 24 Choristers on the St Paul's Roll of Honour. Confusingly, Cyril's father spelled the family name with a hyphen between the Pullen and the Burry but Hilary's mother did not, and the school has decided to follow her lead on its memorial. Hilary joined the 2nd Battalion, the Wiltshire Regiment as a Private (Service Number 10906) while Cyril joined the 6th Battalion, Duke of Cornwall's Light Infantry. By January 1915 Hilary was in France with the 2nd Wiltshires as part of the 7th Division. Sadly, his papers did not survive a fire in a storage depot in the Second World War. However, the February edition of *The Bloxhamist* reported that 'he appears to have had an exciting time in the trenches.' The following month the magazine included the following excerpt from a letter by him, written on 21 January: 'I have not experienced much fighting yet. What with a few shells and bullets flying over me I am quite used to it now. . . . It is very wet and muddy in the trenches, besides being dreadfully cold. We live on bully-beef, cheese, jam and biscuits. Bread when we can buy it.'

Sadly, by the time this was published, Hilary was dead, killed in the battle of Neuve Chapelle. Launched on 9 March 1915, this was the first substantial British offensive of the war, and designed as the BEF's contribution to the major Allied offensive in the Artois region. In a pattern which would become wearyingly familiar over the next three years, Haig's First Army quickly broke through only to find any further progress impossible. Neuve Chapelle cost the BEF nearly 13,000 casualties, of which almost 400 came from the 2nd Wiltshires, including Hilary Pullen Burry, killed on 12 March when the German forces commanded by Crown Prince Rupprecht of Bavaria launched a counterattack. Hilary's body has no known grave, and he is listed on the Le Touret Memorial near where he fell. He was 20 years of age (not 19 as the CWGC has it).

Hilary's mother never informed the school of her son's death – the loss of her only son may well have been too much for a widow to bear given the growing problems of the family business due to foreign competition and the effects of the war. In addition, the family also had to bear the death of Hilary's cousin Cyril near Arras in April 1916. The Pullen Burrys' hopes of passing the running of the family business to the two boys had been shattered. When the Vicar of Sompting asked for names and details to go on the village war memorial, Arthur Pullen-Burry replied on a postcard with the briefest details for both the boys, and it was only an enquiry in May 2013 from Eileen Colwell of a Sussex local history society, the Lancing and Sompting Pastfinders, which alerted the school to the fact that Hilary was missing from its memorial. His name was included in the additional plaque unveiled in a special service in March 2013. Since then, contact has been made with two of Hilary's first cousins (twice removed), Elaine Cottrell and Steph Lynch, who have been very helpful with the complicated Pullen-Burry family history. They were able to inform us that Hilary had a sister, Dorothy, who was twice married and lived until 1982; her second marriage was to playwright Roland Pertwee, father of the Doctor Who actor Jon Pertwee. Hilary's cousin Cyril had a brother, John, who moved to Canada in 1915 to become a railway surveyor, changed his name to George Robinson and enlisted in the Canadian Expeditionary Force in Grande Prairie, Alberta in June 1916. Known to the family as Jack, he survived the war and went on to become a noted palaeontologist, dying in 1982.

The search for a photograph of Hilary was perhaps the most challenging of the 80. He was only at the school for a very short time and there were no known images of him in the school archives. His family in Britain and New Zealand were unfortunately unable to assist. In May 2017 SB finally found a photograph of Hilary among a group of chapel servers in July 1911. It was on a loose page which had fallen out of an album many years ago, and he was labelled as Burry not Pullen Burry, so it was fortunate that it was spotted at all. The dates fit and there was no pupil called Burry in the school's existence. It is definitely Hilary Pullen Burry.

Private Frank Harold May Robertson
5th Battalion, Canadian Infantry Force
Pupil at Bloxham School 1904-1905
Died 12 April 1915, aged 20
Buried in St Omer Cemetery, France
Grave 1.A.78

Frank Robertson was a local boy, the second of four sons of Adderbury doctor James Sprent Robertson and his Brazilian wife Lilian. Frank's uncle was the noted soldier and imperial administrator Sir George Scott Robertson, who was best known for his heroism at the siege of Chitral in 1895, and who later sat as the Liberal MP for Bradford Central between 1906 and 1916. Three of the boys attended Bloxham School. Frank was born on 6 May 1894. His oldest brother James Edward (born 1891) was a pupil at the school between 1901 and 1905, with Frank and Thomas (born 1895) joining him at half term of the Michaelmas Term in 1904. Frank is reported as having taken part in a gymnastic display in the school's new gymnasium in December 1904, alongside Tom, but otherwise they were at the school for too short a time to make much impact. Both left at Easter 1905, meaning that they were only at the school for one and a half terms. It is likely that the boys' departure was connected to their father's retirement. Dr Robertson originally lived at Hill House in Adderbury, a village a couple of miles from Bloxham, but the family then moved to 1, Perham Road, West Kensington. By the time of Frank's death their address is given as 83, Prince of Wales Mansions in similarly well-to-do Battersea Park.

James left Bloxham a term after his brothers and became a bank clerk. In 1912 he was working in Sao Paolo, at the Bank of British South America when he was, according to The Bloxhamist, 'accidentally shot' and killed in June 1912.

Frank moved to Canada, a common decision by Bloxhamists of his generation. At the turn of the century Canada was one of the most underpopulated countries on earth, and the

massive expansion of the urban towns and cities after the Industrial Revolution had reduced the amount of land available in the UK for agriculture. In 1900 the Canadian government passed the Land Aliens Act which speeded up the immigration process for British and Commonwealth nationals wanting to relocate to Canada. With land costing as little as $5 an acre, the opportunities for land holding and agribusiness were huge. The Headmaster at the time, George Ward, told pupils: 'I can strongly advise anyone who has at any time a chance of visiting the country to take it at once, but if a man wishes to make his home there, he should certainly go out in the early years of life, before he is too old to learn and to form new habits.'

Frank was a civil engineer by trade. He enlisted as Private 12616 in the 5th Battalion Canadian Infantry (The Saskatchewan Regiment) on 24 September 1914. He was unmarried at the time of his enlistment, and was described as being 5 foot 8 inches tall, of medium build, with black hair. The 5th Battalion embarked for France in early 1915, and was in training in France when Frank Robertson contracted cerebrospinal meningitis, being treated at the base hospital in Saint Omer. The account of his final days as revealed by his medical records makes for horrific reading as his condition deteriorated rapidly:

6/4/15: LP (lumbar puncture), CSF (cerebrospinal fluid) turbid and under pressure. Upper dorsal puncture – unsuccessful.
7/4/15: Much worse. Complains of mucus collection in throat. Very restless but mentally clear at most times. Purulent conjunctival discharge both eyes. No incontinence.
11/4/15: No improvement. Lies listless all day. Takes a little. Very feeble. Losing flesh rapidly. Incontinent. Later – comatose.
12/4/15: Patient died 7:45 a.m.

Frank Robertson was 20 years of age when he died. He was buried in Longuenesse (St Omer) Souvenir Cemetery, which lies on the town's southern outskirts. The inscription his parents chose for his gravestone was 'In short measure life may perfect be.' It is the last line of Ben Jonson's poem 'The Noble Nature'. Thomas would be killed just over a year later at the Battle of Jutland.

Second Lieutenant Robert Ellis Cunliffe
2nd Battalion, Royal Berkshire Regiment
Pupil at Bloxham School 1906-1909
Killed in action 9 May 1915, aged 21
Commemorated on the Ploegsteert Memorial, Belgium
Panel 7

Robert Ellis Cunliffe was born on 17 October 1893 at 22, London St., Calcutta, to Alfred Ellis Cunliffe and his wife Agnes. He had an older sister, Muriel (born 1890), and a younger brother, Cyril Henley Cunliffe (born 1901). Just as his father had been, Alfred was a member of the Bengal Civil Service. So was his uncle, also called Robert Ellis Cunliffe; the family had a long tradition of government and military service in India. Alfred's grandfather, General Sir Robert Henry Cunliffe CB, had served in the Bengal Army and two of his sons had been killed in the Indian Mutiny in 1857. The family tree is complex, with a profusion of Robert Cunliffes to trap the unwary genealogist, and the Cunliffes were a distinguished family. Alfred's cousin, Sir Robert Alfred Cunliffe, served as a Liberal MP, and if 'our' Robert had survived, he would ultimately have succeeded to the Cunliffe baronetcy. As it was, the 6th Baronet, Sir Foster Cunliffe, lecturer in History at Oxford University and Middlesex county cricketer, died of his wounds at Ovillers on the Somme on 10 July 1916, and as both he and the 7th Baronet, his brother Robert Neville Cunliffe, died childless, the title passed to their second cousin Cyril, the younger brother of 'our' Robert Cunliffe, in May 1949.

Robert was shown on the 1901 census as living at 14-16 Lascelles Terrace, Eastbourne, in the care of Florence Mellish, whose occupation was listed as 'carer of Indian children' (meaning children of British residents of India). He then attended Ascham School, a small preparatory school in Eastbourne founded by the Rev. W.N. Willis in 1889. Ascham had only seven pupils at a time until it merged with St Vincent's in 1908 and became, as Ascham St Vincent's, a larger and very successful preparatory school with a strong track record of gaining places at the public schools and winning scholarships to Eton, Malvern and Eastbourne. As with several of the 80, it is unclear why the Cunliffes should have chosen Bloxham for their eldest son (Cyril would later attend Dulwich College), but that is where he went in January 1906, at the age of 12.

Of the 11 boys who started at the school that term, five would perish in the coming war (in addition to Robert, Basil Brooks, Philip Davy, Laurence Harris and Geoffrey Rawlings). He was one of 20 boys confirmed by the Bishop of Oxford in the school chapel in April of that year. He showed some athletic ability by finishing second in the Junior Long Jump on Sports Day in 1907, although by the sound of the report in *The Bloxhamist*, this was not a contest that took a lot of winning: 'anyone who had taken the trouble to practice (sic) beforehand sufficiently must have won. Few managed to get in more than one jump in three tries, and that a half-hearted hesitating one.' The following year, when he won the same event with a jump of 15 ft. 2 ½ in., it was described as 'a creditable performance'. He also won the Junior 100 yards in a time of 12.2 seconds. He made his first appearance for the 2nd XI at Cricket in the Summer Term in 1908 ('Cunliffe might be quite good at fielding, but he does not take sufficient interest'), and progressed to the 1st XI in both cricket and football for his last year at the school, as well as being awarded his Gym Colours. He also managed to carry off the Drawing Prize in 1909 and served as the Props Master in the school play before leaving at the end of the Michaelmas Term (December 1909), at the age of 16.

After Bloxham, Robert Cunliffe headed for London where he had a job working as a bank clerk in the Cavendish Square branch of Parr's Bank, and he resided at 31, Marmora Road, Honor Oak, a leafy suburb in South London, while his parents were now living at The Flushings, Crawley in Sussex. Parr's had originally been a local bank based in Warrington, but its acquisition in 1909 of Stuckey's Bank, a powerful presence in Somerset, created the sixth largest joint stock bank in England, with 400 branches and combined deposits of £38 million. In 1918 Parr's amalgamated with the London County & Westminster Bank Ltd, which would merge into the National Westminster Bank ('NatWest') in 1970.

Robert enlisted into the Territorial Army on 17 June 1913, as Private 1560 the 16th Battalion the County of London Regiment (the Queen's Westminsters). He was 5'9" tall and of average build and was declared fit for service in the Infantry despite his extremely poor eyesight. His father was a member of the Reform Club, where a fellow member was Lord Kitchener, Secretary of State for War. It was not uncommon for well-connected families to use their influence to ensure that their sons gained commissions when issues such as poor eyesight would normally have precluded them from service. The most famous example of this is John Kipling, son of the poet Rudyard Kipling who had been rejected from military service on five occasions, on account of his terrible eyesight. His father's influence managed to gain him a commission into the Irish Guards, where he was to lose his life at the Battle of Loos in 1915.

Robert was commissioned as a 2nd Lieutenant into the 2nd Battalion, the Royal Berkshire Regiment on 26 September 1914. At this time, the 2nd Battalion were on their way back from active service in India, arriving in England on 22 October 1914. The regiment was transferred to Winchester where it became part of 25th Brigade, 8th Division, before embarking for France on 5 November 1914. Cunliffe's medal index card shows that he landed in France around this time, and therefore it seems likely that he joined the regiment in England. There is some confusion over Robert's service record, as the CWGC states that he 'left for France Oct. 1914, with Queen's Westminsters, having previously joined the regiment as a volunteer', which contradicts his medal index card. One newspaper report of his death suggests that he served with the Westminsters in Flanders until March 1915, when he was gazetted Second Lieutenant on the Special List (officers who possessed a specialist skill which could be of particular use to the military, for example linguists or engineers), attached to the 2nd Battalion of the Royal Berkshire Regiment.

Whatever the case, in May 1915 the Battalion found itself in action at the Battle of Aubers Ridge, an attack by the BEF's First Army on the German line on 9 May 1915. This was the next stage in a costly series of British offensives in French Flanders after the fighting at Neuve Chapelle. Of all the BEF's offensives on the Western Front, it is surely the one which conforms most closely to the stereotype of men sent across No Man's Land to be slaughtered in senseless frontal assaults. Unfortunately for the British infantry advancing across the pancake-flat terrain, the preliminary barrage had been inadequate, the wire had not been cut and the German defenders were ready for them. In the northern sector of the battlefield, the 2nd Rifle Brigade and the 1st Royal Irish Rifles were launched in the first wave of the attack at 05.40 a.m. C and D companies of the 2nd Berkshires were ordered to the front trench in support of the 2nd Rifle Brigade, with A and B companies in reserve.

Captain Charles Nugent of D Company recorded that on his arrival in the front trench, many of the Rifle Brigade were still waiting there, and many of those who had already gone could be seen from the parapet, lying pinned down trying to take cover in the foot-high vegetation. Lieutenant Lipscombe led the first two sections of 15th and 16th platoons over the breastworks, while the other two sections prepared to follow. They found the fire trench and sap, out ahead of the front line, crowded with men of the Rifle Brigade and some Irish riflemen. Confusion was created by reports that an unknown officer had ordered them to remain there, while one junior NCO reported that the order to 'retire at the double' had been given by 'a Captain Dee of the Royal Irish Rifles'. The Battalion War diary entry, which was written by Captain Nugent, advises that after Lieutenant Lipscombe was sent out into No Man's Land it was not clear what happened to him.

At this point, Nugent ordered Cunliffe to go out into No Man's Land and find Lieutenant Lipscombe, to try and establish whether his platoon had made it to the German Lines. Cunliffe followed his orders and was never seen again. It was at this point, in chaotic circumstances, that Robert Cunliffe must have been killed, one of twelve officers of the Royal Berkshires killed that day, including the commander, Lt. Col. H.M. Finch, and his second in command, Major R.P. Harvey, as well as Lieutenant Lipscombe. Another eight were wounded and six reported missing, along with 52 other ranks killed, 185 wounded and 39 missing in what the battalion war diary labelled 'a futile action'. The commander of 25th Brigade, Brigadier General Lowry-Cole, was himself shot and killed while standing on the parapet to rally his men. The attack was an unmitigated disaster, being fought on the same battlefield as the fighting at Neuve Chapelle in March.

In all, the British suffered over 11,000 casualties in 15 hours, and the offensive was suspended after only one day. It had achieved nothing whatsoever, with no ground won and no tactical advantage gained. The French had launched an initially successful attack fifteen miles to the south, but there is no evidence that the British attack helped in any way. Certainly, the Germans felt no need to commit their reserves to stiffen their defences at Aubers.

His commanding officer wrote to Robert's parents saying:

> The machine gun and shrapnel fire was very heavy and I am sure there is little doubt that your son was killed that day. Captain Nugent who commanded your son's company last saw him when he started over our own breastwork, and I can find no one who saw him afterwards. He must have advanced at the head of the platoon part of the way to the German trench and been killed there. Your son fell like many other officers of the Brigade gallantly leading his men against the enemy.

Only four out of twenty-four officers survived. As was often the case, there is a clear contradiction between the letter and the content of the Battalion war diary. *The Bloxhamist* recalled of Robert Cunliffe:

> Looking back to the time when he was here, we have pleasant recollections of a cheerful boy always ready to enter into any fun that might be going on, but always capable of discerning in a moment anything that was wrong and shunning it. We can find no better words in which to express his character than those used by one who knew him well: 'He had the making of a fine fellow, and was a great favourite with all of us. He died in service, and I believe he served his generation as well as his king, and that very humbly he sought to serve the King of kings.'

Like so many of the fallen at Aubers, Robert Cunliffe's body was never found (or identified, at any rate), and he is commemorated on the Ploegsteert Memorial to the Missing. Captain Charles Nugent, now an acting Major, was to die on 19 November 1918 in the influenza epidemic at the end of the war and is buried at Valenciennes Communal Cemetery.

As well as the Bloxham School memorial, Robert Cunliffe is commemorated on a plaque at No. 1, Cavendish Square in London, which records the names of seven employees of Parr's Bank who worked at the branch there and perished in the war. He is also on a memorial in All Souls Church, Eastbourne and on the Ascham St Vincent's Memorial Arch in the town. The school later served as the preparatory school for Eastbourne College but was demolished after closing in 1977, but the archway still stands at Ascham Place. It is about 30 feet high and 25 feet wide, and contains the inscription 'In memory of 49 gallant men who were at school here in their early boyhood and gave their lives in the service of their country during the Great War of 1914-19. At the going down of the sun and in the morning, we will remember them.' The spandrels to the arch are carved with shield and floral motifs. On the obverse side, the arch has an inscription reading 'They went with songs to the battle, they were young, straight of limb, true of eye steady and aglow. They were staunch to the end against odds uncounted. They fell with their faces to the foe.'

The CWGC lists Robert's parents as Agnes Cunliffe, of 'Corylus', Radlett, Hertfordshire, and the late Alfred Edward Cunliffe, though other records suggest that Alfred lived until 1920.

Second Lieutenant Francis Edmund Langton Riddle
2nd Battalion, Oxfordshire and Buckinghamshire Light Infantry
Pupil at Bloxham School 1903-1911
Killed in action 16 May 1915, aged 21
Commemorated on the Le Touret Memorial to the Missing, France
Panel 26

Francis Riddle is a significant figure in Bloxham's Great War story, not least because it is thanks to him that we have a collection of photographs of each of the fallen. He was a local boy, being the third son of the Vicar of Tadmarton, the Reverend Arthur Esmond Riddle and his wife Edith May, and he was born on 10 June 1893. The two sides of Francis' family came from very different traditions. Not only his father was a clergyman but his paternal grandfather Joseph Esmond Riddle was a noted preacher, lexicographer and classical scholar, sufficiently eminent to be invited by Oxford University to deliver the Bampton Lectures in 1852. In contrast, his mother's side of the family was strongly military: his maternal grandfather was a senior officer in the Indian Army, Major General James Kennedy of the 25th Bengal Native Infantry, and James' father had been a major general too.

Francis was one of six children – he had twin brothers, Robert and Arthur, who were three years older than him, as well as two sisters, Margaret (Madge) and Annie and a younger brother, Gerald. Sadly, the family was affected by tragedy when Francis was five years old. His mother died in March 1899, at the age of 44, and his father was left to bring up the family on his own.

The Rev. Riddle would have been familiar with Bloxham School, as it was only two miles distant from Tadmarton, and he had played cricket there regularly since 1891 for a variety of invitation sides. He chose to send his oldest three sons as boarders to Bloxham in 1903, and along with his twin brothers, Francis (Frank as he was known at school) arrived at Bloxham at the start of the summer term, 7 May 1903; at that time the summer term started and ended a good deal later than is now the case. While his brothers were placed in Form IV, Frank started in Form II. A second tragedy struck the family in October 1906, when Frank was 13 years of age. His brother Robert died at the school from appendicitis, as recorded by a plaque in the school chapel. One can only speculate as to the trauma for Frank of the loss of an older brother, not to mention the impact on Robert's twin. It is, surely, significant that Arthur ceased to board at the school and became a day boy at this point.

It soon became clear that Frank was an excellent sportsman, being spotted as a cricketer early on. In May 1907 his younger brother Geoffrey had joined him and Arthur at Bloxham. He was among 23 boys confirmed at the school in March 1908 - six of them would not survive the coming war. He made his mark on Sports Day in April 1908, finishing second to Robert Cunliffe in the final of the Junior 100 yards in a time of 12.2 seconds. The following April, he finished second to Leslie Bowler, the best athlete of his generation, in the school senior steeplechase, with Arthur Riddle finishing fourth. The School Sports took place on Easter Tuesday, April 13th, and according to *The Bloxhamist*, 'the weather was most unpleasant, heavy rain falling till nearly the end of the proceedings.' While Arthur won the mile, Frank carried off the cup for the 220 yards in a time of 27.2 seconds. Now aged 16, Frank was also old enough to make an impact in team sports. He was in the XI which played the school's first ever hockey fixture, in February 1910 against MCS, Oxford and was awarded his hockey colours at the end of the season. *The Bloxhamist* adjudged him to be a useful but erratic forward: 'Has plenty of pace, centres well, but lacks judgment. Has scored some very good goals.' In April 1910 he won the school steeplechase, leading all the way from Ffrench, though unable to shake him off until he pulled away with a sprint in the finishing straight to win by ten yards. The performance was all the more impressive given the continual rainfall in the week before the race which left conditions heavy and meant that 'a fatigue party had to be sent around the course to collect shoes.'

Sports Day in May 1910 was a personal triumph for Frank, and it was fitting that his father was asked to say a few words at the end of the prize giving. He won the Senior Long Jump (17 ft. 2 in.) and finished second in the 100 Yards in a thrilling race during which he managed to get level with his rival, Nicholl. 20 yards from the tape, only for Nicholl to win by 'about a foot'. He also finished runner-up in the 220 Yards, the Quarter Mile, the High Jump and the Mile, though in the latter *The Bloxhamist* was scathing about the standard: 'The Senior Mile was conspicuous for its excessive badness ; the four runners seemed to be trying to keep behind each other all the way. We have had to complain of a similar state of affairs in this event in previous years, and we strongly advise the committee to fix a standard and award no prizes unless it is reached. It is absurd to give good prizes to people who loaf around a mile in 6 mins. 5 secs.' Overall, Frank won the Senior Championship (the 'Victor Ludorum') with a score of 425 points compared with Nicholl's 405.

He passed the Senior Oxford Locals in July 1910; these were the public examinations sat by the school's pupils each summer. He was awarded his football colours in December, scoring the opening goal in a 4-0 victory over MCS the following week. It was reported of him at the end of the season that he was 'a fast dashing forward' who 'employs good tactics and gets well across. Has scored some really brilliant goals.' The School sports for 1911 once more saw Frank carry off the prize for the Victor Ludorum, this time by a convincing margin. He won the 100 Yards in 11 seconds in a close finish, the Long Jump, Quarter Mile and Shot Putt and finished second in the High Jump. At the prize-giving the Rev. Riddle announced his desire to present a challenge cup to be held by the winner of the Quarter Mile, and this fine silver cup is still awarded for the equivalent race, the 400 metres.

In his final hockey season Frank earned praise from *The Bloxhamist* for his pace and hard shooting, while of his cricket it was reported that 'he has come on as much as any member of the team. Very keen and painstaking bat, who puts a great deal of power behind his strokes.' At the end of his final term he was, along with Geoffrey Bowler and Gordon Peecock, one of three pupils selected to accompany the Chaplain and Mr Wilson in representing the school at the dedication of the towering new chapel at Lancing, an event of enormous significance for the Woodard schools.

Towards the end of his school career, the OTC played an increasingly prominent part in Frank's life at Bloxham and would determine his plans after leaving. He was one of six cadets who attended a week-end camp at Shere during the Easter holidays in 1911, and in July he was promoted from Lance-Corporal to the rank of Lance Sergeant. That month he was one of sixteen cadets, who along with the OC and Sergeant-Instructor made up the Contingent which represented the school at the Royal Review held at Windsor. He was awarded the Provost's Cup for the highest score in the OTC's first annual shooting competition and attended the annual camp at Tidworth Pennings after term ended. Even after leaving school, Frank worked with the Bloxham OTC for a term, and was promoted to Sergeant (this was the spelling of the word the school's OTC persisted in employing; the British Army spelt it Serjeant until November 1953).

Frank was an active Old Boy and came back to play football against the school in November 1913. Playing on the opposite team to his brother Geoffrey, Frank had the satisfaction of ending on the winning side, 3-2. On 1 July 1913, he was gazetted as a 2nd Lieutenant in the Special Reserve of officers in the 3rd Battalion of the Oxford and Buckinghamshire Light Infantry. He worked for much of his time as the Assistant Recruiting Officer at Oxford's Cowley Barracks and on the outbreak of war enlisted as a Second Lieutenant in the 2nd Battalion OBLI. He went to France on 25 October 1914 and appears to have spent several months working as the Quartermaster for the regiment in reserve. He spent a brief leave at home in late March before returning to the trenches in time for his first field action in May 1915.

The Battalion went into action on 15 May at the Battle of Festubert, and Riddle seems to have been called up as a replacement early on the morning of 16 May, arriving around 08:00 a.m. The Battalion went into action against the heavily defended German lines opposite Richebourg L'Avoué at around 08:45 a.m. Frank Riddle was reported as having been killed almost immediately. The exact circumstances of his death have caused a number of headaches from a research perspective, but it has finally been established that while he had indeed been in the frontline trenches on occasions, usually accompanying rations, it would appear that the action of 16 May was his first taste of combat.

He was apparently buried near breastworks north of the rue du Bois, but his body was never recovered from the spot. According to *The Bloxhamist*, he was reported missing on 20 May but it was not until 29 May that his father received confirmation that his son had died. Another subaltern wrote to the Rev. Riddle to say that 'he will be missed by his company and men more than I can say, who always relied on him and looked up to him in an emergency', while Frank's Commanding Officer informed him that:

> He had got on so well here, and we were all so fond of him that we shall miss his presence very much. He gave his life fighting for his King and Country and helping to add to the reputation of the regiment with all his might. They for their part have lost a brave, cheery gentleman and one who, from my experience when he was under my command, found no duty too much for him and whose one idea was to help.'

In July 2019 the authors walked the battlefield at Festubert and using modern GPS technology were able to locate the approximate position of the German machine guns that caused such devastation to the OBLI. The pancake-flat fields, devoid of any cover and intersected with wide and deep drainage ditches is most unsuitable for infantry assault. Major Gowen of the Oxford & Bucks LI wrote in his memoirs, 'I can confirm that at least some of the men made it to the German wire, because I could see their bodies caught up in it, fluttering in the wind like mother's washing on washing day.'

The Bloxhamist reflected that 'it is exceedingly difficult to express in anything like adequate terms the greatness of his character – great because so simple. *O si sic omnes.*' The Editor expressed the hope that the Riddle family would derive some comfort from 'the knowledge that a Christian gentleman has given his life in defence of a great cause. In him our motto once more finds fulfilment — *Justorum semita lux splendens.*'

Frank Riddle was 21 when he died. He is commemorated on the Le Touret Memorial to the Missing in France and also on the stone war cross in Tadmarton, as well as a small but beautiful stained-glass window in St Nicholas, Tadmarton. The Rev. Riddle sent the school a photograph of his son so that he would be remembered at his old school – as the school magazine commented, 'This should serve to keep bright the memory of one who was a credit to the British Army, both at School and in the Regular Forces', and this was the start of a tradition which eventually led to the school having photographs of all those who fell in the war. Ironically, his was one of the photographs which was lost in the vestry fire in April 1985, and the poignant photograph of Frank which now hangs in the Egerton Library is taken from a pre-war OTC Camp.

The Rev. Riddle clearly cherished his continuing connection with his son's old school. At the School Sports in 1916 he was back to give away the prizes and pointed out that Sports Day was the anniversary of his son's death in France. He donated a guinea to the fund for a war memorial in chapel and was present when it was unveiled on All Saints' Day, 1920. He continued to contribute to the school's fund-raising, including the fund for a new swimming baths in 1922.

Both of Frank's surviving brothers were to serve in the Great War in the same regiment as him. Gerald, who like so many Bloxhamists of his generation went out to Canada after school, became a clerk in Newfoundland before he enlisted in the ranks in the Canadian Army when war broke out. He rose to became Company Sergeant Major before gaining a commission in September 1918 in his brother's old battalion. Arthur enlisted in the Public Schools Battalion (16th Middlesex Regiment) in 1914 before being commissioned in the 3rd Oxford & Bucks LI in March 1915, two months before Frank's death. Arthur would go on to serve in France, where he was wounded at Le Plantin on 8 September 1915, not far from where his brother Francis had died a few months earlier, and Mesopotamia, where he served for the last two years of the war.

Arthur studied French at Oxford after the war and was ultimately ordained. He also became an author, publishing 'The Vandal' in 1926. The book was advertised as 'an epic on the causes of war', and one might expect the loss of a beloved younger brother to have dominated Arthur's thinking on the recent war, but we should be wary of making easy assumptions: at the end of his book Arthur states that 'Originally I undertook this little work with the intention of expressing the devilish character of war, but all unconsciously there seems to be portrayed in it something of the heroism and nobility of Christ.' Frank's sister Annie married one of his Bloxham contemporaries, the Rev. E.S. Morton, a shell shock victim from the war, in June 1924.

Captain John Carandini Wilson
1st Australian Imperial Force
Pupil at Bloxham School 1896-1898
Died of wounds 21 May 1915, aged 32
Buried in Alexandria (Chatby) Military Cemetery, Egypt
Grave K.20

John Carandini Wilson was the grandson of the opera singer Marie Carandini, who had emigrated to Australia with her parents, where she married Girolamo Carandini, the 10th Marquis of Sarzano, an Italian political refugee, and she went on to enjoy an illustrious career as a noted prima donna in the operas of Bellini and Verdi; she sang for many years in Melbourne and Sydney and toured the United States and New Zealand. She had eight children, and one of whom was Marie Emma Carandini, John's mother. Another was Frank James (originally Francesco Giacomo) Carandini, the grandfather of the distinguished British actor Sir Christopher Lee, who also had Carandini as one of his forenames. John's second cousin was the James Bond writer Ian Fleming.

John was born in Brisbane on 5 January 1882, the eldest of three boys born to Robert Walker Wilson and Marie Emma Carandini. Of his two brothers, Walter would go on to have a distinguished military and sporting career while the youngest, Torrence, served in the Royal Navy but was killed in a railway accident in Roodepoort in South Africa in February 1910. The marriage of John's parents ended in 1899 in divorce on the grounds of desertion. It was reported that Robert was 'cold and indifferent to her', and after his business failed he went to America. The last Marie heard from him was in 1894, when he was believed to be living in London or Scotland. By this time Marie and the boys had also moved to England, and John was a pupil at Bloxham School between September 1896 and April 1898.

He is listed on his school record card as the son of Mrs Wilson of 3 Campden Grove, Kensington. He was obviously something of an athlete – he won the Junior 100 Yards on Sports Day in 1896 and was the winner of the 1/3 of a mile Jubilee Race held to mark Queen Victoria's Diamond Jubilee in 1897, every boy in the school entering and being handicapped depending on the year of their birth; he received a silver cup for his victory. He was confirmed in April 1897 and gave a recitation at a concert in November of the same year. He played for the school's 2nd XI football team as a 14-year old; *The Bloxhamist* reported that 'Wilson centres well and should be a good outside, but he must stand up to everyone, and go for the ball whether the man is there or not.' He made it into the 1st XI the following March but left at the end of that term. By this time his mother had remarried, to a Herbert Stokes, in London.

After he left Bloxham the school lost touch with John for good - the only mention of him after he left is a reference to him being 'probably with the Engineers' in *The Bloxhamist* for March 1900, even though he was not listed in the Bloxham Roll of Honour for the Boer War. In fact, he had joined up as a 2nd Lieutenant in the 3rd Battalion, Loyal North Lancashire Regiment on 5 January 1900. He embarked for Malta to join the battalion, which had been stationed there for garrison duty, and for the next year trained and moved around the island. The Regiment was sent a Farewell Order by the island's commanding officer, praising their good conduct and soldier-like behaviour. On 2 March 1901 the battalion embarked on the P&O transport ship *Formosa* to South Africa. John had been promoted to Lieutenant on 22 September 1900, as noted in the list of officers. The battalion served in South Africa from 1901 to 1902 providing volunteer service companies. The medal rolls for the 3rd Loyal North Lancashire Regiment for the Queens South Africa medal shows that Lieutenant J C Wilson was entitled to the QSA with Cape Colony, South Africa 1901 and South Africa 1902 clasps, though he was not entitled to the King's South Africa medal. The battalion left South Africa from Port Elizabeth and arrived at Southampton on 14 March 1902.

When the Boer War ended, John resigned his commission to take up wheat-growing in the Canadian north-west. This venture did not prosper, and after trying other means of earning a living, both in Canada and the United States, he became a journalist in Los Angeles, working on the *The Los Angeles Times*, and was there in October 1912 when strikers wrecked its offices with a bomb which killed 21 *Times* employees. Returning to his homeland in December 1912, John wrote articles and theatre criticism for *The Sydney Mail* before becoming the military correspondent and dramatic critic for *The Sunday Times* in Sydney. It is likely that John would have known two other Sydney journalists who were shortly to make names for themselves and who would be forever linked with the events of the Gallipoli campaign: Charles Bean, who was to become Australia's official war historian, and Keith Murdoch, father of Rupert. Like John, Bean wrote for *The Sydney Mail* as well as *The Sydney Morning Herald*, while Murdoch spent three years as the political correspondent for *The Age*.

John enlisted soon after the outbreak of war in 1914, joining the 1st Australian Imperial Force on 13 September as a Second Lieutenant, giving 'Bloxham College' as his place of schooling and 'journalist' as his profession. He was described as a single man and a British subject. His address was given as Chatsworth, a mansion in the fashionable Potts Point suburb of Sydney, and his religion listed as Church of England. On his medical certificate, which was signed by the Battalion's MO Captain John Willoughby Bean, Charles Bean's younger brother, he was stated to be 5 foot 9 ¾ inches tall and 12 stone 8 pounds in weight. As a 2nd Lieutenant he was posted to D Company, 3rd Battalion (NSW), 1st Infantry Brigade, one of the first infantry units raised for the AIF. As someone with previous campaign experience John was a valuable commodity, and he was promoted to Captain on 18 October 1914.

Two days later, the 3rd Battalion set sail on *HMAT Euripides* A14 from Sydney and arrived in Egypt on 2 December. After training in Egypt Wilson sailed with his battalion for Gallipoli and took part in the landing at Anzac Cove on 25 April 1915, his battalion coming ashore in the second and third waves. Some 8,000 ANZAC troops landed on Z Beach that day, disembarking further north than intended and under steep cliffs. By the end of 25 April, the ANZACs had established a precarious front on a series of ridges while strong Turkish reinforcements occupied the commanding heights of Sari Bair inland. Strong posts were formed along the second ridge, each soon to be named after their commanders – Courtney's, Steele's, Quinn's.

On the night of Monday 26 April the 3rd Battalion was committed to the firing line on MacLaurin's Hill, and a half-company under Wilson was put in to strengthen the line of the 11th Battalion at Courtney's Post. According to Charles Bean, Wilson was observing through field glasses in a trench forward of Quinn's Post while trying to find out who was on their right flank when he was hit. He was not the only officer to be hit while exposing himself for a better view – Colonel MacLaurin himself would be killed by a sniper's bullet on MacLaurin's Hill the next day. Wilson lay in the trench for 30 hours before he was taken out and sent back to Egypt for treatment. The Australian press reported that 'Capt. John Carandini Wilson, reported dangerously wounded, had a most adventurous career.' He died of the effects of wounds received, recorded as being a perforating wound of the scalp from a gunshot, on 21 May 1915 in No. 17 General Hospital at Alexandria. He was buried at Chatby Cemetery, Alexandria, by Reverend A. V. C. Henderson.

The Army Corps Commander (General Sir William Birdwood) included Wilson among a list of troops who had been brought to his notice for having performed various acts of conspicuous gallantry or valuable service following the landings, and on 5 November 1915 he was mentioned in despatches in the London Gazette.

John Carandini Wilson's will, written on 20 January 1915, stated 'In the event of my death I give the whole of my property and effects to Edith Louise Nelson, care Frank Drummond Esq., 36 Third Street. Bangor, Maine, USA.' We do not know who she was or what her relationship to him was. A note dated 26 May 1915 to Base Records advised that they were letting relatives residing in England know directly of Captain Wilson's death. A parcel and valise containing his personal effects were sent home on 13 August 1915, but the Cairo authorities had clearly mixed things up, as a letter from the Thomas Cook travel agents on 31 March 1916 records that the recipient, an F. G. Wilson of Melbourne, returned the effects as he had no such relative. Eventually John's effects found their way to Edith Nelson. Strangely, his brother Captain Walter Carandini Wilson was listed as John's next of kin rather than Edith or his mother.

Walter, who was educated at Tonbridge School, played rugby on the wing for Leicester and England, winning caps against Ireland and Scotland in 1907, and had a fine war record, serving with the 2nd Battalion Leicestershire Regiment, earning the DSO and the MC. In March 1919 he was awarded the OBE as well as the Medaille d'Honneur by the President of the French Republic. He went on to serve in military missions to Finland and the Baltic States after the war was over. He served as a Group Captain in the RAF during the Second World War and died on 12 April 1968.

Neither Walter nor his mother, who died in 1945, ever notified John's old school of his service in the Great War or his death, and so his name was not listed on the war memorial in chapel and would never have been recorded if it were not for MD's research. He came across the reference to 'Bloxham College' when researching another Old Bloxhamist in the Australian Archives. As a result, John Carandini Wilson's name was added in November 2014 to the memorial below those of two more members of the Bloxham community, Harry Ayres and Hilary Pullen Burry, whose names had only recently been discovered. It was sobering to realise, as the centenary of the Great War was being marked, that names were still being added to memorials all over the country.

Captain Reginald Victor Rylands
1/7th Battalion, Manchester Regiment
Pupil at Bloxham School 1902-1906
Killed in action 29 May 1915, aged 22
Buried in Redoubt Cemetery, Gallipoli, Turkey
Grave IX.D.2

Reginald Victor Rylands was the eldest son of solicitor Richard Walter Rylands and his wife Mary, and was born in Stockport, Manchester on 9 December 1892. He had a younger brother, Harold Bertram, who was also a pupil at Bloxham and was killed on the Somme in 1916. Victor (as he was known at Bloxham) was a pupil at the school between 1902 and 1906 before moving to Shrewsbury School. On leaving Shrewsbury in 1908, he spent some time in Germany, and then at Manchester University where he studied law, taking his Bachelor of Law in June 1912 and frequently taking part in speaking competitions and mock trials. Manchester's School of Law now awards an annual prize, consisting of a bunch of silver keys on a leather fob, known as the Rylands Helm, for the student who produces the most impressive cross examination in the

mock trials known as 'moots' as a part of the final year criminal law course. Victor joined his father's law firm Boote, Edgar, Grace and Rylands, passing his final exams in June 1914.

Having been a member of the OTC at Shrewsbury, the military played a large part in Victor's life, and he served as an officer in the 7th (Territorial Force) Manchester Regiment, becoming a 2nd Lieutenant in May 1910, a Lieutenant in 1912 and being appointed Captain and Company Commander of the 1/7th Battalion Manchester Regiment in September 1914. He served some time at the start of the War in Egypt where he was commanding the massively important railway junction at Atbara. The importance of this cannot be overestimated, and there is a lengthy section about the importance of the Atbara junction in Gayffier-Bonneville's book on the subject. The Battalion also served in Sudan, before taking part in the fighting at Gallipoli in May 1915.

The Battalion landed at V Beach (site of the famous beaching of the River Clyde, a coal steamer that was run aground to provide as close a landing as possible for the men to disembark) on 7 May and progressed inland. This area was dominated by high hills to the north and the fort at Seddulbahir to the south. The battalion was not engaged in any major actions during this time, rather it was fighting the piecemeal skirmishes that characterised this theatre of war. Victor was killed on the night of 29 May 1915, leading an attack against the Turkish lines.

The battalion adjutant, Captain Fawcus, wrote to Victor's parents:

> On the night of the 28-29 May B and D Companies were ordered to advance and dig ourselves in about 200 yards in front of the enemy. We crept to within about 200 yards of the enemy when suddenly the moon came out, which was not to our advantage. Your son was on the extreme left of our advance, commanding half the company, when news came through that he had been hit in the shoulder. A sergeant went to him and gave him water, but the bullet must have hit something vital and he passed away within five minutes.
>
> Attempts were made to retrieve his body, but he remained lying in No Man's Land for three days until the enemy had been controlled enough to allow its safe retrieval. As it was, several men were killed whilst trying to recover him. He was eventually buried just behind the lines with a cross made from a trench periscope which had been shattered by sniper fire. *The Bloxhamist* for June 1915 recorded Victor's death alongside that of Frank Riddle and recalled that 'he left Bloxham rather young in order to go to Shrewsbury School, but in spite of having joined a much larger and more famous school, he always retained a great affection for Bloxham, and signified it by becoming a

member of the OB Society. His contemporaries will be able to recall pleasant memories of a boy of high character.'

On 2 January 1916 a memorial window to Victor was unveiled at the Church of Holy Rood in Swinton, Manchester. Family members attended the ceremony alongside the band of the Royal Engineers and 200 men from his battalion. Such were the crowds in attendance that many were unable to get into the church. In December 1923 his father endowed law scholarships at the University of Manchester for deserving local students. Victor is also commemorated on the University's war memorial and those of his old schools.

Private Harry Ayres
5th Battalion, Oxfordshire & Buckinghamshire Light Infantry
Employed at Bloxham School before 1914
Died of wounds 7 July 1915, aged 18
Buried in St Mary's Churchyard, Bloxham, England

Harry Ayres was born on 7 July 1897, the second son of Solomon 'Gaffer' Ayres and his wife Emma, who lived with their four children in a cottage in Queen's Square in Bloxham, at the time a part of the village notorious for its slum housing. Solomon worked at Bloxham School for many years and was the captain of the village Fire Brigade as well as playing in the Brigade band – it seems to have been a musical family. Their other son Wilfred married Annie Elizabeth Gascoigne Morgan and they also had two daughters, Ada and Amy. According to the family, in August 1914 Harry was in service as a footman at Shipton Court, a country house at Shipton-under-Wychwood whose owner Frederick Pepper was a local magistrate, serving as High Sheriff of Oxfordshire in 1910; it is said that when war broke out Pepper summoned all the male employees and dismissed them, telling them they should enlist. Harry joined the local regiment, the Oxford & Bucks LI, without his parents' permission. They were horrified when they found out what he had done, but decided to let him go. Having only just passed his seventeenth birthday, Harry was below the legal age to enlist (18, commonly flouted by recruiting officers) and two years below the minimum age, 19, at which a soldier could be sent abroad, and so he must have lied about his age, something which cannot have come easily to young Englishmen brought up to avoid falsehoods, but which was often officially connived at, as the following experience of another young recruit reveals:

'How old are you?' asked the recruiting sergeant. I replied, 'Eighteen.'

'Yes, that will do for enlisting but not for service overseas. If you want to join in the war go over there – and he pointed to a table on which lay some newspapers. 'Have a read and perhaps when you return you will have grown another year older.'

Burney, who was with me, being over nineteen, explained this riddle and so I returned and when asked the age question again, I replied, 'Nineteen.'

This practice was so common that it featured as one of the most celebrated cartoons of the Great War in the satirical magazine *Punch*. A small boy in shorts and blazer stands in front of a ferocious sergeant major, who booms 'So you're 18??? Do you know what happens to small boys who tell lies?' The boy looks at him and responds, 'Yes Sir, they get sent to the Front Line!'

A photograph taken in the summer of 1914 at the wedding of Harry's sister Ada includes his parents and his other sister Amy as well as Ada and, in uniform, the groom, but Harry is ominously absent. The Headmaster of Bloxham School, the Rev. George Ward, stands at the right of the photograph. The poignant photograph of Harry in his new uniform shows a proud young man with his bugle – in Bloxham, he is still always referred to as Bugler Ayres – but no regimental insignia on his cap, suggesting he had rushed to have his photograph taken as soon as he signed up; it was common practice for photographers at the time to have uniforms in the studio as props. Harry's battalion, the 5th Oxford and Bucks Light Infantry was part of Kitchener's New Army. Shortly after the outbreak of war, a campaign, spear-headed by the now famous poster 'Your Country Needs You!' was launched to encourage men to enlist – it was successful beyond all expectation with over 100,000 men rushing to enlist by the middle of September. The hope was that groups of work colleagues or sports teams would enlist together, which led to the creation of what were called the 'Pals Battalions'.

The battalion was engaged in training, especially musketry and bayonet training, at Aldershot between August and November 1914, was billeted at Cranleigh before the winter and then returned to Aldershot for further training until May 1915, when the long-awaited order to proceed to France was received. Harry should not have gone with them, as he was still only 17 and so was well under the required age for overseas service, but he and his comrades arrived at Boulogne on 20 May. They were part of the 14th (Light) Division, which was the first of Kitchener's New Army divisions to come into contact with the enemy, and they were engaged in holding onto trenches in the Hooge area in the Ypres Salient – this was the most active sector on the entire Western Front. Within the first six weeks in the trenches, the battalion had lost a third of its strength even though it was not involved in any large-scale engagement. This was 'attrition' in all its ghastly reality.

On 26 June 1915 the battalion was manning trenches in Railway Wood, east of Ypres, when they came under heavy enemy shell fire. Harry suffered severe shrapnel wounds to his left leg and elbow, though family tradition has it that 'half of his body and head were blown away.' Harry's mother Emma visited him in hospital in France and was horrified by the conditions she found there. Thanks to her insistence, Harry was brought back to England on the Hospital Ship HMHS *Asturias*. He was taken to Norfolk War Hospital, Norwich, where he died on 7 July 1915, his eighteenth birthday. His death cast a shadow over the family, and Amy's granddaughter Joy Tilley recalls that neither her grandmother nor her mother could talk about it without becoming upset. Family legend has it that Harry's older brother Wilfred was forbidden by his parents to join up, but we know that this is not the case, as he served in the 94th Siege Battery, and his is the first name on the Roll of Honour in Bloxham's parish church, which lists 'the men from this parish on active service for their King and Country'.

Harry was buried in the village churchyard on 12 July 1915 with the school's OTC providing a firing party and buglers. The vicar spoke 'of the love that all felt for him, the patience and bravery with which he bore his sufferings, and his readiness to serve his King and Country.' *The Bloxhamist* for that month commented that 'we should be lacking in generosity if we failed to express our sympathy with Mr and Mrs Solomon Ayres and their family in their present bereavement.'

Solomon Ayres continued to work at the school, dying in 1936 at the age of 73. His wife passed away in 1943 in her 83rd year. She is buried in the same grave as her husband and their beloved youngest son. For many years the wooden cross made for his grave in 1915 marked the grave alongside an impressive headstone, before the cross was brought indoors to prevent its disintegration due to the elements. The grave was re-made in 2005 thanks to Harry Ayres' great-niece Joy Tilley.

A tragic tale but one all too typical of the experience of so many families in the Great War, and there the story would have ended, at least as far as Bloxham School was concerned, if not for a request for information from two authors of a book on the Public Schools and the Great War. SB was asked whether he knew of any school servants who had perished in the war, and had to admit that he did not, but the question spurred him into research which led to a reference in *The Bloxhamist* for July 1915 suggesting that Harry must have worked for a time at the school alongside his father ('Harry, who a short time ago was also a servant at the School....'), probably working as a serving boy in the dining hall. This led him to ask whether as a member of the school community Harry, whose name appears on the Bloxham Village War Memorial, should not also be commemorated on the school's one, which included the names of masters who perished as well as those of former pupils.

The then Headmaster, Mark Allbrook, spoke movingly about Harry Ayres in his sermon at the school's Service of Remembrance in November 2012, when his name was read out along with those of all Bloxhamists who died in the last century's wars. In November 2013 his name was added to the War Memorial in the school chapel, and Joy Tilley attended a moving service at which the new memorial was blessed. A photograph of Harry kindly supplied by the family was added to the images of the Great War dead displayed in the Egerton Library. Harry Ayres occupies a unique position as the only one of the fallen of both school and village who is buried in Bloxham.

Private Lionel Arthur Harris
9th Battalion, Royal Warwickshire Regiment
Pupil at Bloxham School 1906-1907
Died of wounds 16 August 1915, aged 20
Commemorated on the Helles Memorial, Gallipoli, Turkey
Panel 35

Lionel Arthur Harris was born on 23 April 1895 in Newbury and was the son of Ernest and Marion Ada née Parsons. His father was an ironmonger by trade, and Lionel was the fourth of five sons. His elder brothers were Cecil Edwin (born 1886), Ernest Claude (1889) and Alan

(1891), all of whom attended Bloxham. There was also a younger brother, Paul, born in 1900. A sixth child died in infancy. The family lived at 31, Mount Pleasant in the small village of Cold Ash, a couple of miles from Newbury. Lionel's father had started in Cold Ash with a smithy and village store before moving to Newbury, running an ironmongery business at 3 The Broadway which he later combined with the sewing machine shop next door. He was active in local politics, first as a Borough Councillor and then as Mayor of Newbury.

Lionel arrived at Bloxham in January 1906 along with Alan. Both were placed in Form II, along with two other new boys, Robert Cunliffe and Philip Davy. Lionel made little impression in his brief time at the school; in his obituary, *The Bloxhamist* stated that 'Old Bloxhamists of that period will remember him as a very delicate little boy. He left us in April, 1907, and went to another school, so as to be able to live at home.' This was Newbury Grammar School, and the school magazine *The Newburian* had little to say about him except for noting that 'he was the winner of a record Senior Run.'

When he left Newbury Grammar School in 1912, he became an engineering apprentice at the Humber Motor Works in Coventry, where he was working when war was declared. Within days he signed up for the local regiment, the Royal Warwickshire Regiment, along with many of his workmates. He became a soldier in the 9th (Service) Battalion of Kitchener's Army.

The battalion underwent months of training at Salisbury and Aldershot before being sent out to Egypt prior to leaving the UK on the morning of 17 June 1915 and headed by ship for the island of Lemnos. They were to be thrown into the Gallipoli campaign just four days after arriving in Lemnos when they landed on V Beach in the shadow of the beached freighter the River Clyde. They spent the next two weeks in and out of the trenches, before returning to Lemnos on 29 July. They returned to Gallipoli and landed at Anzac Cove on the morning of 4 August. The following day, they were involved in the heavy fighting towards the dominating ridge of Sari Bair. A spur ran below the crest of Sari Bair, which was known as Rhododendron Ridge and it was here that A Company of the 9th Royal Warwicks were heavily involved. For four days they attacked and defended, in appallingly hot conditions, being constantly raked by shell and sniper fire. During these four days, the casualties mounted and by the time they pulled back on the night of the 9th there was not a single officer left and only 248 men. They lost 15 officers killed, wounded or missing, and of the other ranks 57 were killed, 227 wounded and 115 missing. Lionel was wounded at some point in this operation, and he died from these wounds on 14 August, 'his spine being badly injured', according to *The Bloxhamist*.

The Newbury Weekly News for 9 September 1915 reported that his father was recovering from a recent serious illness and staying at Bournemouth when the sad news reached him, and Lionel's brother Alan, on leave from the 19th Royal Fusiliers, was temporarily in charge of the family business.

Lionel is remembered on panel 36 of the magnificent Helles Memorial to the Missing at the tip of the Gallipoli Peninsula, overlooking the entrance to the Dardanelles. It is unclear why a man who died in hospital does not have a known grave, but it could be that he was buried at sea from a hospital ship on the way to Egypt or Malta. By an amazing stroke of luck when MD visited the Helles Memorial, there were remedial works in progress and every panel was covered except one, which happened to be the one with Lionel's name on. Lionel is also commemorated on tablet 10 of the Newbury Town War Memorial and on the Speenhamland Shrine, the parish memorial for St Mary's, Speenhamland, which is now located in St Nicolas' Church, Newbury following the demolition of St Mary's in 1976, as well as on the Newbury Grammar School memorial at St Bartholomew's School and the one at Bloxham.

Of his brothers, there are no military records for the eldest, Cecil, or the youngest, Paul. Claude saw action in the short but successful campaign in the German colony of German South West Africa (now Namibia) and then served as an electrical artificer in the Royal Navy. Alan served in the ranks in the 19th (Service) Battalion, Royal Fusiliers and then in the Labour Corps. A medical report from August 1916 commented on his insomnia and a severe stutter: 'Is quite unable to answer if spoken to suddenly owing to stuttering. Should be transferred to a mechanical unit as is in danger of being shot at any time by our own sentries.' It would appear obvious to us that he was suffering from what was known as the time as shell shock, and he was eventually transferred to the 349th Agricultural Company as a mechanical engineer.

Serjeant Morris Howard Wilkins
City of London Yeomanry (Rough Riders)
Pupil at Bloxham School 1904-06
Killed in action 21 August 1915, aged 25
Buried in Green Hill Cemetery, Gallipoli, Turkey
Grave II.F.12

Morris Howard Wilkins was born in Ravenhead, Kent, the fourth child of Edward and Ellen Wilkins. His father was an insurance broker and he had three older sisters - Mary, Dorothy and Cecily – as well as a younger brother, Leopold. When he entered the school, the family address was given as Ken Court, Tatsfield. Formerly known as Cold Court, this was the oldest house in the village of Tatsfield, in the north-east corner of Surrey. At the time of the 1911 census the family were living at 17, Edith Grove, Chelsea, the home of Emily Shephard, a vocalist. Curiously, Mary's occupation was listed as 'poultry expert'. Even then, Edith Grove was a bohemian area of flats and apartments, with a transient mixture of residents – between 1912 and 1914, the musical salon of Paul and Muriel Draper at 19a played host to the likes of Arthur Rubinstein, Igor Stravinsky and Pablo Casals, while Nijinsky, Henry James and John Singer Sargent were also regular visitors. Many years later the Rolling Stones lived at 102, Edith Grove when the band was first starting out. Sadly, 17-21 Edith Grove were destroyed by bombing in the Second World War. By 1915, Morris' parents had moved to Richmond Lodge, Sydenham Road in Croydon.

Between 1901 and 1903, Morris attended Whitgift Grammar School in Croydon (known since 1946 as Whitgift School), winning the Challenge Cup for Athletics. He moved from Whitgift to Bloxham in a reversal of the trend of many of the pupils at the time, whose parents used Bloxham as a preparatory school before moving their sons to a bigger and more prestigious institution.

Morris arrived at Bloxham School in January 1904. He was confirmed by the Bishop of Reading in March 1905. His father presented a cup for the Senior Long Jump on Sports Day in 1905; Morris finished third in the event. In May he made his debut for the school's cricket XI against the village, scoring two runs, batting at number ten. In 11 innings for the team that season, he managed to amass the grand total of 29 runs, with a highest score of 13 not out. *The Bloxhamist* judged that he had improved towards the end of the season 'and may be useful another year. At times fielded well at mid-off, but was much too uncertain, both in catching and stopping the ball.' He made more of an impact in the football XI - *The Bloxhamist* reported of his display in a 5-2 defeat at the hands of Jesus College, Oxford in December 1905 that as is usually the case Wilkins played chiefly the part of a spectator, for Campbell seems quite to ignore his wing-man, and when he does pass, the ball generally goes behind Wilkins.' The waspish correspondent added that when he did get the ball 'Wilkins seemed imbued with too much respect for the opposing backs, and did not make sufficient use of his few opportunities.'

Nevertheless, he and Campbell were both awarded their Football Colours at the end of the 1905-6 season. *The Bloxhamist*, recognising his lack of scoring chances, concluded that he was fast but often did not centre the ball quickly enough. In his final cricket season at the school, Morris was promoted to open the batting, making a name for his stubborn defence and hitting scores of 42 and 43 not out. In football too he had made good progress – *The Bloxhamist* recorded in 1906 that he was 'a greatly improved player, and, with increased opportunities, was of great assistance to the team. Is fast and can dribble.....but at times is still inclined to take the ball too far before trying to centre.'

He left Bloxham at the end of the Michaelmas Term in December 1906, and it was recorded that he had gone into business in London. This was the Phoenix Assurance Company, following in his father's footsteps. Phoenix Assurance was a fire insurance company which dated from 1680, and was acquired by Sun Alliance in 1984, which is why Morris' name now appears on the Royal and Sun Alliance Roll of Honour. The day after returning to his old school on All Saints' Day in November 1913 for the annual Old Bloxhamist reunion, Morris joined Rosslyn Park RFC; his brother Leopold was also a member. Bloxham was not a rugby-playing school until

1920, and at Rosslyn Park he would have found himself rubbing shoulders with a preponderance of Old Boys of schools such as Marlborough and Uppingham.

There is no record of Morris playing for the 1st XV at Rosslyn Park, and he does not feature in any annual team photographs, but Leopold does appear in a photograph of the club's tour party to Austria-Hungary in April 1912 – Rosslyn Park was a trailblazer in terms of touring and was the first English club side to play in France.

Morris seems to have been a man of some means, as he is also known to have played polo at the Blackheath Polo Club, located on what is now Charlton Athletic FC's training ground. It was doubtless this equestrian connection which led to his decision to join the City of London Yeomanry, known as the Rough Riders, formed in 1901. The Rough Riders owed their name to the tactics of the Boers during the Boer War, where bands of Boer militia patrolled in an ill-disciplined but largely effective manner. The Rough Riders were members of the Yeomanry sent to South Africa to act as roving reconnaissance troops in an attempt to thwart the guerilla tactics of the Boers. The Yeomanry served with distinction during the War from 1914 through to 1918.

In the Gallipoli campaign the Yeomanry were forced to abandon their precious horses and fight on foot as infantry soldiers. On 21 August 1915, the dismounted cavalrymen found themselves launched into the attack at the Battle of Scimitar Hill. The battle did not go well for the British and the 2nd Mounted Division were called into battle at around 5:00 p.m. Marching inland from Suvla across the dry bed of a salt lake, the advance was soon cut down by accurate and prolonged machine gun fire as it approached Anafarta Ridge and Green Hill. The official history reports that the dismounted cavalry advanced in squadron formation across the salt lake and presented a target that 'artillerymen and machine gunners could only dream of'. The British lost 5300 men on 21 August including Morris Wilkins, who was wounded near to Hill 70 and died of his wounds. He was 25 years old. He is buried in Green Hill Cemetery, Gallipoli.

The Bloxhamist for December 1915 recorded that Morris had joined the Rough Riders 'about four years ago' (in fact it was in 1910), attaining the rank of Serjeant. It went on to assert that 'he was recently offered a commission in the Royal Field Artillery, but preferred to remain with his old friends. He was wounded in the attempt to capture Hill 70, in Gallipoli, and shortly afterwards succumbed to his wounds.' In the December 1915 edition of *The Whitgiftian Magazine*, there is a brief statement: 'The Gallipoli fighting is responsible also for the death of Sergeant M. H. Wilkins (City of London Rough Riders), who was killed in action on August 20th', but the school's Book of Remembrance, published in 1922, recording him as having been killed 'in a Yeomanry charge on Chocolate Hill at Suvla Bay', gives 21 August, the same date as the official records and the Bloxham Roll of Honour. According to the book *Croydon and the Great War*, which mistakenly transposes his two forenames, Morris was mentioned in despatches, but there is no evidence to corroborate this claim.

Morris was confirmed as having been killed in action in the letter sent by Rosslyn Park's Hon. Sec. to members in October 1918, but this letter was not known about when Stephen Cooper listed 84 members of the club on the Roll of Honour in his book *The Final Whistle* in 2012, and so he is missing from the list. The subsequent discovery of the letter in a scrapbook led to 19 further names being added, and there are now 108 names on the club's new memorial, including that of Morris Howard Wilkins.

Private Charles Archibald Walter Quiney
2nd Battalion, Royal Irish Rifles
Pupil at Bloxham School 1882-1884
Killed in action 13 September 1915, aged 43
Buried in Lijssenthoek Military Cemetery, Belgium
Grave III.A.24

Charles Quiney was born on 24 November 1871, the second of three sons of Charles and Mary Ann Quiney, who lived at 66, Loughborough Park, Brixton. He was a pupil at the school between 1882 and 1884, the same time as his elder brother Alfred, but made little mark in his short stint at Bloxham, whereas Alfred was a star cricketer and middle-distance runner. The third brother, Hubert, also briefly attended Bloxham. Few details are known of Charles' life after school, except that he returned to the family home in the Canary Islands, where his father set up a hotel, the Bella Vista, in 1894. For many years this was the most popular hotel on the Islands with Agatha Christie among the regular guests. At the outbreak of war Charles returned to Britain and enlisted in the Lancashire Regiment, before transferring to the 2nd Battalion, Royal Irish Rifles.

According to the Battalion war diary, the 2nd RIR were in trenches around the area of Bellewaarde Ridge near Hooge, just outside Ypres, and were engaged in what was described as 'ordinary trench warfare'. The Battalion war diary records that 'we suffered a spiteful period of German shelling over breakfast, but this soon died down and the rest of day was extraordinarily quiet, with the exception of occasional sniper fire which could be considered an inconvenience.' In other words, like so many of those who died on the Western Front, he did not perish in one of the great battles but was a victim of the daily grind of attritional warfare. Charles was wounded on 11 September 1915 and he died in hospital two days later at the age of 43. He left behind him a widow, Amy, who continued to live in Las Palmas in the Canary Islands; she became the proprietor of another of the family's hotels, the Santa Brigida, which is still in business today. Charles Quiney is buried in Lijssenthoek Cemetery, and his grave is one of those visited by the school's regular Western Front trips. Sadly, as of 2020 his headstone is almost illegible.

**Brevet Major Philip Stafford Gordon Wainman
6th, attached 2nd Battalion, Worcestershire Regiment
Pupil at Bloxham School 1891-1892
Killed in action 26 September 1915, aged 35
Buried in Vermelles British Military Cemetery, Loos, France
Grave VI.D.12**

The next of the 80 to lose his life did so in one of the most important but now little-known battles of the First World War. Philip Stafford Gordon Wainman was killed on 26 September 1915 in the Battle of Loos. This was the British Army's largest effort of the war up to that point, with 75,000 men involved on the first day alone. It saw the first British use of poison gas and also the first deployment of battalions formed of inexperienced wartime volunteers. It became known at the time as 'the Big Push'.

While many of the 80 Bloxhamists to perish in the Great War were ordinary citizens who had never intended to follow a military career but volunteered to 'do their bit' for their country after the war broke out, the next three to die were all long-term professional soldiers for many years before 1914. Philip Wainman had left the army after eleven years of service but returned to the colours when war broke out. He was born on 27 September 1879, the only son of Lt. Gordon Wainman, late of the Lincolnshire Regiment, and Evelyn Charlotte née Harding of Northallerton. The Wainmans were an old Yorkshire gentry family, and Philip enjoyed a comfortable upbringing. He attended Bloxham School from 1891 to 1892 but made little impact in the short time he was there. He was, however, an active Old Boy, and kept the school fully informed of his movements and family news over the next two decades. After Bloxham he went on to Fettes College in Edinburgh and then entered the Royal Military Academy, Sandhurst in 1897. He was known for his excellence in polo, riding and shooting. He obtained his commission in 1898 and served in the Boer War from 1900 to 1902. He was wounded in action in Kwa Zulu Natal and received the Queen's and King's Medals with two clasps. He was promoted to Captain in 1902 and became Adjutant of the 1st Devonshires in 1906.

Philip was married on 14 January 1904 in Philadelphia to Miss Christine Ledlie Wheeler of Bryn Mawr, Pennsylvania. The Wheelers were one of Philadelphia's leading families; Christine's father, Charles Wheeler, owned two iron works in Pennsylvania and a bank in New York, and left a fortune of £7 million (1883 values) on his death. Christine's sister Mary had married a Bavarian nobleman and became Countess Pappenheim – the family was part of a prevalent pattern at the time of rich Americans marrying into hard-up European aristocratic families. Other examples would be Nancy Astor, Consuela Vanderbilt (who married the Duke of Marlborough) and Winston Churchill's mother Lady Randolph Churchill. Viewers of the enormously popular television series *Downton Abbey* could cite the fictional Lady Grantham as another example of the trend.

After postings to Bermuda, Jamaica, Malta and Devon, where he acted as Adjutant to the 4th Volunteer Battalion of the Devonshire Regiment, Philip left the Army in 1909 and settled down with his young wife to the life of a country gentleman, residing in Otterington Hall, a large country house in North Yorkshire. *The Bloxhamist* reported the birth of a son in August 1905, another in April 1907 and a third, who would never know his father, on 11 May 1915.

When war broke out, Philip Wainman immediately rejoined his original regiment, but was sent to France on 1 October 1914 along with five other officers as replacements for the heavy casualties already suffered by the Worcester Regiment. They were sent to Flanders, and Philip had not been there long when he was involved in one of the most crucial actions of the war. By this point the British were engaged in desperate fighting east of Ypres in an attempt to hold the German onslaught which sought to capture the last segment of Belgium before driving onwards to the strategically vital Channel ports of Dunkirk and Calais.

The 2nd Worcesters were almost the last available reserves in the British defensive line, and the loss of the village of Gheluvelt on 31 October prompted the preparation of orders for a general retreat. Only the launching of a heroic counterattack by the Worcestershire Regiment, which succeeded in retaking the village, prevented the Germans from heading on to Ypres before breaking through to the Channel ports. Credit for this decision is generally given to Brigadier General Charles FitzClarence VC, commanding the 1st (Guards) Brigade, the senior general on the spot. FitzClarence was killed in action at Polygon Wood a fortnight later, and it was not until summer 1915 that Field Marshal Sir John French made it clear that it was FitzClarence who 'rallied the troops and directed the successful onslaught'. Lieutenant Colonel (Major at the time) E.B. Hankey of the 2nd Worcesters agreed that 'by shoving us in at the time and place he did, the General saved the day.'

However, a letter to *The Worcester Chronicle* argued that the credit should be shared. In it, Major Spencer Scott of Battenhall, Worcester, wrote as follows:

> I have no desire to decry the credit due to anyone, but in justice to one who has made the ultimate sacrifice, I feel bound to express at once that if the evidence of men of the Worcestershire Regiment is to be relied upon the officer who, acting on his own initiative, gave the order on which the Worcesters advanced, and thus by their indefatigable courage saved Calais, was Captain Philip G. Wainman of the Worcestershire Regiment.

Whatever the truth of the sequence of events on that confused and desperate day, Wainman certainly led the unit (A Company) which advanced and prevented the enemy from advancing up the Menin Road, an action for which he was mentioned in despatches for his 'gallant and distinguished services in the Field'. The Germans never came so close to breaking through on the Western Front again. It is difficult to overestimate the importance of the stand made by the Worcesters at Gheluvelt. While it did not win the war, it certainly had a decisive impact on the final outcome. Had the Germans broken through Ypres and seized the Channel ports, the outcome of the war could have been very different indeed.

The following September, Captain Wainman led his men into action once more, this time at the Battle of Loos. This was part of the Anglo-French offensive known as the Third Battle of Artois and marked the first British use of poison gas. It was undertaken reluctantly by Field Marshal French and General Haig, who regarded the ground as unsuitable. On 26 September, Wainman led his men in an advance on the German lines near the heavily fortified quarries near Hulluch. The entire battalion advanced in open order across 1000 metres of flat fields, in the face of prolonged and accurate machine gun fire. By the time the attack ground to a halt on the evening of the 26th, nearly half the battalion had been killed or wounded, including the second in command and all four company commanders. Phillip Wainman was shot down on the parapet of the German front-line trench.

On a visit to the Loos battlefield in July 2019, the authors used a combination of trench maps and modern technology to navigate their way to the location of the British trench occupied by the Worcesters. It was a remarkably poignant experience to be standing on the exact spot where one of the Old Bloxhamists stood on the day he was killed, and it is certainly something that will stay in the memory of the authors for some time to come. According to the regimental history Wainman 'led his men forward, waving his stick till he fell riddled with bullets.' Further right, the divisional commander, General Thompson Capper, was killed in the same attack, one of three major generals killed during the Battle of Loos. The offensive was a costly failure which taught the British some painful lessons and ultimately led to the replacement of Field Marshal French by Sir Douglas Haig as commander of the BEF.

Philip Wainman's epitaph reads that he was 'killed in action whilst leading his men into battle on the eve of his 36th birthday.'   He was appointed Brevet Major (a substantive but un-gazetted rank) on the day he was killed. He is buried in Vermelles Cemetery and is also remembered on the war memorial outside Worcester Cathedral and the war memorial of Fettes College as well as the one at Bloxham School, for which his widow donated 10 shillings to the fund. His sword was auctioned by Dix Noonan Webb in 2010; sadly MD was pipped to the post by another bidder. Through a family member we managed to obtain a wonderful photograph of Philip in uniform, smoking a cigarette. Compared to his portrait picture, the strain of war is clear to see on his face.

Lieutenant Colonel Cyril Compton Jackson
110th Mahratta Light Infantry
Pupil at Bloxham School 1883-1885
Killed in action 22 November 1915, aged 47
Commemorated on the Basra Memorial, Iraq
Panel 48

The next name on the list of the 80 Bloxhamists to have perished in the Great War provides a valuable reminder of the fact that this was very much a global war. He died not in Flanders but in Mesopotamia (modern day Iraq), and is commemorated on a memorial in Basra, where British troops would find themselves fighting once more, in 2003.

While most of the 80 were young men who would never have dreamt of a military career if it had not been for the Great War, Cyril Jackson, like the men before and after him on

the list, was already an experienced soldier by the time war broke out. He was born on 22 December 1867 in the Staffordshire Potteries town of Hanley, one of eight children of the Reverend Charles Bird Jackson and Mary Jackson (née Compton). He had three older brothers, three older sisters and a younger sister, all of whom were born in Hanley. The family then moved to Wold Newton in Lincolnshire, where his father was the Rector, and Cyril was sent to various boarding schools, including Queen Elizabeth Grammar School in Horncastle, then Newark and finally Bloxham. He was a pupil at Bloxham between January 1883 and July 1885, winning the Senior History Prize and becoming a Prefect and Secretary of the prestigious Committee of Games. He was the school's leading athlete in 1884, winning the quarter mile, 120 yards hurdles and the 100 yards on Sports Day, and played football for the 1st XI, occasionally as a goalkeeper. He was at Bloxham with two future generals of the Great War, Wilfred Ellershaw and Thomas Beach.

While his brothers all pursued careers in either medicine or law, Cyril enlisted in the Army, at first as a subaltern in the militia in 1887, then being commissioned as a 2nd Lieutenant in the Border Regiment in 1888. The following year, he was stationed in Malta with the 2nd Border Regiment. In February 1890, he sailed from Malta on *HMS Malabar* bound for his posting at Chakrata in India. This initial stay in India did not last long, however, as he contracted a 'fever' and had to return to England on sick leave. After convalescing, he returned to India in March 1891. The following year, he was attached to the 27th Madras Native Infantry in the Indian Army based at Mahidpoor in Lucknow. He transferred to the Indian Army in April 1893 and was posted to the Bhopal Battalion, in Sahore, Bhopal. On 9 March 1899, the 31-year-old Major Jackson married Beatrix Clara Grey at St Thomas Church in Calcutta. He next saw service in Afghanistan and Kashmir before being stationed in Allahabad for several years as adjutant to the local levies.

When war broke out in 1914, Cyril, now a Lieutenant Colonel, was given the command of the 103rd Mahratta Light Infantry which formed part of D Force in the Mesopotamian Campaign. He was subsequently transferred to take command of the 110th Light Infantry, part of Force B. In November 1915, the regiment was in action in Mesopotamia, and involved in fighting near Baghdad in what would become known as the Battle of Ctesiphon. A British force under the command of General Townsend was advancing slowly towards Baghdad and by early October was nearing the ruins of the ancient city of Ctesiphon, whose arch, 85 feet high, was said to be the largest ancient standing arch in the world. Political vacillation between London and Delhi prevented Townsend from launching his attack until 22 November, by which time the Turks had prepared strong defences and received reinforcements from Baghdad. Captain Spink of the 103rd Mahratta Light Infantry, later wrote of the advance:

> I shall always remember this march as I rode with Colonel Jackson of the 110th Mahrattas, and one of the best, who with his wife used to drive out from 'Nagar to my dam on Sundays. The colonel was one of the few who took an interest in the country and its prospects, and being a first-class artist himself, spent all his spare time sketching. As we rode along he spoke eagerly of the Arch and other ancient monuments we hoped shortly to see and how pleasant a rambling tour around Baghdad would be, little realising that within three days he would be lying dead on the field of Ctesiphon.

Four columns of British troops converged on well dug-in Turkish positions in a complex operation which failed when B Force, including Jackson's regiment, was halted by fierce machine gun fire. The British were forced to retreat to Kut-al-Amara after a bloody two-day engagement in which the British lost 4,600 men and the Turks 6,200. There is some disagreement about how Cyril Jackson died. According to one account, a shell landed on a tent during an orders meeting and killed several senior officers, although other accounts imply that he died after being hit by fire from Turkish machine guns. His regiment sustained casualties of 560 out of a strength of 700. The 110th lost all its officers bar one. Ironically, if he had remained with the 103rd, Jackson would probably have survived as they were held in reserve all day and sustained very few casualties. The fact that the battle was followed by a long and difficult retreat explains the lack of any British graves at Ctesiphon.

As well as the Bloxham School war memorial, Cyril Jackson is commemorated on the Basra War Memorial in Iraq and the parish memorial in Wold Newton. The authors are exceptionally grateful to JB, a serving member of the UK military who very kindly made a visit to the Basra Memorial and obtained a picture of Jackson's name. He reported back to the authors that even in 2020, when peace had supposedly descended on Iraq, his visit to the memorial was interrupted by a bomb explosion on the road adjacent to the Memorial, followed by a prolonged gun battle. Given the circumstances, any picture is a real bonus. There is a brass plaque in the church at Wold Newton in his memory which states 'Of your charity, please pray for the soul of Lt Col Cyril Compton Jackson, CO 103 Maharatta Light Infantry, killed in action at Ctesiphon on 21st November 1916', and he is also listed on a memorial in Malvern Library, as this is where his mother had settled after the death of her husband in 1895.

Wold Newton's memorial was in effect a private one, put up by the local squire, William Maurice Wright, a childhood friend of Jackson. On October 2009, the fact that Jackson's name on the memorial was almost worn away was used in a House of Commons debate by the local MP, Shona McIsaac, as evidence for the poor condition of Britain's war memorials, although residents of Wold Newton strongly disputed her contention that the memorial was illegible or in need of repair.

The school's Roll of Honour indicates that Cyril Jackson had been awarded the DSO (Distinguished Service Order), the most significant gallantry medal after the Victoria Cross, and it was therefore placed on the caption beneath his photograph, but there is no evidence of this award in his service record. Full checks of the London Gazette also reveal no record of the award of the DSO and it must therefore be assumed to be a mistake within the archives.

Major Henry Ball Holmes
2nd Royal Irish Fusiliers
Pupil at Bloxham School 1885-1887
Died of wounds 27 November 1915, aged 43
Buried in Lower Fahan Churchyard, Donegal, Ireland

Henry Ball Holmes was a professional soldier who had already been in the army for twenty years when the First World War broke out. He was born in Hong Kong on 23 July 1872. His father was a solicitor and his mother a doctor who was one of the first western women to practise medicine on the island. He was educated at Bloxham between 1885 and 1887. The *Find a Grave* website gives a florid account of his sporting exploits at Bloxham, where he apparently scored a record-breaking 33 tries in his final season in the 1st XV and took over 40 wickets as a fast bowler in 1887, including five against Eton. Sadly, this is all pure invention – Eton was not on Bloxham's cricket fixture list at that time and Bloxham was not a rugby-playing school until 1920. A salutary example of the perils of genealogy and relying on the Internet for information! In truth, Henry made little impression at school, leaving at the age of 15 to go on to a military college in Oxford. After serving in the militia, he was gazetted as a Second Lieutenant in the Royal Irish Fusiliers on 2 June 1894. He progressed quickly through the ranks, becoming a Lieutenant on 22 May 1897, Captain on 12 March 1902 and then Major on 14 March 1904.

Henry Holmes saw service in the Boer War from 1899 to 1902 and was severely wounded on two occasions. He took part in operations in Natal in 1899, including the engagements at Lombard Kop and Nicholson's Nek, in the Transvaal in 1900, Orange River in 1901, Natal in 1902 and operations on the borders of Zululand between 1902 and 1903. He was the officer commanding the Machadodorp Rest Camp between May and September 1901. He was awarded the Queen's medal with three clasps and the King's medal with two clasps. He was also mentioned in despatches twice during the war.

In 1911 Holmes' unit, the 2nd Battalion Royal Irish Fusiliers, was in Quetta in India; when King George V went to India for the Delhi Durbar, the magnificent gathering which marked his coronation as Emperor of India, Henry acted as an equerry on the Royal Train and at the Durbar. In appreciation of this service the King presented him with a splendid diamond encrusted monogrammed stick pin, which is now in the regimental museum in Armagh. When war broke out in August 1914, the battalion returned to the United Kingdom, arriving at their barracks at Winchester on 20 November. On 19 December 1914 they embarked at Southampton on the SS *City of Benares*, disembarking the next day at Le Havre.

On the afternoon of 15 May 1915, it was a relatively peaceful day in the trenches where the 2nd RIR were posted between Bellewaarde Ridge and Sanctuary Wood. The war diary reports that the front was very quiet and a German attack from the previous night resulted in large numbers of German dead lying in front of the British lines. The diary had remarked that a particularly troublesome sniper had been harassing the Irish lines for a few days. At the time, Holmes was commanding A Company in the lines, and on the 15th a relief took place. The diary remarks that Holmes was wounded, and his medical records show he was admitted to a CCS with a gunshot wound to the head. It seems likely that he was probably shot by a sniper. He was evacuated from the trenches and eventually found himself at the War Hospital at Ludden Camp, Buncrana in Ireland. It was here that he died seven months later, on 27 November 1915, of what was described as 'septic blood poisoning of the brain'. He was buried at Lower Fahan churchyard in County Donegal and a memorial was erected to him by his brother officers, one of whom wrote of him 'All the Regiment, past and present, mourn with you; he was a perfect gentleman, a gallant soldier and a staunch friend to all.'

The Ball-Holmes family are very well represented online from a genealogy perspective, with the family being prominent Irish landowners, but despite their standing, there is almost no reference whatsoever to Henry in any records or archives. He was mentioned in Field Marshal Sir John French's despatch published in the London Gazette on 1 January 1916. Henry married Violet Mabel Ryles of The Hermitage, Stevenage on 1 July 1914 at Totnes, Devon – Violet was the daughter of the late Henry Wingfield Figgis of Dublin. The couple set up home in Chalfont St Peter and had one son who was still born, posthumously, on 28th December 1915. Henry Ball Holmes was 43 when he died.

1916

Of all the years of fighting during the Great War, it is 1916 that has taken up more pages, analysis, argument and debate than any other. It was the worst year of the entire war for the Old Bloxhamists, with twenty-eight old boys losing their lives. While the fighting on the Somme, and the casualties of the first day in particular, dominate the history of the war, there is much more to 1916, than just this one famous battle.

1915 had been a bruising year for the Allies. The Germans remained firmly encamped on Belgian and French soil, and tens of thousands of soldiers had been sacrificed for little to no material gain. The planning conferences of early 1916 decided that 1916 would be the year of the offensive, offensives on a scale never seen before. The plan was to launch simultaneous assaults against the Germans using millions of troops on three fronts simultaneously, in the West in France and Belgium, in the southern front against the Austrians via Italy, and on the Eastern Front against the Turks and the Germans by the Russians. By summer 1916 it was hoped that Kitchener's volunteer armies would be trained and ready to take the offensive.

The first few months of 1916 were taken up with preparations for the massive Anglo-French offensive that was due to take place in Northern France later in the year. While the Allies were preparing to go on the offensive, all across the Western Front the Germans were putting into practice the principle of 'Verteidigung in der Tiefe' – defence in depth. They spent months bolstering the defences in their existing lines, fortifying and strengthening their reserve and second lines, and unbeknown to the Allies, they began the construction of a formidable line of defences several miles behind the current front line. This second line, which was known as the 'Siegfriedstellung' or the Hindenburg Line, was to play a significant role in the German withdrawal from the Somme in late 1916. As well as strengthening the lines, the Germans went underground and along the length of the Western Front constructed deep dugouts, many metres underground, big enough to shelter entire companies of men, and impervious even to the heaviest of Allied shells. It was this troglodyte world and the protection they offered that was to have significant and far-reaching impacts on the British preparations for the Somme.

In February the Germans seized the initiative and attacked the French 2nd Army at Verdun. The German plan, devised by General Erich von Falkenhayn, was brutally simple – to bleed France white. Falkenhayn knew that the French would defend Verdun to the last man, and by simple attrition he would wear the French army down to breaking point. Initially the attack was a huge success with the fort at Douaumont falling in just three days, before the offensive ground into stalemate. Such was the toll in men on the French and the conditions so appalling, that it is estimated that over three quarters of the French Army served at Verdun at one time or another, and the battlefield became known as the 'Mill on the Meuse'. As French casualties at Verdun reached 300,000, it became apparent that the French could not sustain these levels of loss much longer, and in consequence the British were under pressure to bring their planned offensive forwards in order to relieve pressure on the French.

It was not just on land that the war was raging. At the end of May, the Navy got its long-awaited chance for a show down with the German High Seas Fleet at the Battle of Jutland, where 151 British ships engaged in combat with 90 German ships. Two Bloxhamists were to lose their lives in the battle, and the British limped home having lost 14 ships and over 6000 men killed. German losses stood at a third of the British total, though in the long-term Jutland must rate as a strategic victory for the British.

On 5 June 1916, one of the most significant events of the entire war took place, when HMS Hampshire, carrying Lord Kitchener to Russia, struck a mine off the Orkneys and sank. Kitchener's aide-de-camp, Brigadier General Wilfred Ellershaw, lost his life when the Hampshire went down, becoming the highest ranking Old Bloxhamist to die during the Great War. Like Kitchener he is commemorated on the Holybrook Memorial in Southampton.

The pressure on the French at Verdun led the British to speed forward with their preparations for their great offensive to be launched on the Somme. The men were told that it would be a walk over, a week-long artillery bombardment would have pulverised the German lines and any Germans who survived the bombardment would be in no fit state to fight. In some places British soldiers were ordered to walk towards the German lines, running being a waste of energy. More words have been written about 1 July 1916 than any other date in British military history, but the bare statistics remain shocking. Three Bloxhamists were among the 19,000 men killed on that first day, two losing their lives in the diversionary attacks at the village of Gommecourt, and one attacking with the Barnsley Pals against the heavily defended village of Serre.

Despite the abject failure along most of the British lines, there were some successes on the first day July, most notably in the southern sector of the British attack, with the villages of Maricourt and Mametz falling to the British.

The fighting on the Somme ebbed and flowed for the next four months, with land being gained and then lost in a series of attack and counterattack between the protagonists. The scale of losses were appalling and between 7 July and 23 November, seventeen Old Bloxhamists were to lose their lives on the Somme. It is testament to the nature of the fighting that many of them have no known graves and are commemorated on the various memorials to the missing that stand on the Somme battlefield.

It was in 1916 that Bloxham had its first air war casualty, when Oswald Nixon, in his first week as a qualified pilot, had the great misfortune to come up against one of Germany's greatest air aces in the skies above Serre. Nixon lost his life when his plane was shot down, an event that was recorded in macabre detail by the Germans in a series of photographs which lie in the German archives to this day. The Somme campaign continued until November 1916.

By this time the fighting at Verdun had also ground to a halt, with the French and Germans losing over 600,000 men between them for very little material gain, but the city hadn't fallen and Falkenhayn's tactical gamble had failed. The desired breakthrough did not materialise and with German losses running higher than those of the French, the battle quietly petered out in December.

The war continued in other theatres as well throughout 1916, and it was in the Middle East that one Old Bloxhamist lost his life, fighting against the Turks in the Yemen. The campaign in this part of the world was one of the most forgotten about theatres of war, but this loss was to continue into 1917 and beyond.

As the year closed in 1916, the Allied efforts had been largely a failure and the death toll on all sides neared a million men, and the Germans remained ensconced in France and Belgium.

Lieutenant James Clement Smith
4th Royal Fusiliers
Pupil at Bloxham School 1899-1900
Died of wounds 27 March 1916, aged 33
Commemorated on the Menin Gate Memorial to the Missing, Ypres, Belgium
Panel 6

James Clement Smith was the sixth of eight children born to Bryan Hinton Smith and his wife Mary Anna, who lived in the village of Ashwood Bank in Worcestershire. He had three sisters and a brother, as well as a half-brother and two half-sisters from Bryan's first marriage. When his father, a needle maker by trade, died in 1892, his widow and her children went to live with her sister, Frances Tysoe Smith, who owned the Montpellier Hotel in Llandrindod Wells. Frances was also a prominent member of the St Ives colony of artists, noted for her oil paintings of maritime life and a regular exhibitor at the Royal Academy.

James arrived at Bloxham in May 1899 and within a month had played cricket in the 2nd XI's match against Banbury Night School, though for the opposition when they turned up with only ten players. He was the top run scorer that season in Division II (for those not in a school team), but was unable to force his way into the 2nd XI. James came into his own in the football season, representing the 1st XI and being adjudged by *The Bloxhamist* to be a 'useful player at left-half, though rather inclined to dribble too much; always plays a very hard game, can use his head well, and never forgets his forwards.' The editor went on to opine that 'with more weight (he) will prove a useful man', an apposite comment given that he weighed just seven stone and two pounds at this point. By April 1900, he was reported to have 'improved very much. Tackles and feeds his forwards well.'

James made his first appearance on stage at All Saints' Tide in November 1899. An outbreak of German measles and the departure of some of the school's leading actors dictated the choice of a less ambitious play than the Shakespeare productions of recent years. In the farce *Cox and Box*, which only required a cast of three, James played the part of the landlady Mrs Bouncer, and according to the play's reviewer, he showed himself quite equal to the occasion, 'and though he had not a great deal to do he was quite successful in his part.'

While James was at Bloxham, the Boer War had broken out, and he would have taken part in the celebrations for the relief of Ladysmith in March 1900, which resulted in the cancellation of that evening's preparation, which was replaced by an impromptu concert, and the granting of a half-holiday the next day. For James there would have been additional cause for celebration in that his half-brother Charles was serving in South Africa with the Worcestershire Imperial Yeomanry.

After leaving Bloxham in April 1900, James became an electrical engineer by profession, working for the National Telephone Company. At the outbreak of war, he volunteered into the 16th Battalion the Middlesex Regiment (The Public Schools Battalion), enlisting in London on 7 September 1914. James was later commissioned as a 2nd Lieutenant in the 4th Royal Fusiliers.

By 1916 he was the bombing officer (bombs were hand grenades) for X Company, 4th Royal Fusiliers, who on 25 March found themselves in trenches near St Eloi. This area had been heavily mined by both sides and the battlefield was a morass of water-filled craters. The area was dominated by an earth bank known as The Mound, which formed part of a nasty German salient which poked into the British lines and dominated the surrounding area. For six months, the British had been digging six mines under the German lines, four finishing under the German trenches, and two finishing in No Man's Land. The idea was to detonate the mines with no warning and no preliminary artillery bombardment, before sending in the infantry, to capitalise on the surprise. The 4th Royal Fusiliers attacked to the right, the 1st Northumberland Fusiliers attacked to the left. The mines were exploded at 4:15 a.m. on 27 March 1916, and the infantry attacked some 30 seconds later. As soon as they left the trenches, the 4th Royal Fusiliers were sprayed with machine gun fire, and less than one minute after the mines had detonated, intense and accurate German artillery fire began to fall amongst the men. They were disorientated, being decimated by bullets and shell fire, and were lost in the featureless wilderness of shell holes and craters.

As Private S. Williams of Z Lewis Gun Company reported, 'We came to a place called the Mound of Death, or The Mound, it lies between Vooremezeele and St Eloi and is to the right of The Bluff. Lt. Smith was a brave man and led us forward without hesitation. The following morning we were making our way back to the lines, and I saw the dead body of Lt. Smith lying on the German side of the crater. A few more yards and he would have made the German lines.'

Although his commanding officer wrote to James' parents to say that 'He was killed whilst so gallantly leading his men, in such a successful attack', it was in fact a failure which cost the battalion losses of five officers and 255 other ranks. James was counted as missing, and his body was never recovered. Consequently, his is one of the 54,395 names inscribed on the Menin Gate in Ypres. He was 33 years old when he died. He was single and left everything in his will to his mother. James' brother Ernest, himself an Old Bloxhamist, gave 10 shillings to the newly launched fund for a Bloxham war memorial, and in December 1916 James' mother made a further donation in his memory and that of his half-brother Charles, who had been killed in action the following month.

As well as his commanding officer, James' parents also heard from the Rev. Noel Mellish VC, who sought to reassure them that 'his life was not given in vain, for a life sacrificed is a life – a splendid, glorious life – won.' They also received a letter from his servant, who told them that 'he died like a hero in action, shouting "Come on, lads, follow me!" It was his last wish that I should send you the enclosed.' Two days before he died, James had written the following letter home: "We are taking part in a *great* attack in a few hours from now. It *must* be a success. I can't think of any other result. If I don't come through alive, my servant will send you a final letter, which I am writing before we move off from camp. But whatever happens we are in the best of spirits and as happy as sand-boys, and we would not have it different for anything in the world.' The letter ended on a strange note at variance with what had gone before: 'I cannot say anything more, but you must read between the lines.'

It is in the research into James Smith that the authors are extremely proud of the detective work they carried out. Over a period of 17 years, searches were made through hundreds of pages of biographical information in an attempt to find a photograph of James Clement Smith. Trying to find an image of a man named Smith, in a regiment that had over 47 battalions was a challenging task. However, one afternoon while in the National Newspaper Archive in Colindale, MD came across a copy of *The London War News Illustrated*. This periodical used to produce a supplement entitled 'He nobly fell on the field of battle' which contained pen portraits of various officers who died. There was normally a period of between 7-11 weeks between a date of death and the publication of an image, and sure enough in the supplement of 23 June 1916 was a small portrait of James Clement Smith. It shows that no matter how challenging the task, genealogy always has the ability to provide wonderful results if you have the patience to look long and hard enough.

Private Alexander Eardley Wilmot Chimms Nairne Samson
Royal Fusiliers (1st Sportsman's Battalion)
Pupil at Bloxham School 1884-1889
Died on active service 10 April 1916, aged 44
Buried in St Mary's Churchyard, Northolt, Middlesex, England

The splendidly named Private Alexander Eardley Wilmot Chimms Nairne Samson was a sugar trader living in Kingston, Jamaica, where he was born, according to the 1901 census. There appears to have been a family connection with the Eardley-Wilmot baronets of Warwickshire on his mother's side.

Alexander made a massive impact in his time at Bloxham between 1884 and 1889 as a sportsman, captaining the 1st XI at football and playing for North Oxfordshire in 1889 and

being crowned Senior Champion on Sports Day in 1887 and 1889. He held the junior long jump record (19ft 2in) until 1892 and his winning height of 5ft 2in in the high jump was still a school record when he died. The cup awarded for the Senior High Jump was presented to the school by his mother in Alexander's memory. He was a sub-prefect in his final year in the school. When he left Bloxham in December 1889, the editor of *The Bloxhamist* declared that 'the loss of E. W. Samson—who was probably the best forward the School has ever possessed, and who also played extremely well for this county-—will be greatly felt.'

He was an extremely active Old Boy, regularly attending the annual London dinner and turning out for the Past v the Present. In 1897 he went out to South Africa big game shooting and later became a partner in the Phoenix Gold Mine. Later he returned to England and married Alice Hannah Schofield at the Croydon Registry Office on 23 February 1902. They had a daughter Clarissa May, who was born on 25 July 1903 in Montreal, Canada. According to *The Bloxhamist* he had first gone out to Canada in 1901, shooting in the Rockies.

When war broke out, he enlisted on 14 October 1914 at the advanced age of 42. He joined one of the Pals Battalions, the 23rd (Service) Battalion the Royal Fusiliers, better known as the 1st Sportsman's Battalion. This was formed by Mrs Emma Cunliffe-Owen, a well-connected society lady who decided to set up a battalion similar in ethos to the Pals Battalions being formed all over the country, but one for men who excelled in sport. Her position in London society was such that Mrs Cunliffe-Owen soon had permission from Lord Kitchener to start the formation, and had installed herself in headquarters in the Hotel Cecil on The Strand. Because of their fitness, Mrs Cunliffe-Owen was granted permission to recruit men up to the age of 45, well over the maximum age for enlistment which was 38.

In October 1914, the Battalion commenced training at a purpose-built camp at Hornchurch in Essex, to a great deal of public interest from press and public. Quickly christened the 'Hard as Nails Battalion', they were then transferred to 99th Brigade, 33rd Division, but when they landed in Boulogne in November 1915, Samson was not with them. Of all the 80, his war service is probably the one of which we know least, but it appears that he never served abroad. He certainly had an operation in December 1915 and was discharged as medically unfit in March 1916, dying the following month of unknown causes at the age of 44. He was buried in St Mary's Churchyard, Northolt, Middlesex. He was one of the comparatively few Old Bloxhamists to have served in the ranks, though he was apparently recommended for a commission before his operation.

Lieutenant Archibald Herbert Horner
Eastern Ontario Regiment (Princess Patricia's Canadian Light Infantry)
Pupil at Bloxham School 1890-1898
Killed in action 13 April 1916, aged 37
Buried in Menin Road South Military Cemetery, Belgium
Grave I.J.25

Lieutenant Archibald Herbert Horner was the son of Edward and Blanche Mary Horner. He was born on 5 March 1879 and was a pupil at Bloxham between 1890 and 1898. Archie was the second of five brothers who all attended Bloxham; three served in the war, but he was the only one to perish in it. The family had strong ties with the school: Edward Horner's sister, Annie, was married to the Founder's brother, Hubert Decimus Egerton, the school's Bursar between 1872 and 1896. The Horners lived in Pebmarsh in Suffolk, and Archie's name is one of 12 on that village's war memorial.

Archie was an outstanding sportsman, excelling at both the school's major team games, cricket and football. He captained the Football XI for three seasons (two of his brothers followed him as captain) and played for Oxfordshire, as well as being captain of Tennis and Fives. In Cricket, he topped the school's batting averages in 1897, with a highest score of 145*. Another brother, Frederick, played 29 games in goal for Watford, and Archie himself became the ABA's Heavyweight Champion of England in 1904 (the same title later won by the likes of Frank Bruno (in 1980) and Tony Bellew (2004-6). With no surviving photograph of him in uniform, the school had to provide one of him in football kit, which is appropriate given his sporting prowess. Archie enjoyed a highly successful school career, and it is noticeable that his is the longest of all the obituaries of the 80 in his old school magazine, in which one of his schoolmates described him as 'honest, truthful, kind to all, absolutely unable to do anything mean or underhand, good at games and sporting in everything, and above all, deeply religious in the highest sense.'

Archie was seriously injured playing football against the Britannia Works at Banbury in October 1894, breaking his leg and dislocating his ankle, and his importance to the school can perhaps be gauged from the fact that his recovery from injury was marked by a half-holiday requested by his mother and granted by the Headmaster in March 1895.

Like so many Bloxhamists of their generation, all five of the Horner brothers left the shores of Britain to seek their fortune after school. Four went out to Argentina; the eldest, Jack, (born in

1876) went there in 1895 and worked on a cattle ranch until he accidentally drowned in March 1920. Fred (born 1882), the Watford goalkeeper, joined Jack but died in Argentina in 1911. Humfrey (born 1889) served in the Great War as a Lieutenant in the Norfolks, being wounded in 1918. At the end of the war he returned to Argentina to farm. The youngest brother, Geoffrey (born 1892), went out to Canada just before the war, and served during it as a Trooper in the 2nd Canadian Mounted Rifles, seeing action at the Somme, Vimy Ridge and Passchendaele and being mentioned in despatches and twice wounded. After the war he went back to Alberta.

Archie left school a year before the outbreak of the Boer War and served in South Africa in Paget's Horse (19th Battalion Imperial Yeomanry), an elite cavalry unit made up of public school-educated men recruited through advertisements in gentlemen's clubs in Pall Mall. Wags suggested that the battalion's PH badge stood for 'Piccadilly Heroes' or even 'Perfectly Harmless', though Archie's old teacher Charles Wilson suggested that this was changed to 'Punch Hards' once they had been proved in combat. The battalion arrived in Cape Town in April 1900 and Archie saw action at Haartesbeestfontein in February 1901 – this was described by *The Bloxhamist* as a battle, but in reality was a skirmish, though Archie's letter describing the action gives a graphic sense of the dangers he faced – 'very hard work it was, all the time hearing the bullets singing and whistling around.' His commanding officer wrote to him after the war to tell him 'how much I admired your splendid endurance and your cheery disposition and fine example.'

Following the South African War, Archie enjoyed considerable success boxing for Belsize Amateur Boxing Club. In 1904 he won the ABA Heavyweight Championship, beating the redoubtable Fred Parks, who had already won the title three times and would go on to win it again in 1905 and 1906. Archie's father presented a photograph of the champion to adorn the school's brand-new gymnasium, and it must have been a matter of considerable pride for a small school with no boxing tradition to boast a national champion, especially when he was part of a team of seven boxers who represented their country in an international match against France in Paris in December 1904.

Having made his mark in both sporting and military spheres, Archie went to Argentina to join Jack on his ranch, before emigrating to Canada as so many Old Bloxhamists at the time did, to make his fortune, also as a rancher. He bought 320 acres of land near Lumby in a remote part of British Columbia and set about clearing it of trees and bushes and building a wooden home with his brother, Geoffrey. When war broke out in August 1914, Archie volunteered to join Princess Patricia's Canadian Light Infantry, a unit named after the daughter of the Governor General of Canada, Prince Arthur of Connaught. Archie enlisted at Port Levis, Quebec and was recorded as being aged 35 years 4 months, height 5 feet 11 inches, girth 41 inches, complexion fresh, eyes blue, hair fair; religious denomination Church of England.

Remarkably, the battalion was recruited and formed in just eight days and was ready to leave Canada less than a month after the war broke out, arriving in Bustard Camp on Salisbury Plain for training in October 1914. Archie joined as a private soldier, but as a Boer War veteran in an expeditionary force short of officers and NCOs, was soon promoted to Serjeant in 1915 and then obtained a commission as a Lieutenant on 11 June 1915. Despite his powerful physique and sporting prowess, Archie was not immune from the perils of trench warfare and spent much of 1915 invalided at home suffering from trench foot. This gangrene-like disease was caused by continual immersion of the feet in cold water, which led to swelling, intense pain and in some cases amputation. Archie seems to have been fortunate in recovering from this, only to then suffer a knee injury. He did eventually rejoin his regiment in the trenches near Ypres in April 1916.

The Hooge area in which he now found himself was considered 'hot', in other words a dangerous sector of the line. On his first day back with the regiment, and while temporarily commanding his company, he exposed his head above the parapet, and a German sniper shot him through the head. He was killed on 13 April 1916 and is buried in Menin Road South Cemetery in Ypres. As well as at Bloxham, his name is on the war memorial at Pebmarsh in Essex, close to the border with Suffolk.

His commanding officer, Lieutenant Colonel Herbert Buller, wrote to Archie's father Edward to tell him that 'he always proved himself a most cheery and capable officer, always ready to help in anything that was required, and was popular with everyone.' Buller would himself be killed in action at Ypres within six weeks of writing. One can read beyond the conventional platitudes of this sort of letter to see that Archie Horner does appear to have been an exceptional individual. *The Bloxhamist* recorded that his name would be 'handed down to future generations with the honour due to him who was so splendid an exponent of *Justorum semita lux splendens*' (the school motto, 'The path of the just is a shining light', from the Book of Proverbs). One of Archie's contemporaries asserted that 'I know that the whole moral tone of the school was far higher when he left than when he entered it. This was very largely due to him, and I believe I am right in saying that it was due more to him than to any other individual among either the boys or masters.' In today's more cynical age, such language would seem sentimental and out of place, but it reinforces just how highly esteemed Archie Horner was, and what a blow his death was to his family and his old school.

For MD in particular, Archie Horner holds a special place. When the odyssey of researching the school's fallen began back in 2000, Horner's grave was the first one of the 80 visited on a very wet day in Belgium.

Trooper Charles Howard Smith
Worcestershire Yeomanry
Pupil at Bloxham School 1883-1889
Killed in action 23 April 1916, aged 42
Commemorated on the Jerusalem Memorial, Israel and Palestine
Panels 5 and 6

Charles Howard Smith was the elder half-brother of James Smith, killed less than a month earlier, but whereas James died at Ypres, a name synonymous with the British contribution to the fighting on the Western Front, Charles was killed in battle a few miles away from the Suez Canal in Egypt in a little-known campaign against the Ottoman Empire generally remembered, if at all, for the involvement of T.E. Lawrence, 'Lawrence of Arabia'.

Charles was born in April 1874 at Astwood Bank, a village just south of Redditch. He was a pupil at Bloxham between 1883 and 1889, playing for the school's 1st XI at both football and cricket. He fought in the Boer War, enlisting in the Worcestershire Imperial Yeomanry, a volunteer cavalry unit. He was in the same unit (now officially the Queen's Own Worcestershire Hussars) when war broke out in August 1914, and was still a Trooper, so either did not merit promotion or did not want it. He served along with his regiment in the 1st South Midland Mounted Brigade, first seeing action at Gallipoli, where they were landed at Suvla Bay in

support of the Anzac landings there, and then being sent to Egypt, where the regiment was part of the force protecting the eastern side of the Suez Canal from Turkish attack.

At dawn on 23 April 1916, both St George's Day and Easter Sunday, a force of 3,000 Turkish troops commanded by the German General Kress von Kressenstein, including a machine gun battery of 12 guns, advanced across the Sinai Peninsula and raided the British defences at Oghradine. The Turks' initial attack was repulsed but the defenders' only machine gun was put out of action at an early stage and all the gunners were killed or wounded. The weight of their numbers eventually pushed the Yeomanry back after two hours' fierce fighting. The Turks then advanced and captured the outpost at Qatia. Anzac troops, who reoccupied the two positions four days later, testified to the ferocity of the battle and paid tribute to the valour and tenacity of the defenders. Almost all of the men of the three and a half Imperial Yeomanry squadrons at Oghradine and Katia were killed, wounded or captured. In all nine officers and 102 NCOs and men of the Worcestershire Yeomanry were killed, among them Charles Howard Smith, who died at the age of 42. He has no known grave and is remembered on the Jerusalem Memorial as well as the war memorial in his home village, Astwood Bank. The Smith family were instrumental in the creation of the Astwood Bank Cricket Club, which was set up for workers at the family pin factory to play cricket during the summer months. The Club still exists today and is part of the Worcestershire League.

Private Herbert Raymond Standage
20th (Service) Battalion, Royal Fusiliers
Pupil at Bloxham School 1905-1909
Killed in action 17 May 1916, aged 22
Buried in Cambrin Extension Cemetery, France
Grave M.44

Herbert Standage was a pupil at the school from 1905 to 1909 and was the eldest son of the Reverend Samuel Standage who was the Vicar of Great Bourton, a village just north of Banbury. His father was a regular visitor to the school as a member of the cricket team fielded by the clergy of the district. As a junior boy at Bloxham, Herbert showed promise as a batsman, playing in the same 2nd XI as another six boys (Brooks, Sawyer, Bolton, Davy, Riddle and Hill) who would perish in the Great War. He was confirmed in 1907 and joined the editorial

staff of *The Bloxhamist* in 1909. He left the school in the same year when he was still only 15. Little was heard of him at Bloxham after he left school, though the 1911 Census shows Herbert as living at Ingram House Residential Club, which was located at 46 Stockwell Road, in Stockwell, London.

The Bloxhamist magazine of November 1914 recorded Herbert as serving as a Private in the 20th (Service) Battalion Royal Fusiliers (part of the Universities and Public Schools Brigade). While most of his Bloxham contemporaries chose to serve as junior officers, Herbert had joined a unit which contained a great many young public school men who preferred to serve in the ranks. He would have trained with the battalion at Clipstone Camp near Mansfield, and then at Tidworth in Wiltshire, before landing in France in November 1915. Nothing more was heard from him at his old school until notice of Herbert's death was given in the July 1916 edition of *The Bloxhamist*, which recalled that 'we remember him as a quiet retiring boy at school', adding that he was known to his army comrades as 'the man who never grumbled'. Herbert Standage was killed by shell fire on 17 May 1916 at the age of 22. *The Bloxhamist* recorded that he was killed 'instantaneously', but that was wishful thinking on behalf of his commanding officer, as so often in these letters of consolation to parents. His name appears in the record of admissions to the CCS, which indicates that he was dead on arrival – he must therefore have been alive when the ambulance collected him. The letter from his CO was clearly the far more palatable option for his parents to read. He is buried in Cambrin Extension Cemetery, north of Arras. The Rev. Standage and his wife Edith attended the unveiling of the school's war memorial in November 1920, one of only six sets of parents of the fallen to be present.

Second Lieutenant Harold Dudley Long
1/7th City of London Regiment
Pupil at Bloxham School 1910-1913
Killed in action 21 May 1916, aged 20
Commemorated on the Vis-en-Artois Memorial, Arras, France
Panel 9/10

Harold Long was born in 1896, the only child of Henry and Emmeline Long. Henry was an auctioneer by trade. Harold was christened in the parish church at Winchmore Hill, Middlesex on 8 February 1896. The 1901 census shows Harold living with his mother in a shared house at

94 Inderwick Road, Hornsey, at the home of Albert Mager and his wife Marie. Emmeline is listed as 'wife' but there is no mention of Henry Long, so we can only guess that he had either died, or he and Emmeline had separated.

Harold attended Bloxham between 1910 and 1913 and was described as being 'a thoroughly good fellow in every way'. *The Bloxhamist*, went on to note that 'seriousness was probably his chief fault, if that can be described as a fault', and all of the photographs of him at school feature the same serious expression, including one which shows him as one of the servers assisting Chaplain Hugh Willlimott. He would be the first, but not the last, chapel server to lose his life in the war. He was also a server at his home church of St Mary's, Camden. He joined up in late 1914 and arrived in France with his battalion on 18 March 1915, serving in the Arras area and suffering a gunshot wound to the head from which he recovered, returning to the front at the start of 1916. By this time he had been gazetted as a 2nd Lieutenant on 22 October 1915, being promoted from the rank of Serjeant.

In May 1916, Harold's battalion found themselves in the Arras sector facing Vimy Ridge, an area that had been taken over from the French in March 1916, as the French needed to focus on the defence of Verdun. The Londons found poorly constructed trenches and the ground littered with thousands of decaying and poorly buried bodies. The sector was one where the two sides had a 'quiet' relationship with each other and adopted a so-called 'live and let live' policy, but this changed when the British arrived and started to employ regular trench raids and shelling. In May 1916, noticing an enormous build-up of British troops in the area (the preparations for the forthcoming Somme offensive) the Germans decided to launch an attack.

On the morning of 21 May, the 1/7th Londons were in trenches between Givenchy-en-Gohelle and Neuville-Saint-Vaast when the Germans commenced the heaviest artillery bombardment of the war up to this point. In four hours, over 70,000 shells were fired on a front of only 1800 yards, hitting communication and reserve trenches as well as the front line. The Germans attacked that evening. The 1/7th and 1/8th Londons bore the brunt of the attack and were forced to retreat. The 1/7th made an unsuccessful attempt at a counterattack, and the following day, the 1/6th and 1/7th Battalions pushed forward 250 yards to reoccupy an old French trench which they consolidated, thereby preventing any further enemy advance. They were relieved in the evening of 22 May, having suffered heavy casualties. Harold Long was killed during the initial bombardment. His body was never found and he is commemorated on the Arras Memorial, which the Bloxham School Western Front trip visited in October 2015.

He is remembered at his church, St Mary's in Camden, with a plaque which records the gift of a figure of the Holy Mother and child given in his memory.

A brother officer, writing to his mother, said: 'Your son was placed in charge of a very important and dangerous detached post. It may console you somewhat to know that he died bravely defending this position. He clung to his post until the end and died like a hero.'

Sub-Lieutenant Thomas Robertson
Royal Navy
Pupil at Bloxham School 1904-1905
Killed in action 31 May 1916, aged 21
Commemorated on the Portsmouth Naval Memorial, England
Panel 11

On 31 May 1916, the British Grand Fleet and the German High Seas Fleet met off the Danish coast in the long-awaited clash which the British public confidently expected to be a decisive 'Second Trafalgar'. A total of 274 warships and 70,000 seamen were involved, but in the end the battle proved to be something of an anti-climax, and certainly not the crushing victory for British naval power which the public took for granted. Two Bloxhamists perished in the battle.

What happened at Jutland (or Skagerrak as the Germans called it) was in truth only the first stage in a battle which was never completed, as after their initial successes the Germans made their escape and made it back to harbour. Admiral Scheer was able to tempt the British Admiral Beatty into engaging in an action where the superior German gunnery and the flaws in British ship design led to the loss of three British battlecruisers. These ships had been designed to combine the speed of a cruiser with the firepower of a battleship, but their defensive weakness was demonstrated in a confused action in which hazy visibility was made worse by gun smoke, while the position of the late afternoon sun helped the German gunners. Three British ships were badly damaged before *HMS Indefatigable* received five hits and blew up at 16.03 p.m. At 16.25 p.m. a full broadside from the German battlecruiser *SMS Derfflinger* straddled *HMS Queen Mary* and it exploded, disappearing completely within ninety seconds. It was at this point that Beatty famously turned to his flag captain Chatfield and remarked, 'There seems to be something wrong with our bloody ships today.'

There were only ten survivors from *Queen Mary's* crew of 1,276, and among the 57 officers who died was Sub-Lieutenant Thomas Arthur May Robertson. He was the son of Dr James Sprent Robertson, who was a GP in Adderbury when his three sons attended Bloxham, but by the time of the Great War he and his Brazilian wife Lilian had moved to Battersea. Tom had been at Bloxham School between October 1904 and March 1905. He initially served as a Sub-Lieutenant on the battlecruiser *HMS New Zealand* before securing an even more glamorous berth as the Senior Sub Lieutenant on board *HMS Queen Mary*, the most modern warship in the Royal Navy. His elder brother Harold served in the Canadian army and died in France of meningitis in April 1915. Tom was 21 years of age when he died. He is remembered on the Portsmouth Naval Memorial at Southsea.

Naval Surgeon George Shorland
Royal Navy
Pupil at Bloxham 1887-1890
Killed in action 31 May 1916, aged 40
Commemorated on the Portsmouth Naval Memorial, England
Panel 14

By the time *HMS Queen Mary* sank at Jutland, taking Tom Robertson with her, the arrival of the main British battleship fleet (24 Dreadnought battleships and three battlecruisers) under the Commander in Chief, Admiral Jellicoe, was threatening to turn the battle in favour of the British, but before the Germans turned away for home, there was one more disaster for the Royal Navy when Admiral Horace Hood's flagship, *HMS Invincible*, was struck by a shell which penetrated the ship's Q turret at 18:33 p.m. It has often been asserted that what doomed Invincible, the world's first battlecruiser, was not so much faulty design as human error. Rapid fire was a central part of British naval strategy, and in order to speed up the rate of fire, the British were prone to remove the air-tight safety interlocks in the ammunition hoists, allowing bags of cordite to be left lying around and risking any fire in a gun turret reaching the magazines. Naval historian Lawrence Burr has observed that leaving tons of cordite charges with their igniters exposed, stacked up outside open magazines was an accident waiting to happen.

There is little doubt that *Invincible's* safety devices were extremely inadequate - what was meant to be flash tight simply wasn't. However, whether it is possible to ascribe the loss of the battlecruisers to one single factor is highly debatable, and the answer probably lies in a combination of complex factors. In the resulting massive explosion, the ship was ripped apart and sank within 15 seconds, the moment of the explosion apparently being caught on camera on a nearby ship. For some time bow and stern were left clearly visible, each resting on the shallow bottom. In a few seconds, 1,026 men had been killed. Only six officers and men, most of them high up on the ship's foremast, survived. Among those to die was another Old Bloxhamist, Surgeon George Shorland.

Unlike Robertson, Shorland was an experienced professional man by the time of Jutland. He was born at Westbury in Wiltshire on 18 March 1876, the son of Dr. Edward Peter Shorland, a surgeon, and Caroline Anne Elizabeth (née Bluett) Shorland of Church Street, Westbury. He was christened at Westbury on 15 May 1876.

George was a pupil at Bloxham from 1887 to 1890 before moving onto Lancing College where he was in School House from January 1891 to July 1893. It was not unusual at this point in Bloxham's history for parents to use it as a 'preparatory school', sending their sons to a bigger and more prestigious school for their final years. George went on to King's College, Cambridge to study medicine and Guy's Hospital, taking MRCS and LRCP Lond. in 1901 and graduating as MB ChB in 1906. He worked for a while at the Cambridge Infirmary before moving to London where he worked at the City Hospital in Whitechapel.

George was married to Gertrude Harriett (née Adams) and they had three sons. At the time of his death the family was living at Park View Cottage, Berkhamsted in Hertfordshire. He was in general practice at Mill Hill and worked occasionally as a locum at St Pancras Station where he was medical officer of the Clearing House in Euston Square. He was also honorary surgeon to the Railway Benevolent Institution up until he accepted a commission in the Royal Navy. He was appointed as a Surgeon in the Royal Navy on 3 November 1915 and was posted to *HMS Invincible*, part of the 3rd Battle Cruiser Squadron.

Most of those Old Bloxhamists who died on the Western Front received some form of burial, whether or not their bodies could be identified, but George Shorland's remains went to the bottom of the North Sea along with his crewmates as did those of Thomas Robertson. As well as their old school's memorial in chapel, both men are commemorated on the Portsmouth Naval Memorial. Having been involved in a number of communities during a busy career, George was additionally commemorated in a further five places, the war memorial at Lancing College, the war memorial at Mill Hill, on the memorial at St Mary's Church, Northchurch, Berkhamsted and on the memorial at Guy's Hospital in London, as well as on a carved wooden plaque at All Saints Church, Westbury.

Queen Mary's wreck was discovered in 1991 and rests in pieces, some of which are upside down, on the floor of the North Sea. *Invincible's* wreck is lying on a sandy bottom at a depth of 180 feet; her stern is right-side up and the bow upside-down, and the 12 - inch guns in Q turret remain loaded although its roof is missing, supporting the theory that the ship was blown apart by an explosion in the magazine. Both wrecks are protected sites under the Protection of Military Remains Act 1986.

Brigadier General Wilfred Ellershaw
Royal Artillery
Pupil at Bloxham 1884–1886
Died at sea 5 June 1916, aged 44
Commemorated on the Hollybrook Memorial, Southampton, England
Panel 1

Five days after the Battle of Jutland, the British public was shattered to learn of the death of the country's most celebrated soldier, Lord Kitchener, whose face was familiar to all through the iconic and ubiquitous recruiting poster, which featured his pointing finger. When Kitchener drowned off Scapa Flow in the sinking of *HMS Hampshire* on 5 June 1916 when about to sail to Russia, he was one of 650 men to perish, including nine members of the Field Marshal's staff. The most senior of these was Brigadier General Wilfred Ellershaw, the most senior Old Bloxhamist to die in the Great War.

Wilfred Ellershaw was the son of Rev. John Ellershaw of Chew Stoke, Somerset. There is some confusion over the spelling of his Christian name, with Bloxham School's records listing him as Wilfrid, a spelling also favoured in his obituary in *Wisden Cricketers' Almanack*. We have decided to follow the spelling used by the Army. He was born on 16 July 1871 and followed his elder brother Edward to Marlborough College in 1883, but left the following year, moving to Bloxham School in September 1884; neither school has been able to explain the change, but it was not uncommon in Victorian times for pupils to move schools in the middle of their schooling.

Edward, born in 1867, served as a Captain with the South Wales Borderers in the Boer War, staying on in South Africa to become a barrister in the Transvaal. A third brother, Arthur, born in 1869, attended Westminster School and also entered the Royal Artillery, retiring as Brigadier General in 1925. Arthur served on the Northwest Frontier of India (1897-8) and then in South Africa, where he was severely wounded and was awarded four Queen's Medals with clasps. He became a Major in 1909 and Lieutenant Colonel in 1916 and was awarded the DSO in 1915. The existence of two brothers who were both senior officers in the Royal Artillery was to cause considerable confusion in June 1916, when newspapers initially reported Arthur to have been the Ellershaw brother to have drowned. To add to the potential for mistaken identity, there was a third Ellershaw in the Royal Artillery, Brigadier General Walter Ellershaw, who was Chief Instructor at the School of Gunnery at Larkhill and would go on to command the heavy artillery of three different corps between February 1917 and the end of the war.

Whilst at Bloxham Wilfred played football for his dormitory (the forerunner of houses) and cricket for the 2nd XI and was appointed a sub-prefect, but when he left in December 1886 he was still too young to have made any great impact at the school. Ellershaw proceeded to the Royal Military Academy, Woolwich, where he was a member of the 1st XI in 1891, when he made 226 runs at an average of 14.12 and scored 33 against Sandhurst. He went on to play a good deal of military cricket, especially for the Royal Artillery, and he was a member of the MCC from 1904. His obituary would appear in the same edition of *Wisden* as that of W.G. Grace. He was commissioned into the Royal Artillery in 1892. He served on the North-West Frontier between 1897 and 1898 and was promoted Captain in 1899, when he became an Instructor at the Royal Military Academy as well as marrying Catherine Ingles, daughter of Rear-Admiral John Ingles on 22 June 1899. They had four daughters, Katherine, Phyllis, Ruth and Mary.

After his service at Woolwich, Wilfred then served as an Instructor at the School of Signalling. Following service in Aden he was Adjutant of 27th Brigade RFA between 1906 and 1912. In 1914 Ellershaw was a Major on the Artillery staff; the outbreak of war saw a rapid expansion of the Army with new batteries and brigades being formed from the regular cadres. One of these was 113th Battery which Ellershaw was appointed to command. In August 1914, they were embarked for France as part of 25th Brigade RFA equipped with 18-pounder guns, each pulled by six horses. As part of Major General Lomax's 1st Division in Haig's I Corps, they took part in the Retreat from Mons and the counterattack on the Marne.

Wilfred's battery saw plenty of action – he wrote home on 5 September and reported 'I am writing this in the middle of a terrific battle, it has been awful slaughter and has been going on since yesterday morning and seems likely to go on for some days.' He remarked on the devastating effect of modern artillery fire – 'At last I got six splendid shrapnel on to a wood and cleared a heap of them out and then got into them with shrapnel; it is awful', adding that even his Serjeant-Major had put his hands up to his head and said, 'Oh, sir, it's terrible!' On 12 September, his battery crossed the River Aisne at Bourg and on the 14th came under heavy fire in an action near Vendresse, with Bombardier Horlock receiving the Victoria Cross for his bravery in remaining with his gun when his entire crew had been killed. Ellershaw was mentioned in despatches for his part in the campaign.

As Ellershaw himself had observed, 'It is a war of artillery so far', and his expertise was required at home, being ordered to report to the War Office. Convinced that Russia's critical shortage of shells was due to the incompetence of Tsarist officials, Lord Kitchener asked the War Office to find 'a thoroughly up-to-date gunner of sufficient standing to be able to keep his end up when dealing with superior Russian officials'; he must also have business capacity, tact and energy, as well as being a French speaker. Ellershaw was selected and set off for Russia in May 1915, returning from his meeting with the Russian commander, the Tsar's cousin, Grand Duke Nicholas, convinced that if supplies were not found quickly, Russia would collapse. He then headed to the USA, placing orders on Kitchener's behalf for 12 million shells and 200,000 rifles, all done via J.P. Morgan, who refused to deal directly with the prickly Russian officials. The Americans had offered 25 million rounds, but the complacent Tsarist High Command insisted that Russia was in no danger of running out of shells.

By the end of the year Kitchener was being told by his representative in St Petersburg that 'Ellershaw is working wonders', despite encountering Russian bureaucracy, corruption and political infighting at every step. Russian appreciation of his efforts was reflected in the award of the Order of Saint Stanislas (First Class). Before taking up a permanent post in the USA, he was asked to accompany Kitchener on his fateful mission to Archangel to keep Russia supplied and fighting. On the night of 4 June 1916 Ellershaw joined Kitchener on the night train to Thurso, on his way to Scapa Flow, anchorage of the British Grand Fleet. There they boarded the fast armoured cruiser *HMS Hampshire,* which had just returned from the Battle of Jutland. At about quarter to nine in the evening, in stormy conditions and within two miles of Orkney's northwest shore, she struck a mine which had been laid by German submarine *U-75* a week earlier and sank within twenty minutes, officially with the loss of 650 lives, though recent research by local historians Brian Budge and Andrew Hollinrake has suggested that the final death toll was 737. Only twelve members of the crew survived, and of Kitchener's staff of ten only Fitzgerald's body was washed ashore. As with Kitchener, Wilfred Ellershaw's grave is the sea off Marwick Head, Orkney. *HMS Hampshire* capsized as she sank and lies with an upturned hull on the seabed, in approximately 60 metres of water.

The impact of the death of Lord Kitchener cannot be overstated – it was that generation's 9/11 or Kennedy assassination. There remains to this day, however, much controversy and intrigue about the events of that evening. The RNLI rushed to launch the Stromness lifeboat, but to their surprise their offer was strenuously rejected. Further up the coast armed soldiers stood guard preventing locals from reaching the stricken ship. The Hampshire had been down for almost four hours before the first lifeboats reached the shore. The first raft which had forty men in when it left the ship, picked up thirty more from the sea, but by the time it reached the shoreline only six men remained alive. A second craft carrying fifty men later arrived on the shoreline and only four men remained alive. Many of those who made it were unable to haul themselves up the rocks and most died on the shoreline. Of the 667 men who left Orkney only twelve survived the sinking, and Kitchener was not among them, dying on board with his staff.

The actions of the authorities that night inevitably led to intense speculation about the sinking. Questions were asked about why the Hampshire left Orkney in such a hurry with such bad weather forecast. Why were locals prevented from helping and why were armed soldiers found warding them off? If people had actively been discouraged from trying to rescue the stricken craft, there must have been a reason for this. Theories circulated that Kitchener had been deliberately killed or that he had not actually been in the boat at all, or a body double was lying dead in the sea in his place.

To this day, no one is really sure what happened on the night that the Hampshire sunk. What is likely, is that during the confusing aftermath of the fighting at Jutland, no one from Naval Intelligence or the Coastal Protection Division noticed U-75 penetrating the waters off Orkney. On the night itself, officials weren't sure which ship had sunk, indeed whether it was a British or a German vessel.

Whether the Kitchener mission would have made any difference we cannot tell, but we know that nine months later the Tsar was overthrown and within a year of that, the Russians had left the war as Ellershaw had predicted. One expert on the subject judges that the loss of Ellershaw was a greater blow to the Anglo-Russian war effort than that of Kitchener, given the Field Marshal's 'arbitrary leadership and tendency to operate outside official channel' General Callwell judged that Ellershaw 'proved himself to be absolutely made for the Russian job.'

Ellershaw is commemorated alongside Kitchener on the Hollybrook Memorial at Southampton and at his parish church in Wymering in addition to memorials at Bloxham School and Marlborough College, as well as the MCC memorial at Lord's. His name is also listed on the Kitchener Memorial at Marwick Head, on the west coast of the Orkney mainland, a beautiful but desolate spot which SB was fortunate enough to visit in the summer of 2021.

Second Lieutenant Kingsley Meredith Chatterton Fradd
2nd London Regiment, Royal Fusiliers
Pupil at Bloxham School 1908-1914
Killed in action 1 July 1916, aged 18
Buried in Hébuterne Military Cemetery, France
Grave IV.A.10

As for so many schools, the first day of the Battle of the Somme, 1 July 1916, was the single most disastrous day of the war for Bloxham School. The three Bloxhamists who died that day stand as a fair representation of the volunteer mass army, which faced its first great test on the Somme. Kingsley Fradd was an 18-year-old subaltern, the epitome of the fresh-faced public schoolboy junior officer of popular imagination. William Potter was two years older, a Lance-Corporal in the London Rifle Brigade. Tommy Guest was a good deal older than the other two, a 41-year-old Major and Boer War veteran commanding a company of the Barnsley Pals.

Kingsley Fradd was born on 24 August 1897 in Highgate, London, the oldest of five children of Martin Meredith and Ada Fradd née Chatterton. His father is listed in the 1911 census as an author and journalist, and may be the same Martin Fradd who was the first editor of *The Evening News*, the first popular evening paper in London, which was priced at one halfpenny. In his time at Bloxham, Kingsley was a sergeant in the Officers Training Corps, a chapel server and a keen actor; typically for boys' schools through the ages, he was condemned to a succession of female dramatic roles by his short stature – his enlistment papers reveal him to have been 5 feet 4 ¾ inches tall (the minimum height was 5 feet 3 inches). When the one act play *The Silent System* was staged in July 1910, *The Bloxhamist* judged that 'as the cockney servant girl, Fradd made a decided hit'. After leaving Bloxham in July 1914, he emigrated to Canada, starting in the main branch of the Bank of Nova Scotia in Cobourg, Ontario on 14 September 1914. A year later he returned to Britain, sailing from Montreal aboard the *Sicilian* and arrived in England in October 1915. He enlisted in the 4/2 Battalion, the London Regiment (the Royal Fusiliers), his experience in the Bloxham OTC guaranteeing him a commission despite his youth. He gave his address as 41 Fitzroy Street in Fitzrovia, a fashionable area of London which before the war was home to a group of artists led by Walter Sickert.

On 1 July 1916 Kingsley Fradd's battalion was part of the 56th (London) Division, tasked with launching a diversionary attack on Gommecourt in the north of the German line. The 2nd Londons were held in reserve, lying in the open until 2.30 p.m. They were ordered to attack a German line known as Ferret Trench; three attempts were made, each foiled by German artillery and machine gun fire. The attack at Gommecourt, represents one of the most disturbing aspects of the Somme battle. The sole purpose of the attack was to distract the Germans and to prevent them from sending reserves down to the strategically important village of Serre, which lay to the south. There was no tactical or military sense in attacking the heavily defended woodland of Gommecourt, and those officers and men must have been under no illusions that they would be sacrificing their own lives in this operation.

During one of these attacks, Kingsley Fradd was killed. He lies buried in the beautiful cemetery at Hébuterne, north of Albert, in the same row as ten men of his battalion. His name is recorded on the war memorial of the parish church of St. Mary Magdalene in Munster Square, close to his old family home, and on the memorial which stands in the entrance lobby to the headquarters of his old bank, now known as Scotiabank, in Ontario, as well as in its Book of Remembrance.

Sadly, the school does not have a photograph of Kingsley in army uniform, as his was one of those lost when the fourth board was burnt in the fire of 1985. Most of the photographs taken of him at school tended to show him in costume in female dramatic roles, but we have unearthed a fine image of him as a smart young man in a suit.

Lance Corporal William Henry Potter
3/5th Battalion London Regiment, the London Rifle Brigade
Pupil at Bloxham School 1908-1912
Killed in action 1 July 1916, aged 20
Commemorated on the Thiepval Memorial to the Missing, France
Panel 9.D

William Henry Potter was a pupil at Bloxham between September 1908 and July 1912. His parents were William Godfrey Potter and Mary Pyne Potter, of 29, Warnborough Road, Oxford, just off Walton Street in a smart part of North Oxford. He was a keen cricketer, playing for the 2nd XI in the 1911 season. When they played Abingdon School, they travelled 'by means of a motor hired from Banbury', as reported by *The Bloxhamist*. 'As this vehicle sustained a few punctures on the road, it was somewhat late before the team arrived, and the result was that the match was left drawn decidedly in our favour.' The following season he broke into the 1st XI, batting at number six. When Bloxham played Magdalen College School, Oxford in June 1912, he made 36 and shared in a sizeable partnership with Basil Brooks, another Bloxhamist and resident of North Oxford to perish on the Somme. They are shown together in a photograph of the 1912 1st hockey XI, with Potter standing directly behind Brooks.

When war broke out in 1914, the two schoolmates followed very different paths; Basil Brooks was commissioned as an officer, while William Potter became a private soldier in the 3/5th Battalion London Regiment (the London Rifle Brigade). The difference between the two might have something to do with the fact that unlike Brooks, and most of his Bloxham contemporaries, Potter had not been a member of the OTC while at school. Judging by his service number (2803), William joined up at some time in September 1915. By 1916 he was

a Lance-Corporal, one of only two among the 80 to hold that rank at the time of their death. Most were officers, with several others enlisting as privates, some of them choosing to serve in the ranks when they might have obtained a commission.

William was killed on the first day of the Battle of the Somme, when the London Rifle Brigade was deployed in the diversionary attack at Gommecourt. William was hit by a sniper's bullet which killed him instantly, or at least that is what *The Bloxhamist* said. The gruesome but more likely reality was that he was killed near to Gommecourt Wood. The Germans had dug a massive pit which they lined with barbed wire and covered with turf, so it was effectively invisible. Those men who fell into it were decimated by two well sited German machine guns Whatever the case, his body was never found, and he is now commemorated on the vast Thiepval Memorial to the Missing. William was 20 years old when he died.

Major Thomas Heald Guest
13th York and Lancaster Regiment (1st Barnsley Pals)
Pupil at Bloxham School 1886-1889
Missing in action 1 July 1916, aged 40
Commemorated on the Thiepval Memorial to the Missing, France
Panel 14.A

Thanks to the attention given to the much-studied phenomenon of the Pals battalions and to their assault on Serre on 1 July, we know a comparatively large amount about Thomas Heald Guest, generally known as Tommy Guest.

Thomas Heald Guest was born in 1875 in Rusholme, Lancashire, the son of Thomas Guest senior, a prosperous Barnsley grocer and confectioner and JP, as his father, another Thomas, had been before him. Thomas's middle name, Heald, was his mother's maiden name. The Guest family shop on Market Hill in Barnsley was an impressive three storey building and included a warehouse, a restaurant and a wine cellar. The business closed in 1973 after 134 years on Market Hill and the store is now an Irish themed pub. Guest's was remembered by one Barnsley resident as 'THE shop to patronise if you were well off. Ladies with big hats, long gloves and their pearls used to visit for afternoon tea, this was in the 50s. Sometimes as a treat, (we) used to go in our walking out days.' The confectionery business was clearly a lucrative one, as the family firm is recorded in the 1881 census as employing 79 people. It seems likely that the reason Thomas attended Bloxham School was because it was the old school of his uncle Arthur

Guest, who from 1877 was the vicar of Lower Peover, near Knutsford in Cheshire. Thomas' three years at Bloxham (1886-1889) were undistinguished, though he did play some cricket for the school at a junior level.

Thomas married Ethel Fountain, the daughter of a colliery owner from Haigh in Yorkshire. They had no children. The marriage was conducted by his uncle Arthur and took place at Darton parish church on 3 October 1905. Tom's residence is given as Bowden, which is near Altrincham in Cheshire. By this stage in his life Thomas had served in the Boer War in the Cape Mounted Riflemen, earning three wound stripes and two medals, including the South Africa Medal and Clasps (1901) for Cape Colony, Orange Free State and the Transvaal. In 1911 he and Ethel were recorded in the census as living in Brighton, when under Occupation he is recorded to have 'private means', but he may have been working in the family business when war broke out, which would explain why he volunteered in Barnsley in the local regiment.

In 1914 he was made a temporary Second Lieutenant in the 13th York and Lancaster Regiment, the so-called First Barnsley Pals, and was promoted to Major in 1915. His photograph, with cap at a rakish angle, gives us an impression of someone who was not one for standing on ceremony. In his book *The Barnsley Pals* John Cooksey gives one example of the sort of gesture which made Tommy such a popular officer with his men while they were training back in Yorkshire. According to Private Harry Hall, 'We used to march out as far as Kexborough and on the way back along Walefield Road we'd have a stop at "The Sportsman", Smithies. Tommy Guest used to have a barrel laid on outside. There'd be a pint for all of us – he was a good old stick!'

The two Barnsley Pals battalions (the 13th and 14th York and Lancaster Regiment) were placed in the 94th Brigade of the 31st Division along with the Sheffield City Battalion (the 12th Battalion) and the Accrington Pals (11th Battalion, East Lancashire Regiment). The Division was sent to Egypt to guard the Suez Canal and then shipped to France in March 1916 as preparations for the forthcoming 'Big Push' intensified. Following a week-long bombardment, the Sheffield City Battalion and the Accrington Pals were to take four lines of German trenches before pushing through Serre behind a creeping barrage, while the 1st and 2nd Barnsley Pal took care of clearing-up operations as well as guarding the west flank and providing the Brigade reserve. However, the bombardment had failed to destroy the deep underground bunkers where the Germans took shelter. Crucially, there were not enough high explosive shells used, and shrapnel failed to clear the barbed wire in front of the German trenches – as one of Major Guest's soldiers later commented, 'the German wire hadn't been cut and it should have been.' The ending of the bombardment gave the Germans warning that the British advance was coming. The Germans had machine guns ready to set up and concealed artillery in place behind the village of Serre. As the troops left their front line at 07.30 a.m., all the ingredients were in place for a disaster at Serre. This was the assault for which the attack at Gommecourt, in which Fradd and Potter lost their lives, was meant to be a diversion.

When the Accrington Pals set off, two platoons of A Company followed them, while Guest's B Company was ordered to follow the Lancastrians' fourth wave in their advance ten minutes later; as company commander, Guest was given the option by Colonel Wilford whether to lead his men over the top or stay in reserve, but for someone who had risen from the ranks in a previous war, the decision was an easy one. He is said to have addressed his men as follows: 'Now boys, we have to uphold the honour of the old town and remember, I am the first over the top. Over boys and give them hell.' He led his company across No Man's Land, but they soon started to take heavy casualties from the German machine guns. Guest pressed on, and in company with Lieutenant Hepstonstall and three Pals he made his way through a gap in the wire and almost reached the German trenches. Hepstonstall then fell, wounded in the side, into a shell crater, noting as he did so the three men falling and Guest being shot in the right leg just as he was reaching the German front line. He was never seen again.

Private Harry Hall, one of those who made it back to the British front line, later recalled that 'somebody had seen Major Guest fall but didn't know if he was hit and wounded or hit and killed.' Hall was one of only fifteen who attended roll call later that morning out of about 300 men. Others drifted back as the day went on. Hepstonstall, pinned down by German snipers in a shell crater, was only able to crawl back across No Man's Land when night fell and reported that he had seen a bullet strike the company commander. Such was Guest's popularity that several men volunteered to search for him – Harry Hall reported that 'they decided to go out and find him that night. There were about four or five of them. They went out but they never came back.' The Battalion's War Diary records that 'the night was spent in collecting wounded & dead within our line and from No Man's Land, and in repairing our much battered trenches and consolidating our position.'

In all, the 1st Barnsley Pals lost approximately 290 men that day, while the 2nd Barnsley Pals suffered 270 casualties. When the news of the battalions' losses started to appear in newspapers back in South Yorkshire, Guest was still listed as missing, with the *Barnsley Chronicle* insisting that 'there is still hope.' Private Crossley, who had cut the Major's hair the day before as he was keen to appear well turned-out for the 'Big Push', remembered, 'I picked up a paper with Major Guest's photo in it. He is a man who will be greatly missed by the Battalion as he was a fine soldier and a proper gentleman. It was fine to see the lads go over the top as if on parade; not one faltered, but straight on for a noble cause.' There are letters in the Major's file at the National Archives from a Lieutenant de Commarque and from Christopher Needham, Liberal MP for Manchester South West and a family friend, asking the War Office for news of him. Ethel, waiting anxiously for news at home in Port Erin on the Isle of Man, was finally informed by Colonel Wilford at the beginning of August that her husband was presumed to be dead. He assured her that 'Our Brigadier, who has seen many fights, remarked that he had never seen anything more splendid than the way your husband led his men through the heavy artillery barrage and intense machine gun fire. He showed an example of bravery and devotion which has been unequalled.'

Thomas' name was placed on St John's Memorial Tablet in the church in the Barebones area of Barnsley, but this was sadly lost when the church was demolished in the 1960s. Towards the end of the war, Thomas Guest senior, along with his son's widow, paid for work in St Oswald's Church, Lower Peover, replacing the chancel floor with black and white marble and erecting a brass plaque on the oak panelling of the chancel in memory of his son, as reported in the *Liverpool Daily Post* for 10 October 1918. The plaque is a beautiful piece of work and includes his old school crest. He also contributed £1 to the War Memorial, which was to be erected in Bloxham School's chapel, and on the same list of contributors appears the name of the mother of William Henry Potter, also killed on 1 July and commemorated on the Thiepval Memorial.

Second Lieutenant Edward Gordon Peecock
9th Battalion, Royal Fusiliers
Pupil at Bloxham School 1908-1911
Killed in action 7 July 1916, aged 22
Commemorated on the Thiepval Memorial to the Missing, France
Panel 8.C

Edward Gordon Peecock was the second son of Edward Beck Peecock and his wife Elizabeth, who lived at 65, Westbury Road in Brentwood, Essex. His father was a commercial traveller, and he had an older brother, Percival. He was born on 26 February 1894 and was a pupil at the school between September 1908 and July 1911. We have followed the school's practice by referring to him by his second name, Gordon.

Gordon was not a prominent team player, but was a speedy runner, and was probably unfortunate to have been at Bloxham at the same time as a number of outstanding athletes. He competed in the 120 Yards Handicap on Sports Day in 1910, winning his heat in the first of four rounds, but failed to make it through in a strongly contested event featuring such talented performers as Frank Riddle and the Cain brothers. His talents lay perhaps more in the field of music. Of his performance of Roubier's *Menuet Impromptu* at the All Saints Day concert in November 1910, *The Bloxhamist* observed that 'Peecock's pianoforte solo was all too short'. He was also an active member of the school's Debating Society, speaking in February 1909 against the reintroduction of conscription and in December 1910 in favour of a motion that 'in the opinion of this House, aeroplanes will be the ruin of Great Britain's supremacy.'

Along with Arthur Stevens, he was one of the first 22 boys to join the OTC on its formation in 1910 and was rapidly promoted to Lance-Corporal along with Basil Brooks. He was also a Prefect in his final year at the school.

Leaving Bloxham at the end of the Summer Term in 1911, Gordon studied to become a Chartered Accountant. He was an active member of the Old Bloxhamist Society, attending their annual dinner at the Trocadero Restaurant in January 1912 and again in 1913, and subscribing to the appeal for the new altar and reredos which served as the school's memorial to its recently deceased Founder, P.R. Egerton. He also contributed the substantial sum of £5 to the chapel organ fund.

When war broke out, Gordon Peecock enlisted on 1 September 1914 as Private 2482 in the 28th (County of London) Battalion, London Regiment (the Artists' Rifles), a territorial unit which was particularly successful in attracting recruits from the public schools and universities as well as the arts. He landed in France on 17 January 1915 and is shown as being commissioned as a Second Lieutenant on 6 November 1915 into the 9th Battalion Royal Fusiliers. For eight months he acted as the battalion's Sniper Officer - this was the officer responsible for training men from each battalion to be sniper. The officer would not be a sniper himself.

In July 1916, the battalion was heavily involved in the fighting on the Somme, and on the evening of 7 July, the 9th Battalion were involved in an attack on Ovillers. The battalion's official history recounts the massacre that took place, with every officer of the 8th Battalion and the majority of officers of the 9th Battalion being reported as either killed, wounded or missing. Of the two battalions, only 180 men remained alive at the end of the fighting on 7 July. Amongst the dead was Edward Peecock, killed by enfilading machine gun fire coming from positions held by the Prussian Guard to the north of Ovillers. According to Charles Quinnell, an NCO in the same battalion, two traversing machine guns 'played on us like spraying water with a hose.'

A letter to the school from a fellow officer and Old Bloxhamist (which by deduction was clearly Arthur Stevens) stated 'He was leading his men in a most gallant manner when he was shot down by machine gun fire, mortally wounded. His men were very fond of him and he was very popular amongst the officers.' Stevens had a request for the Chaplain, Hugh Willimott: 'As his closest friend out here, I would ask you to remember him at the altar.' The death of Gordon Peecock would have struck the Chaplain especially hard as he was one of his servers. Along with Frank Riddle and Geoffrey Bowler, Gordon had been selected to represent the school at the dedication of the Chapel at Lancing in July 1911, an event of great importance for the Woodard schools.

The commemoration in chapel was duly done on the first Saturday of term in September 1916, though by that point the name of Arthur Stevens had been added to the toll and repeated the following week in the presence of his mother. Mrs Peecock was also present in the school chapel in November 1920 when the war memorial was unveiled.

Gordon Peecock was 22 years old when he died and is commemorated on the Thiepval Memorial to the Missing, as his body was never found.

Captain Basil Benjamin Burgoyne Brooks
4th Battalion, Oxfordshire and Buckinghamshire Light Infantry
Pupil at Bloxham School 1906-12
Killed in action 23 July 1916, aged 21
Buried in Pozières British Cemetery, France
Grave I.C.44

Basil Brooks was born on 11 March 1895 and was a pupil at Bloxham School from January 1906 to July 1912. He was the eldest son of Edmund and Elizabeth Brooks. Elected Mayor of Oxford in 1906-1907, Alderman Edmund John Brooks (himself an Old Bloxhamist), was an auctioneer and estate agent whose firm was based in Magdalen Street, Oxford. The firm of EJ Brooks & Son (Auctioneers, Surveyors, Valuers, and Estate Agents) survived into the 1980s, being later situated at 13 Beaumont Street, with branches in Summertown, Cowley, and Bicester.

Edmund Brooks was a prominent member of the local community. He became Sheriff of Oxford in 1903 and a JP in 1907 and was for many years a churchwarden at St Michael's in Summertown. His year as Mayor of Oxford coincided with the celebrated 1907 Oxford Historical Pageant. This remarkable event involved 4.600 performers in a spectacle organised by Frank Lascelles, and Edmund Brooks, a 'shy and reserved man' according to his son Humphrey's recollection seventy years later, had a central role. He played the Earl of Leicester and Mrs Brooks Queen Elizabeth I. The pageant, which took place at the end of the Broad Walk, where the Cherwell divides Christ Church Meadow from Magdalen College School's playing fields, was blighted by bad luck – on 29 May a group of Christ Church undergraduates set fire to one of the marquees and dumped Lascelles' desk in the river before heading back to their colleges, some of them sporting policemen's helmets. Worse than this was the wet weather, which continued throughout the rehearsals and performances - on 1 June nearly an inch of rain fell in 25 minutes. In the end an event expected to raise £7,000 for the Radcliffe Infirmary and other worthy causes made just £809 6s 8d.

Basil was the fifth child of Edmund and Elizabeth – there were two other brothers, Humphrey and Edmund John, and five sisters: Dorothy, Christobel, Gwendolen, Margaret and Gretchen. An older boy, Edward, had died aged four before Basil was born. The family lived in a large house, Athelstan Lodge, in Hernes Crescent, an affluent area of North Oxford, and their photograph albums portray an idyllic Edwardian childhood of garden parties and boating on the Cherwell – they had their own boathouse on the river. He was known among the family as Bam or B4 thanks to his initials.

While at Bloxham, Basil shone on the sports field, playing football, cricket and hockey for the school's 1st XI and became a Prefect, though making less impression in academic terms, never making it out of Form IV. He gained his coveted colours blazer for cricket and in his final season was awarded the bat for the player with the best batting average, though *The Bloxhamist* was somewhat grudging in its praise: 'Rather unsteady as a bat; cannot get out of a habit of drawing away from his wicket. Hits well when set.' As a bowler, he 'bowls well when he can keep off the leg. Quite fast.'

Although he did not shine in the classroom, Basil was an active member of the School Debating Society, speaking in favour of Atlantic liners – this was less than two years before the Titanic disaster – and against a motion supporting compulsory military service (the motion was defeated). He was appointed Lance Corporal in the school's newly founded OTC in 1911, was one of sixteen cadets who represented the school at the Royal Review at Windsor in July of that year and attended camps at Tidworth in 1911 and Bordon in 1912, when he was promoted to Lance Sergeant. On leaving school he became a pupil in his father's office. He joined the Oxford University OTC in 1913.

At some point before the war, Basil met a beautiful young Belgian exchange student by the name of Germaine Deru, who was probably learning English in Oxford, where he worked as a manager at the city's market. When war broke out, Basil joined the 4th Battalion, the Oxford & Bucks LI and was commissioned on 29 August 1914. By 1916 he had been promoted to the rank of Captain.

While on leave in June 1916, Basil married Germaine in London. The Brooks family believe that his father – a pillar of the Anglican Church – was horrified at his eldest son having married a Roman Catholic and would have nothing to do with Basil's young wife. One member of the family later recalled that Basil 'went off and got married without the family's knowledge to a French lady'.

Three weeks after the wedding he was sent to France where he was killed in action on the Somme on 23 July 1916, at the age of 21. *The Oxford Times* reported him missing on 30 July – 'The battalion went into action on Saturday night, and the last that was seen of Captain Brooks was when he was leading his men against the German trench.' The paper gave some grounds for hope – 'There is a report that he was wounded, but this is not confirmed. There is still a chance that he managed to get in and passed through to one of the dressing stations' – but this proved to be illusory. The account of Basil's death in *The Bloxhamist*, written the following month, gave more details:

> We hear that he led his men into action during a night attack on July 23rd. They took a first line trench and went on to the next one, Brooks arriving there first. He was lost sight of on the parapet, and must have been shot there, for he did not return with his company. He was reported missing and it was some days later that his body was found when our troops attacked and finally got possession of the same trench.

The Battalion war diary describes the day's events in some detail, with the battalion attempting in a confused night attack to capture ground near the Pozières railway line. The day's attack had been a disaster for all units involved, with very heavy casualties throughout. The diary records the following: 'Captain Brooks attempted to reach a small party of our men who were trapped by enemy fire. He did this successfully, and on reaching them he straightened himself and a sniper shot him through the head' – in fact he appears to have been mortally wounded by shell fire. The line about being shot cleanly through the head was one often told to families to make the details of the death sound less brutal, and this may have happened in this instance. He was buried two days later where he fell and now lies in the British Military Cemetery at Pozières, a few yards from his schoolmate Arthur Stevens.

Inside a bible owned by the Brooks family, an account was stuck, cut from a local newspaper entitled 'Killed in Action': 'In our issue of 4th August, it was reported that Capt. Basil B. B. Brooks, Oxford and Bucks LI, eldest son of Ald. E.J. Brooks J.P. and Mrs Brooks, of Athelstan Lodge, Summertown, was missing. Numerous inquiries were made and it is now officially reported that Capt. Brooks was killed.' The newspaper went on to recount a letter sent by another officer:

> I am sorry to say, any hope of Capt. Brooks being still alive must now cease. Early yesterday morning, two of my officers went for another search and found his body. He must have been killed instantaneously, from the wounds they found in his head. Yesterday evening the same two officers and our Chaplain went up and buried him and put a cross over his grave. I am awfully sorry for Mrs Brooks and his sister, the surprise must have been terrible. You will quite understand, I am sure, that it is very difficult to get definite news after an attack in the dark, and as the battlefield is being constantly shelled, a very minute search is impossible till the battle line has advanced sufficiently to allow it. Please convey my deepest sympathy to Mrs Brooks.

Lieutenant Gamlen, also a North Oxford resident, wrote on 28 August to say that the body had been found that afternoon, adding 'Your only consolation can be in the thought of your son's devotion and his glorious end. He was highly thought of out here.'

In an earlier letter, a lieutenant in the same company as Basil wrote 'I have found one man in the Company who was near Capt. Brooks at the time he was wounded. The man enquired if he could do anything for him, and the Captain's reply was 'No, I am quite alright, you get on!' He was seen to get up and move away, but in the awful confusion of the moment it was extremely easy for him to lose his way and unwittingly stray into the German lines. His orderly, unfortunately, was killed quite early in the fight.'

Basil's last letter home was sent on 14 July, nine days before his death. Towards the end he employs a racial epithet which reflects the very different world he inhabited:

All's well and cheery. We had great fun at daybreak today: we gave the Wily Hun an awful strafing and frightened him out of his life. Our guns expressed a murderous fire, while we let off smoke at him. It was a gorgeous sight, one not to be missed. The Hun retaliated like wildfire, but we sat under cover and laughed at his efforts. We leave this neighbourhood soon, for what you must guess. It's very obvious, as here we are not out of the fighting. I am very fit, but rather tired, due to lack of sleep. The noise of the guns is awful and we are working like n------s. We have had two very good reports from down South. Things here are slow, but sure. The Wily Hun must be getting shaky.

The family donated a stained-glass window in memory of Basil and his parents in 1937 to their local church, St Michael's, Summertown, where there is also a brass memorial to Basil on the South wall of the nave. The family do not appear to have had anything to do with Germaine, widowed after three weeks of marriage, though one of Basil's sisters, Mary, did keep in touch with her. The young widow's photograph shows Germaine proudly wearing the three pips from Basil's captain's uniform as a brooch. She donated a crucifix in Basil's memory to the local Catholic church, Saints Gregory and Augustine, Oxford, and when this was blessed and rededicated in a solemn mass by the Bishop of Birmingham in May 2011, members of the Brooks family, including his nephew, Major Richard Moore, were present at the service, as well as representatives of his old regiment and his old school.

Her niece Bernadette, who remembered her as Tante 'Maine, recalled that Basil's widow, Germaine was a lively and outgoing lady. She told Bernadette that when Basil went 'over the top' that day on the Somme, he was one of the first over and he went up shouting 'Hallo Boys!' at the Germans, shortly after which he was killed. Germaine later married a wealthy sheep farmer called Kelly and went off to live in Rhodesia, after which the Deru family lost touch with her. Germaine and her husband had no children but adopted a boy, Dennis, the son of a wealthy Englishman. During the Second World War Dennis came from Rhodesia as a soldier and stayed with his Great Aunt Mary, Basil's aunt, in Oxford. He served with the Green Howards and landed in France on D Day.

As well as the Bloxham School memorial, Basil is commemorated by the cross outside Summertown's parish hall, along with the other men from Summertown who fell in the war, although no names are listed on the cross. Basil's father was the one responsible for the purchase of the parish hall, which is itself a war memorial, and he was photographed laying a wreath at the memorial in 1922. It would appear that at least one member of the family visited Pozières in the 1920s, as there is a photograph of his grave in one of the family albums, rendered all the more poignant by its being surrounded by images of the family enjoying holidays and celebrations, while all the time mourning their lost son and brother. There is also a remarkable photograph of the cemetery in its original form.

When the school staged '79' in November 2014, the director Sam Brassington chose to make Basil Brooks the play's central character, focusing on the love affair between him and Germaine, and the experience of watching it with members of the Brooks family in the audience was an extremely emotional one. After the final curtain they met Bertie Fisher, who played Basil.

Second Lieutenant Reginald Funge Potter
4th Battalion, North Staffordshire Regiment
Pupil at Bloxham School 1894-1899
Died of wounds 24 July 1916, aged 33
Buried in Corbie Communal Cemetery, France
Grave I.F.33

Reginald Funge Potter was the fifth son, and sixth of eight children of Frederick William Potter and his wife Clara Louise, and lived at 246 Nelthorpe Road, Uplands Park in Enfield, North London. Frederick's occupation was listed as a director of a public company. Reginald was a twin, born on 5 November 1882 and baptised along with his brother Douglas on 17 January 1883. The twins arrived at Bloxham at the start of the Lent Term in January 1894, joining their brother Cecil, who was three years older than them. Cecil was a talented tennis player and cricketer, opening the bowling for the 1st XI in his final season in 1895. Reginald never reached

the same heights as a sportsman as either Cecil or Douglas, who won his football colours in 1899. He made sporadic appearances for the 1st XI in football and cricket, but was injury-prone, as *The Bloxhamist* for December 1898 hinted: 'being rather fragile, he has been hurt on several occasions, necessitating his retirement from the team. Plays with dash and sometimes centres well but should pass more and quicker.'

Reginald enjoyed more success in the classroom, gaining school prizes for Divinity and German and the Form IV prize in 1897. He was also an actor, appearing as Bassanio in *The Merchant of Venice* in one of the school's earliest forays into Shakespeare, although as *The Bloxhamist* explained, 'the whole play would have been too great a tax both on our own resources and also upon the patience and forbearance of our audience, so only those scenes were chosen for representation which give the story proper of the Merchant himself.'

Reginald and Douglas left Bloxham at the end of the Summer Term in 1899, by which time they had been made sub-prefects and been joined by their younger brother, Bernard, a pupil at Bloxham between 1896 and 1901. The 1911 census shows Reginald living with Cecil and Douglas, and sisters Violet and Mildred at 12, Nelthorpe Terrace in Enfield, and his occupation was shown as being a travelling printer. Cecil and Douglas were both shown as being managers at a local smelting works. In August 1914, he enlisted as Private 1944 in the 10th Battalion of the Royal Fusiliers ('the Stockbrokers' Battalion'), although *The Bloxhamist* reported that he and Douglas had joined one of the Public Schools Battalions (the 18th-21st Battalions of the same regiment). On 11 May 1915 Reginald was commissioned into the 4th North Staffordshires and was followed into the battalion by Douglas on 16 May and Bernard on 1 October. It has been very difficult to piece together his service record, and there is an anomaly which has been thrown up, since the records that do exist state that he served in the 4th Battalion of the North Staffordshire Regiment and died whilst serving on the Somme. The 4th Battalion, however, was based in the UK at the time of the Somme offensive, so he can only have been serving with another battalion at the time. Extensive checks of the war diaries of all North Staffordshire Regiments make no mention of Potter by name, but the Roll of Honour for the 8th Battalion includes his name, and so it would appear that he took part with this battalion, part of 19th (Western) Division in the attack on La Boiselle, when half of the village was captured, on 3 July and the fighting to the east of La Boiselle on 8 July. By 21 July they were engaged in the Bazentin-le-Petit sector, and it is here that he was wounded on 23 July, the same day that Basil Brooks was killed.

Reginald died the next day and was buried in Corbie Communal Cemetery Extension. Corbie was a medical centre east of Albert, with no. 5 and no. 21 Casualty Clearing Stations based close by, and most of the 918 graves in the cemetery extension are of officers and men who died of wounds in the Battle of the Somme. Reginald's grave is adjacent to that of Major Billy La Touche Congreve VC DSO MC. He is remembered on the memorial in his local parish church of St Mary Magdalene, Enfield, as well as that in his old school chapel. The day after he died, Reg's twin brother Douglas was wounded, probably at Bécourt Wood, but he recovered and was promoted to Lieutenant on 1 July 1917. Douglas was wounded a second time, this time much more seriously, when he was shot through the lung and upper part of the chest during the Ludendorff Offensive in the last year of the war (31 March 1918). He survived this wound too and died at the age of 55 on 17 March 1938. Douglas contributed £5 to the Bloxham School war memorial, specifying that the donation was made 'in mem. R.F.P.' This was a very substantial sum, the largest of the 138 contributions made to the fund between March and July 1917. The third brother to have served, Bernard, was also promoted to Lieutenant (4 July 1917) and also survived the war, going on to serve in the Pay Corps during the Second World War.

Private Harold Robinson
20th Battalion, Royal Fusiliers (3rd University and Public Schools Battalion)
Pupil at Bloxham School 1905-1908
Died of wounds 3 August 1916, aged 23
Buried in St Mary's, Chitterne Churchyard, Wiltshire, England

Most of the 80 Bloxhamists who perished in the Great War present a straightforward if time-consuming task to a researcher, with no doubt over their identity or final resting place. In some cases, however, there is considerable confusion over names and circumstances of death. Harold Robinson is an outstanding example of this, as there has until recently been doubt over where he died and where, or whether, he was buried. The Commonwealth War Graves Commission appears to have made an error in recording that he has no known grave.

Harold Robinson was the older of two brothers born to William and Lucy Robinson of Pendleton, a village a few miles from Manchester (now swallowed up by the Manchester suburb of Salford). There were also two sisters, Nora and Amy. William was a builder by trade; he was born in 1861 and was from Lincolnshire, while Lucy was from Yorkshire. Harold was born on 9 September 1892. He and his brother Cecil both started at Bloxham School in September 1905; Harold made an immediate impression on the games field. *The Bloxhamist* reported of the 1907 Sports Day that 'H. Robinson ran very well for his size.' He was a talented opening bowler, *The Bloxhamist* opining that 'Robinson is distinctly promising, but at present is apt to bowl short and too much on the leg side; could he but cure himself of the latter fault he would be of great assistance to the team.'

Harold left the school in December 1908 at the age of 16 and went out to Canada to farm, but returned to England in 1914 on the *SS Lusitania*, arriving at Liverpool on 10 November from New York (six months before the ship's sinking by the Germans). By this time his parents had moved to nearby Eccles. Harold joined up with his brother Cecil in Manchester as a private in the 20th Battalion Royal Fusiliers (the 3rd University and Public Schools Battalion) and after training on Salisbury Plain (close to Chitterne) he went out to France on 15 November 1915, serving in the ranks along with another Bloxham contemporary, Herbert Standage, who was to die in May 1916.

Harold took part in 33rd Division's attack on High Wood on 20 July, the third British attempt to take that strong defensive position since 14 July. High Wood was said by the British troops to be 'ghastly by day, ghostly by night, the rottenest place on the Somme.' He was wounded, died on 3 August 1916 in Chatham and was buried in the churchyard of St Mary, Chitterne, in Wiltshire on 5 August. An article in *The Eccles Journal* of 1 September 1916 reported Harold's death and burial in Chitterne as well as the fact that his brother Cecil had been wounded in the same attack. Despite what Robert Graves wrote in *Goodbye to all That*, where he suggested that the 20th Royal Fusiliers had performed poorly at High Wood, 397 men (two thirds of the effective strength of the Battalion) had become casualties – dead, wounded or missing – by midnight on 20 July. This included every single officer as well as the two Robinson brothers. It would take several more attacks before High Wood was finally secured on 15 September. It is estimated that the remains of 8,000 men may still lie in the wood.

There are several mysteries about the circumstances of Harold's death and burial. First, how did he die in Kent if he was wounded at the Somme? Second, why was he buried in Chitterne in Wiltshire when his family were from Greater Manchester? Third, why is his name on the Thiepval Memorial to the Missing if he has a known grave? The first two questions can be answered thanks to the contribution of his great niece to an online Great War forum in December 2010. She reported after speaking to her aunt that Harold was shot in the arm at High Wood and no medical pack was applied at the time (though his death certificate records his shrapnel wounds as being in the left thigh). He contracted tetanus, or lockjaw as his family termed it, and was shipped back to Fort Pitt Hospital in Rochester, Kent where he died of the infection on 3 August 1916. The death certificate gives as the cause of death 1) shrapnel wounds and 2) tetanus and 'exhaustion'.

As for the connection with Wiltshire, his parents had bought Harold a property in Chitterne, Clump Farm, a mixed arable and livestock farm with pigs and milking cows, for him to make a go of farming on his return from Canada, and we must assume that it was his parents' wish to have him buried in Chitterne. The family believes that at least one of the children was born in Chitterne, and William was certainly one of the biggest landowners in the village, albeit an absentee one – Clump Farm was leased to the Bazell family, with Charles Bazell's son Alfred acting as the farm bailiff in 1911.

The Warminster and Westbury Journal for 11 August 1916 provides more details of Harold's death and burial. The reference to a 'Jack Johnson' describes a type of German trench mortar which produced a distinctive cloud of black smoke – Jack Johnson being the first African-American heavyweight world champion boxer.

We regret to state that Mr Harold Robinson, aged 23, of Clump Farm, Chitterne, who joined the Royal Fusiliers soon after coming to reside in the village, was severely wounded on July 20th in France. After receiving his wound and before he could receive any help he was buried by the explosion of a 'Jack Johnson' and it was several hours before he could extricate himself. This greatly aggravated the wound and caused gangrene. He was conveyed to Chatham, and died there. Mr James Feltham kindly undertook the challenge of getting the body conveyed to Chitterne, and was met at Codford railway station with a gun carriage provided by the Heytesbury Camp on Saturday last. The first part of the Burial service was taken in the Parish Church, in the presence of a large number of inhabitants and friends, and then the body, preceded by the firing party as escort, was laid to rest in St. Mary's Churchyard, the Vicar (The Rev. J. T. Canner) conducting the service.

There is now no doubt over the fact that we have the correct Harold Robinson, as his great niece has confirmed that the photograph on MD's Bloxham School War Dead website is the same as the photograph she has of her great uncle. The third question remains a mystery but is probably down to a bureaucratic oversight, unsurprising and certainly not unique in a vast citizen army suffering an utterly unprecedented scale of loss – Harold's regiment, the Royal Fusiliers, alone raised 47 battalions during the war. The sheer scale of the operation confronting the Imperial War Graves Commission and its successor, the Commonwealth War Graves Commission, is mind-boggling, and it cannot be surprising that a few errors were made. Those wanting an insight into the extraordinary work they did, should read David Crane's excellent book *Empires of the Dead*.

It has been suggested that the Harold Robinson on the Thiepval Memorial was not the same Harold Robinson as the one who lies buried in Chitterne, and one of the arguments employed to support this was that 'our' Harold Robinson was from Manchester and so would not have joined the 20th Royal Fusiliers, a London battalion. In fact over half the casualties from High Wood on 20 July were from what is now Greater Manchester, both the city itself and suburbs like Salford. Although the Royal Fusiliers was known as the City of London Regiment, the 20th battalion had strong connections with Manchester in general and its University and Grammar School in particular. The other three public schools battalions of the Royal Fusiliers had been disbanded by July 1916 in order to provide much-needed young officers for the army, and disquiet was expressed by local MPs that men of the 20th Battalion were not similarly being given commissions, which might explain why the Robinson brothers and Standage all served in the ranks, unlike the majority of their Bloxham contemporaries.

Harold's brother Cecil became a cotton salesman after leaving Bloxham in July 1910. He enlisted in Manchester in the same battalion as his brother and went out to France in November 1915. He was wounded in the same attack in which his brother received his fatal wound and recovered in hospital in Edinburgh. He returned to the front and was taken prisoner in May 1917, remaining in a German Prisoner of War camp until the armistice. After the war he became a building contractor, living in the family home in Eccles.

The confusions involved in this tale (Harold's medal card states that he died of wounds on 25 July, though he was actually still alive at this point) provide a good example of the painstaking research required to tell the stories of those who died in the Great War.

Lieutenant Arthur Reginald Ingram Stevens
9th Battalion, Royal Fusiliers
Pupil at Bloxham School 1909-1913
Killed in action 6 August 1916, aged 19
Buried in Pozières British Cemetery, France
Grave IV.J.9

Arthur Stevens is an interesting individual who conforms to the classic image of the young public schoolboy who joined up as a subaltern, only to be cut down at the Somme. Arthur's birth certificate shows his date of birth as 13 April 1897, and this is the same date that appears on the record card filled in for him when he joined the school. However, a letter, dated 14 August 1916, from his father to the War Office, states that 'I am in receipt of your telegram announcing the death of my son 2nd Lt A.R. Ingram Stevens, 9 RF. As the boy was underage, would you let me know what mode of procedure you require to settle his affairs? I assume the Government pay compensation to the parents in such circumstances.' It is hard to see what his father had in mind, unless he was referring to Arthur's age when he joined up (he was 17 at the outbreak of the war) or when he went out to France.

Arthur was the eldest son of Arthur Herbert and Florence Jane Stevens. According to the Bank of England's meticulous records, Arthur Stevens senior joined the Bank as a junior clerk when he was 18, in June 1886, on the nomination of Sir Mark Collet, who would become the Governor of the Bank of England the following year. Arthur Herbert Stevens would eventually rise to become a Senior Clerk on a salary of £725 p.a. the family was clearly comfortable off; when Arthur junior joined Bloxham their home address was listed as 54, Duke's Avenue, Chiswick, a wide, leafy avenue in a rapidly developing area of west London (the same house would apparently have fetched over £5 million in 2016). By 1916, the family address had changed to 27, Woodstock Rd., Golders Green (not then the centre of a large Jewish population that it would later become). The house was known as 'Bradda', possibly named after the headland of that name on the Isle of Man.

Arthur joined the school in April 1909, swiftly earning the Form III Mathematics Prize and promotion to Form IV B. He was one of 21 candidates who were confirmed in March 1910.

Arthur passed the Oxford Locals with Honours in July 1910 and earned further promotion to Form IV A alongside his friend Gordon Peecock. When Bloxham's OTC was founded at the end of the year, and *The Bloxhamist* was complaining of the dilatoriness of some pupils in getting permission from home to join, Arthur was one of the initial 22 members of the corps.

By October 1911 Arthur had become a member of the Sixth Form. He was an active member of the Debating Society, opposing a motion in favour of conscription that month. He argued that conscription would place too great a burden on the country and would hinder emigration. In Arthur's eyes 'England did not need a large conscript army since she had her navy, which forms ample protection from her enemies.' He was supported by Basil Brooks and by the commander of the school OTC, Arthur Child, and the motion was narrowly defeated. A month later, he was once again on the winning side, when he was the proposer of the motion that 'Wellington was a greater man than Napoleon'.

Arthur was made a Prefect in September 1912, when he would have only been 15 years of age. He won the VI Form Divinity Prize in July 1912 as well as those for Latin and English.

By now Arthur was Lance Corporal in the OTC and was promoted to Lance Sergeant at the start of 1913. That summer he turned out for the school's 2nd XI, opening the bowling but making little impression. In September 1913 he was promoted to Sergeant in the OTC, the most senior cadet in a corps of 53. The highlight of the term came on 29 September, when fifteen cadets were chosen to mount a guard of honour for the 2nd Battalion of the Oxford & Bucks LI who were marching through the village. Arthur was in command of the guard of honour and must have felt considerable pride when the battalion's CO, Lieutenant Colonel H.R. Davies, wrote to express his appreciation, writing to Captain Child that 'your lads looked very smart, and it was a pleasure to us to see them.' With the OTC expanding, Arthur Stevens was kept busy that term with night exercises and drill, and he finished second in that year's musketry course, just behind Kingsley Fradd. Once again he won the Divinity prize, this time coupling it with the History prize.

He left in December 1913, and it was announced that he had joined the University of London OTC, though this does not mean that he had any other connection with the university. He wrote to *The Bloxhamist* in February 1914 to give a detailed report on an OTC camp he had attended at Shere the previous month, and from his account one gets a clear picture of someone who enjoyed the military life. So, it can have been no surprise to his old schoolmates when, on the outbreak of war, he was offered and immediately accepted a commission into the 9th Battalion the Royal Fusiliers, finding himself serving alongside his old friend from Bloxham, Gordon Peecock. The regiment proceeded to France in May 1915, but owing to ill health, he was unable to join them until December 1915. During this time of illness he was working in England in reserve on the staff at Shoreham - this must have been a challenging time for an eager young man who wanted to be in the thick of the action.

The 9th Royal Fusiliers were in action almost constantly throughout 1916, and eventually Arthur found himself thrown into the maelstrom of the Somme. A report in *The Bloxhamist* for July 1916 reported that he had received a wound in the leg, 'which, although not serious, necessitated his return to England for a short period in order to recover. He has now rejoined his regiment.' On 22 July he had the melancholy duty of writing to his old school chaplain to inform him of Gordon Peecock's death, asking Willimott to 'remember him at the altar.'

There is considerable confusion over the date of Arthur Stevens' death. On his headstone it is given as 4 August, though the telegram from the War Office stated 8 August. The Battalion war diary is quite clear that he died on 6 August, and it is this that we have chosen to follow. On the night of 6 August, Arthur's company were charged with making a night attack on the heavily defended German line known to the British as Ration Trench. The attack, as documented in the war diary, started in the early hours of the morning of 7 August, whereby the 9th RF attacked in conjunction with the Royal West Kents. The war diary reports that between 1:00 a.m. and 4:00 a.m. all was going well, until a sudden counterattack by the Germans.

A Company of the 9th RF found themselves in No Man's Land between Sulphur Avenue and Ration Trench when they were caught in a sudden artillery bombardment. The panic of this caused them to swing eastwards and they were trapped in an area of exposed ground. Without warning they were attacked with German flamethrowers and heavy machine gun fire and the battalion suffered appalling casualties. The bombardment carried on for several hours before the regiment was finally relieved by the Royal Sussex Regiment. H.C. O'Neill's history of the Royal Fusiliers in the Great War gives a vivid account of the horror of this attack: 'For some it was their first experience of actual fighting, and their bearing was admirable. The assault was made by flammenwerfers, supported by bombers using smoke as a screen. The flames burst through the clouds of smoke from various directions, and all the conditions of panic were present. The fumes alone were sufficient to overpower some of the men. But no panic took place.'

During this engagement the 9th RF suffered heavily with five officers killed, including Arthur Stevens, seven officers wounded and 281 other ranks killed, wounded or missing. Arthur's colonel spoke of him as being by far the youngest officer in the battalion and showing a capacity and tact in dealing with his men in advance of his years, and informed Arthur's parents of the keen loss which the battalion had suffered 'by the death of this gallant young officer'. His parents may have been able to derive some comfort from hearing of 'the great popularity and respect in which he was held by the men in his platoon'.

Arthur Stevens is commemorated on the Golders Green War Memorial as well as at his old school. He is buried in Pozières British Cemetery, a few yards from the grave of his old schoolmate Basil Brooks, killed a fortnight earlier. The next of kin could choose an inscription for the gravestone, as long as it did not exceed 66 characters. For Arthur's gravestone, his mother chose a verse from Robert Louis Stevenson's 'Requiem':

> *Glad did I live and gladly die,*
> *And I laid me down with a will.*

Lieutenant Alan William Russell Cowan
Canadian Black Watch
Pupil at Bloxham School 1901-1905
Died of wounds 20 August 1916, aged 29
Buried in Lijssenthoek Military Cemetery, Belgium
Grave IX.B.6

Alan was the son of Robert David Russell Cowan and Catherine Florence Cowan (née Scroggs), of Bushley Vicarage; Bushley is a small village two miles north-west of Tewkesbury. Robert Cowan was the 'Perpetuate Curate' who discharged the duties of Vicar and lived in the vicarage which was adjacent to St Peter's Church. Alan was born in Upwell in Norfolk on 5 March 1887. He was the second of the Cowans' three sons; his brothers were Denys, who was killed in a London air raid in 1941, and Philip, who died in 1985. Denys was posted to Havana as British Vice Consul and then appointed Consul there in 1918, along with the award of the MBE.

There were also three sisters, Marjorie, who married Philip Bayly of Pershore in 1918, Barbara, who died unmarried in 1987, and Lydia, who married Denys Boyd-Carpenter in 1929 in Upton and died at Alderton in Gloucestershire in 1992. The Rev. Robert Cowan would continue in office until his death in June 1935, with his wife living in the Gloucestershire village of Gretton until her death in 1941. According to the 1911 census, the Cowans lived in the vicarage along with a maidservant, a pageboy and two boarders of independent means.

Alan was a pupil at Bloxham between April 1901 and June 1905. He made his first appearance for a school team, the 2nd XI in cricket, against Abingdon in May 1903, and was appointed a prefect in September that year. Sports Day in 1904 was held on two days, Saturday 21 May and the following Tuesday, and according to *The Bloxhamist*, 'we had the bad luck to pitch on two of the very few wet days we have had this term.' Fortunately 'our visitors pluckily braved the elements and turned up in great force', and Alan Cowan dominated proceedings, winning the 100 yards (in a time of 11 1/5 seconds), 200 yards, quarter mile and mile, while in the school steeplechase, held the same month, he led for most of the race but was overtaken by his rival, Yonge, towards the end and ultimately lost by twenty yards.

The Bloxhamist for June 1905 provided its usual mixture of good and bad in its appraisal of Alan's play at left half for the football eleven: 'A useful player possessing both weight and pace. A good tackler, but inclined to dribble too much. Does not follow his forwards closely enough. His individual play, though brilliant, is often detrimental to his side, but, occasionally, he played a splendid game for his team. Intercepts passes skilfully.' The same tendency to combine praise with caustic criticism was evident in a summary of his cricketing skills in a later issue: 'Batted very nicely in the nets but quite failed in the matches; would perhaps have done better had he hit more. A good field, but not always safe, and is inclined to be too showy.'

Alan emigrated to British Columbia in 1905, though he was apparently back in Britain for the Old Bloxhamist Dinner at the Trocadero Restaurant in Piccadilly in January 1906. Alan ran a fruit farm in British Columbia for nine years. He married Emily Harris Gostling at Kelowna on 24 August 1910, and the couple had two children, Molly and Reginald. Emily was the youngest daughter of Charles R. Gostling, Esq., JP, of Gravesend, England.

Four days before the outbreak of war, Bloxham's Headmaster, George Ward, embarked from Liverpool for a trip to Canada organised by the British Columbia Church Aid Society, and he arrived in Winnipeg to find 4,000 Canadian troops marching through the city en route to Valcartier on the way to Britain. While at Kelowna, on the Ohanagan Lake, he came across Alan Cowan, camping out in a tent by the lake side with his wife and child. Even before the war Alan was a member of the Canadian militia in the shape of the 30th British Columbian Horse, but he enlisted into the 103rd Battalion of the Canadian Expeditionary Force on 17 July 1915, and was eventually commissioned as a Lieutenant into the 13th Battalion Canadian Infantry (the Canadian Black Watch). It seems possible that the delay in his progressing overseas was that he was one of the 'unwanted', that is to say an officer from a colonial force deemed by the British as not fit to lead men in battle.

Robert Cowan was a keen photographer, and took a photograph of his son during a 36 hour leave before he crossed to France on 14 August. Alan's last letter home was posted on 19 August 1916, and arrived with the official telegram announcing his death. While marching along a road on the afternoon of 20 August, Alan was hit by a shell fired in the area around Mount Sorrel, near Ypres, and he was horrifically wounded, his left leg being partially amputated with the left femur protruding, as well as suffering serious arm injuries. He was in an ambulance en route to CCS no. 10 when he died. His superior officer, in writing to his parents, spoke very highly of Lieutenant Cowan's capabilities as an officer and regretted that he had been so short a time with the battalion. He left a widow and two children. *The Bloxhamist* recorded that Mrs Cowan left one guinea to the school's war memorial fund in her husband's memory.

He was buried at the time in a temporary grave before being finally interred in the massive cemetery at Lijssenhoek (IX B.6). The cemetery contains 9,901 graves. The original wooden cross which marked his battlefield grave can be found on the wall of his father's church, St Peter's, Bushley, and his name is also on a memorial at Salmon Cove, British Columbia. He was 29 years old when he died on 20 August 1916.

Second Lieutenant Walter Rowland Heath
1/1st Battalion, Oxfordshire and Buckinghamshire Light Infantry
Master at Bloxham School 1902-1904
Killed in action 23 August 1916, aged 37
Commemorated on the Thiepval Memorial to the Missing, France
Panel 10.A

Walter Rowland Heath was a master at Bloxham between September 1902 and July 1904. He was born in 1879, in Strood, Kent, the son of Richard and Jane Elizabeth Heath, née Waller, of 'Handford', Salisbury Road, Herne Bay in Kent. He attended Hatfield Hall, Durham University, on a Lightfoot Scholarship, and was granted a BA (1901) and then an MA (1904) in Classics and Philosophy. In welcoming him to the school in October 1902, *The Bloxhamist* expressed the hope that, given that he had played for the Cricket Club and the Rugby Club, which he captained in 1900, as well as being President of the University Boat Club in 1900 (he had also played football, fives and chess at university), Mr Heath would be a valuable addition to the Bloxham staff, 'equally popular both in the classroom and the playing field. We sincerely trust that he may be with us for some time and may be both happy and successful in his life and work here.'

He was certainly to prove popular, playing football for the school's 1st XI in club matches, and scoring four goals in a 6-0 win over the Hook Norton village side in March 1903. When the decision was taken to start an appeal for a new gymnasium, Walter Heath was put in charge of organising the subscription list. His tireless efforts led to an obvious improvement in the standards of gymnastics at the school. As well as playing football, cricket and fives, he was also keen to get involved in other areas of school life. In December 1902 he acted as Stage Manager for the school's production of *A Pair of Spectacles,* put on for the last day of the Michaelmas Term. *The Bloxhamist* judged that 'the play was distinctly a great success, and the staging of it says much for Mr. W. R. Heath, to whom we offer our very sincere thanks for his kindness in acting as stage manager.'

However, the other hope expressed by the school magazine on his arrival proved to be forlorn, as Walter Heath left after only two years at the school, at the end of the Summer Term in 1904. He departed for Cairo, to take up a post in the Education Department of the Egyptian Government and was not heard of again (other than occasional telegrams on Old Bloxhamist days and subscribing to an appeal for a new window in the chapel) until June 1915, when it was reported from Cairo that he had heard of the death of another OB at Gallipoli. By this time he was recorded as being a Second Lieutenant in the Oxford & Bucks LI, and for a time he held a staff appointment as inspector of physical training and bayonet drill, with the temporary rank of Captain. He was promoted to the temporary rank of Lieutenant on 8 June 1916, and, according to his obituary in *The Bloxhamist*, he was killed on 23 August after only four weeks at the front.

That day, the battalion relieved the 6th Gloucestershire Regiment in the trenches between Ovillers and Thiepval, with A and C companies detailed to carry out an attack on the enemy's forward positions near the formidable strongpoint of the Leipzig Redoubt. This attack was timed for 3:05 p.m. From 1:00 p.m. to 2:45 p.m. the heavy artillery carried out a bombardment which was not only ineffective but actually made obvious to the enemy the exact limits of the objective. At 3:00 p.m. a final intense bombardment was put down for five minutes by the Field Artillery, in order to provide cover for the assault. Although the barrage was effective, it was too short, as it lifted while the attacking troops had still some way to go, and the enemy was able to fire hard at them from the heavily manned German trenches.

The German barrage opened up as soon as the British ended, inflicting heavy casualties and making progress impossible. Second Lieutenant Bates, who was commanding C Company, ran forward to try to take the position, but was instantly killed. On the left, Walter Heath of A Company met with the same fate, and both companies were forced to lie where they were until dark. According to *The Oxfordshire & Buckinghamshire Light Infantry Chronicle 1916-1917*, 'the losses in the two companies ... were irreparable, and in 2nd Lieuts. Bates and Heath the Battalion lost two very able and gallant officers.'

Having no known grave, Walter Heath is commemorated on the Thiepval Memorial to the Missing. His name is also on a plaque at Hatfield College. His service medals came up for auction at Dix, Noonan Webb in December 2011.

Second Lieutenant Lawrence Arthur Barrow
10th Battalion, Royal Sussex Regiment
Pupil at Bloxham School 1907-1912
Killed in action 31 August 1916, aged 21
Buried in Englebelmer Communal Cemetery Extension, France
Grave D.3

Lawrence Alfred Howard Barrow (the school incorrectly recorded his name on arrival as Laurence) was born on 21 April 1895 in Billinghurst, Sussex. He was the son of Emily May Barrow and her husband the Rev. Alfred Henry Barrow of St Paul's Vicarage, East Molesey, though by the time the war broke out he was rector of All Saints, Hastings. Lawrence had two brothers, Bernard Isaac and Gerald Forster and a sister, Hilda Mary; Bernard served as a Private in the Army Service Corps.

Lawrence was a pupil at Bloxham between September 1907 and July 1912. He progressed to Form IVa in September 1909, then a year later to Form V and passed the preliminary Oxford Locals in the same cohort as five other boys who would perish in the war (Brooks, Cunliffe, Marshall, Harold Rylands and Sawyer). Whereas Brooks, his exact contemporary, was a star on the games field whose exploits were regularly described in *The Bloxhamist*, Lawrence appears to have been an indifferent sportsman, and mentions of him in the pages of the school magazine are few and far between, beyond occasional appearances in Sports Day heats. After leaving school in 1912, Lawrence went up to Oxford with a view to ordination, but there is no record of him as a student. He enlisted as a private in the 5th Battalion of the Royal Sussex Regiment in August 1914 and was pictured in uniform in *The Hastings and St Leonards Pictorial Advertiser's* Roll of Honour in November of that year.

Lawrence was commissioned as a Second Lieutenant in January 1915 in the 10th Battalion of the same regiment. This was a reserve unit based in the UK, and he was transferred to the 11th Battalion, which was sent out to France that year. A cryptic reference in *The Bloxhamist* suggests that he was in Ireland at the time of the Easter Rising – 'He took part in suppressing the disturbance in Ireland' – but this cannot be substantiated from his service record. From the Battalion war diary it is clear that in late 1915, Lawrence serving with the poet Edmund Blunden and in December was involved in a trench raid where he and Blunden led a platoon which successfully captured a German officer and some valuable intelligence documents.

He was killed by shell fire in Englebelmer Wood on the night of 31 August 1916, during the Battle of the Somme. According to *The Bloxhamist*, he and two other officers were killed simultaneously by a shell bursting at their feet. He was 21 years of age when he died. Lawrence Barrow was buried in Englebelmer Communal Cemetery Extension. His name is recorded on the East Wall of St Leonard's Church in Flamstead, near St Albans in Hertfordshire, as his father became the parish priest there in 1916. He remained there until 1923 and officiated at the unveiling of the war memorial in 1920; though his son's name was not on the memorial, the occasion must have been suffused with grief at the loss of Lawrence. Along with the plaque on the wall of the church, which records that Lawrence 'fell fighting for his country, in France', his parents, brothers and sisters donated a cross and candlesticks to the church in his memory. Five years after the death of his old comrade, Edmund Blunden wrote of his time serving with the Royal Sussex Regiment :

1916 seen from 1921

Tired with dull grief, grown old before my day,
I sit in solitude and only hear
Long silent laughters, murmurings of dismay,
The lost intensities of hope and fear;
In those old marshes yet the rifles lie,
On the thin breastwork flutter the grey rags,
The very books I read are there—and I
Dead as the men I loved, wait while life drags

Its wounded length from those sad streets of war
Into green places here, that were my own;
But now what once was mine is mine no more,
I seek such neighbours here and I find none.
With such strong gentleness and tireless will
Those ruined houses seared themselves in me,
Passionate I look for their dumb story still,
And the charred stub outspeaks the living tree.
I rise up at the singing of a bird
And scarcely knowing slink along the lane,
I dare not give a soul a look or word
Where all have homes and none's at home in vain:
Deep red the rose burned in the grim redoubt,
The self-sown wheat around was like a flood,
In the hot path the lizard lolled time out,
The saints in broken shrines were bright as blood.

Sweet Mary's shrine between the sycamores!
There we would go, my friend of friends and I,
And snatch long moments from the grudging wars,
Whose dark made light intense to see them by.
Shrewd bit the morning fog, the whining shots
Spun from the wrangling wire: then in warm swoon
The sun hushed all but the cool orchard plots,
We crept in the tall grass and slept till noon.

Second Lieutenant Reginald William Harris
4th Battalion, West Yorkshire Regiment
Pupil at Bloxham School 1906-1909
Killed in action 3 September 1916, aged 23
Commemorated on the Thiepval Memorial to the Missing, France
Panel 6.A

Reginald Harris was the only son of Herbert and Claire Harris and came from Sidmouth in Devon. He was a pupil at the school between 1906 and 1909. At Prize Giving in July 1906 he carried off the Form III Latin and French prizes. For the next two years he won the Divinity Prize for Form IVA. He was a keen member of the Debating Society. In February 1907 he spoke against the motion that the time had arrived for the building of a Channel Tunnel and in April, he spoke in favour of a motion condemning the Liberal government of the day as 'a failure and a menace to the nation' – the motion was passed unanimously, which tells us something of the pupils' political leanings. The following year he spoke in favour of conscription.

On leaving school he went to South Africa where he engaged in farming, before he became a mounted police officer in Rhodesia. He returned to England in April 1914 and was due to take up a position in Uganda when the war broke out. He was commissioned as a 2nd Lieutenant into the 4th Battalion the West Yorkshire Regiment and served with them throughout, although at the time of his death he was attached to the RFA.

He was gazetted as a Lieutenant in 1916 and joined Z Company, Trench Mortar Battery on the Somme, where he was killed by shell fire on 3 September 1916. His body was never found and he is commemorated on the Thiepval Memorial to the Missing. A fellow officer in the same battery, writing to Harris' young wife, whom he had only recently married, says 'He was hit by an enemy shell whilst in pursuance of an important piece of work, and was killed immediately.'

Reginald Harris' photograph was one of those lost in the vestry fire which destroyed one of the original boards. The search for a replacement picture of Reginald Harris is one of the pieces of research of which we are the most proud. Recourse to the school archives and the regimental museum yielded nothing. There were many publications appearing during and immediately after the Great War which contained portrait pictures of deceased officers. Baron de Ruvigny created a roll of honour whereby the families of soldiers could send in obituaries of their relatives. It ran to five volumes before the money sadly ran out, and so no more were published. *The Illustrated London News* ran a feature entitled 'Died on the field of honour' which featured portraits primarily of officers who had been killed. Neither of these sources was of any help in our search.

Bloxham School in 1896.

Bloxham's Founder, Philip Egerton is on the right on his Otto dicycle in this photograph from 1886. The boy marked with the number 10, Wilfred Ellershaw, would become a Brigadier General in the Great War.

The cast of 'The Silent System' (1910) – the two boys standing in the centre, Frank Hart and Kingsley Fradd, would both die on the Somme six years later.

Hugh Willimott, Chaplain of Bloxham School at the outbreak of war.

The 1914 Hockey 1st XI. Both masters in charge, James Pastfield and John Nuthall, were to perish in the war.

Gymnastics in the new gymnasium, c. 1914.

The Chaplain and Charles Wilson with chapel servers, July 1911.

Bloxham School OTC, December 1911.

Bloxham cadets at Shere Camp, April 1911. Of these six boys, four would lose their lives in the coming war, Riddle, Brooks, Hart and Peecock.

Bloxham OTC at Tidworth, August 1911. Five of the 15 cadets would not survive the war – the four at the back in the middle (Stevens, Brooks, Gepp, Riddle) and Peecock (sitting with a plate on his knees.

OTC Field Day, Wytham, February 1913.

OTC Field Day, Garsington, October 1913.

The chaplain and members of the chapel choir at Warwick, July 1913.

OTC Camp at Rugeley, August 1913. The extreme youth of many of these cadets is noteworthy.

Camera Club outing to Shipton-under-Wychwood, 1 July 1914, three days after the assassination of the Archduke Franz Ferdinand.

The quarter mile on Sports Day, 1912. Harold Long, the athlete nearest to the starter, would die near Arras in May 1916.

The Cricket 1st XI, 1916. Several of these boys, including the captain, Douglas Cain, would see action before the war ended.

Basil Brooks at home in North Oxford with members of his family.

Philip Wainman on leave in England.

Keith Bidlake on leave – the epitome of a
subaltern's fresh-faced enthusiasm.

Alick Sawyer at home on leave in the summer of 1917. The strain of the conflict is clearly evident.

The Headmaster, Rev. Roy Grier, with his prefects, 1916.

The headstone of Second Lieutenant Kingsley Fradd in Hébuterne Cemetery. He was killed on the first day of the battle of the Somme.

Mourning card for Harry Ayres.

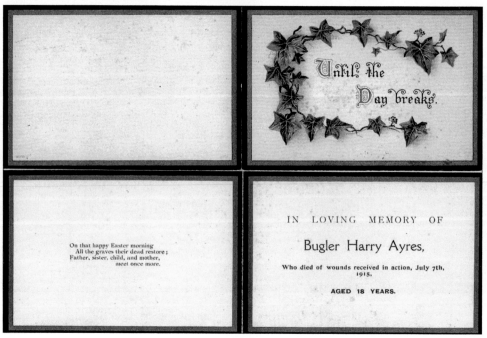

Bugle and drums presented to the school OTC by the Old Bloxhamists after the war.

The OTC band with its new instruments, Armistice Day 1927.

Junior cadets at the village war memorial,
Armistice Day 1930. Many of them would serve
in a Second World War.

The original photographs of the fallen in the
Chapel Corridor, c. 1930.

The opening of the new memorial gateway by Lord Saye and Sele, 1933.

Armistice Day at Bloxham, 2015.

Sounding 'Last Post', 1960. This
tradition continued every evening
until the early 1970s.

Bertie Fisher (centre) as Basil
Brooks in the school production
'79', November 2014.

The war memorial in the school chapel, with the extra board added in 2014.

The difficulty of finding a picture of Reginald Harris was compounded by his position in a trench mortar battery which was attached to an infantry battalion. MD carried out a search of the National Inventory of War Memorials and discovered that Harris was commemorated on the Sidmouth war memorial in Devon. He went to the National Newspaper archive in Colindale and by searching the records, found a copy of *The Western Gazette*, which confirmed that Harris' family were indeed from South Devon. Through modern media we located the names and addresses of 32 families named Harris still living in Sidmouth. A speculative letter was sent to each one asking if they were related to Reginald. In due course, a lady called Sally Clark emailed back, saying she had been passed the letter by an elderly lady called Hilda Harris who was a distant relative by marriage of the Harris family.

Sally suggested contacting the Vicar of Sidmouth, which MD duly did. This enquiry led him to the Sidmouth History Society. They confirmed that in 1922, the South Devon Fisherman's Benevolent Society mounted a campaign to erect a cross on the quayside in memory of the 66 men from Sidmouth who died in the Great War. As part of the original exhibition they included pictures of the dead, and thankfully the pictures remained to this day. Reginald was number 44 and MD duly found the superb image shown above.

It is very hard to convey the range of emotions one feels, having spent seven years searching for a photograph of a single officer, but it is the sort of elation that makes historical research so rewarding.

Second Lieutenant Frank Arthur Selwyn Hart
9th Battalion, Somerset Light Infantry
Pupil at Bloxham School 1904-1911
Killed in action 16 September 1916, aged 22
Commemorated on the Thiepval Memorial to the Missing, France
Panel 2.A

The youngest son of the late Mr W.H. Hart, MVO, of 41 School Road, Moseley in Birmingham (a road along which MD used to walk the beat!), Frank spent an unusually long time at school (1904-1911), and during his later years served as a prefect and as an NCO in the OTC. After a long apprenticeship in the second team at cricket, he eventually forced his way into the 1st XI as a batsman; *The Bloxhamist* harshly adjudged that he was 'rather a disappointing bat', though conceding that he was 'much improved in fielding and is a very safe catch.'

By now he was also a regular in the school's football XI, playing in goal and captaining the side, and made his stage debut in a one act farce, *The Silent System*, in October 1910. Three of the four pupils in the cast would lose their lives in the coming war. He was an active member of the school's debating society, opposing a motion against Atlantic liners in November 1910 and speaking on the Portuguese Republic the following week. He was also Captain of Hockey and Fives. Frank was School Captain for his final year at Bloxham.

After war broke out, he enlisted as a private in the 16th Middlesex Regiment (the Public Schools Battalion) on 14 September 1914. He was promoted to Serjeant-Major and fought in the trenches between November 1915 and March 1916. He was then commissioned as a 2nd Lieutenant in the 9th Battalion Somerset Light Infantry and returned to Britain for training. He became the Assistant Bombing Officer for B Company, in charge of the unit's hand grenades, an important element of trench warfare, and arrived back in France on 8 September

1916, while the Battle of the Somme was still raging. By 1916 the development of hand grenades had improved immeasurably from the fighting in late 1915, where it was found that German grenades were vastly superior to those of the British. The Mk 1 Mills bomb, which resembled what we would recognize as a hand grenade today was a fragmentation device that exploded approximately seven seconds after the pin was pulled, and unlike earlier grenades didn't need to have the fuse lit. Over 100 million were produced, and at last the British had a grenade to rival the Germans. Northern soldiers affectionately called them 'Co-op Bombs' – because when they went off, everyone got a bit.

On 16 September 1916, eight days after arriving on the Somme, the Somerset Light Infantry was heavily involved in fighting north-east of Flers, where tanks had been employed for the first time in history the day before. There is some dispute over exactly with which unit Frank was serving at this point; *The Bloxhamist* and the Commonwealth War Graves Commission both have the 9th Battalion, but his name appears on the Roll of Honour of the 7th Battalion, and it was the 7th, along with the 6th, both 'pals battalions' of Kitchener's New Army, which was involved in the attack at Lesboeufs.

As part of the Battle of Flers-Courcelette the Guards Division, reinforced by 61 Brigade of 20th Division, renewed its attack north of Ginchy at 9: 25 a.m. on 16 September. 7th Battalion, Duke of Cornwall's Light Infantry and 7th Battalion, Somerset Light Infantry moved forward from Trones Wood before dawn and formed up 200 yards in front of 2 Guards Brigade in Serpentine Trench. At Zero Hour they advanced and captured the section of the Ginchy-Lesboeufs Road that had been the Guards' third objective the day before. Between them the two Somerset battalions lost 231 men on that day, and 16 September has been dubbed Somerset's Day of Remembrance.

The toll among the battalion's officers was especially heavy. Its temporary commander, Major Edward Lyon, was mortally wounded during the attack. According to *The Bloxhamist* magazine, Frank Hart's Captain was lying wounded in a shell hole in No Man's Land. Frank crawled out to help him and was shot dead by a German sniper as he crawled back. He was 22 years old when he died. His body could never be identified and he is commemorated on the Thiepval Memorial.

Second Lieutenant Oswald Nixon
70 Squadron, Royal Flying Corps
Pupil at Bloxham School 1908-1911
Missing in action 17 September 1916, aged 21
Buried in Serre Road Cemetery No. 2, France
Grave XXIX.O.10

The next of the 80 marks a significant milestone in their story, with the first death of an Old Bloxhamist in the developing war in the air; Oswald Nixon was a pilot in the Royal Flying Corps, killed in combat while carrying out a reconnaissance mission over the Somme battlefield on Sunday 17 September 1916. Oswald Nixon was the youngest of the six sons of Colonel Francis Nixon of the Royal Engineers and Edith Eliza Nixon of Cape Town, where Oswald was born on 3 May 1896; the couple also had six daughters, all older than Oswald. Four of Oswald's brothers saw action in the Great War, and all survived – Captain Edmund Nixon in Jacob's Horse (Indian Army), Lieutenant Commander George Nixon in the Royal Navy, Serjeant Richard Nixon in the 88th Canadian Infantry Regiment and Second Lieutenant John Nixon (10/Royal Sussex Regiment).

He grew up at the family home, Commonside at Reigate, Surrey, and was educated at Dulwich College Preparatory School (1907-1908), at Bloxham (September 1908-July 1911) and then at Felsted School in Essex September 1911-July 1913. At Bloxham he made an immediate impact on the sports field; in the 1909 Junior Steeplechase, he crossed the line first, but, according to *The Bloxhamist*, 'having carefully gone the wrong side of the last flag, he had to go back again, and, meanwhile, Marshall won.' He made no mistake in the same event the following year, winning easily. He also won the Under-16 Mile at the 1910 Sports Day. By now he was playing for the school's 2nd XI at football, which was not bad going for a 14-year-old, and he also played cricket for the 2nd XI in his final term. He won the Lower School Drawing Prize in 1910.

There was much anticipation of the 1911 Junior Steeplechase, for which there was a big field of 27 runners – the seniors' race, run beforehand, only attracted 12 entrants. Following the previous year's races, there had been complaints that the courses were too easy, 'so several improvements were made by digging out and widening the jumps. They certainly looked more formidable and interesting developments were expected.' However, *The Bloxhamist* reported, 'in this we were disappointed, as most of the newly made difficulties were successfully surmounted and jumps negotiated without much discomfort or damage to personal appearance.' A close race was expected between the two favourites in the junior race, Nixon and Herbert Cain, and the two set off together and cleared the first jump together, but Cain then led the rest of the way and won a good race. Nixon came in second, minus a shoe.

Oswald once again performed well on Sports Day in 1911 (held on Wednesday 29 March – at that time athletics was a sport for the Lent Term). He won the half mile handicap and finished second (to Cain once again) in the junior half mile, losing out to the same opponent in the rather less prestigious sack race. In the high jump and the quarter mile he was unplaced (four of the field in the latter race would perish in the Great War, Nixon, Riddle, Long and Roberts). In his final term he was awarded his gymnastic colours and was an active member of the OTC.

On leaving Bloxham, Oswald moved onto Felsted School in Essex for two more years. There he distinguished himself in fives and boxing and was a member of their OTC. After leaving Felsted he attended Hampshire County Agricultural School in Basingstoke but left to enlist as a private in the 11th (Territorial) Battalion, the Royal Sussex Regiment. He was swiftly selected for officer training and was commissioned as a Second Lieutenant in the 4th Battalion, the Royal Sussex Regiment on 5 October 1914 and promoted to Lieutenant in December. He arrived as a replacement officer in the 10th Battalion of the same regiment in the trenches outside Loos on 23 March 1915. The Battalion war diary records:

24th March: Battalion subjected to a persistent and spiteful bombardment of HE and shrapnel shells, and many casualties were inflicted by this bombardment. A further draft of replacements were received including 2nd Lt J.E. Compton, 2nd Lt O.S. Nixon, 2nd Lt L.K.R. Bakewell. Bombardment lasted until 4am, and trenches were relieved by 2 Royal Berkshires. Battalion moved into reserve and the relief was completed by 5.35 am.

Oswald was wounded on 1 May 1915 and hospitalised suffering from a gunshot wound to his left hand. After recovering from his wounds, he left the infantry, being tempted like so many young infantry officers to join the Royal Flying Corps. He would have quickly learnt that their distinctive winged 'O' badges earned them the cruel nickname of 'Flying Arseholes'. A fast route into the RFC was to become an observer in two-seater aircraft, which entailed much less training than a pilot, and Oswald headed to Nieupoort in Belgium as an observer on 25 October 1915. He returned to Britain in May 1916 for training as a pilot, taking the time to visit his old school, Bloxham, on 14 June, before graduating as a flying officer on 23 August. Two weeks later he was back in France, where he was posted to 70 Squadron, which flew long-range reconnaissance missions, employing two-seater Sopwith Strutters to observe artillery positions and troop movements far behind enemy lines.

By September 1916 the Germans had caught up with the Allies in the air war thanks to reinforcements of men and new fighter biplanes. Oswald Nixon was unfortunate to have been a pilot on the Western Front for only six days when he and his observer, Second Lieutenant Ronald Wood, encountered the Albatros DIIs of Jasta 2, the elite fighter unit created by Germany's greatest ace, Oswald Boelcke. Among the newly arrived pilots Boelcke had recruited from the Eastern Front were Manfred von Richthofen (later immortalised as 'the Red Baron') and Erwin Böhme, and it was Leutnant Böhme who shot down Nixon's Sopwith 1 ½ Strutter, No. A1913, at 7:45 a.m. (8:45 a.m. British time) on 17 September. The British tended to prefer individual patrols whereas the Germans grouped their planes for mass attacks, and Nixon stood little chance in this aerial combat. Böhme reported that 'Our new aircraft border on the marvellous......their rate of climb and turning radius are amazing.'

At first Oswald was listed as missing, and Colonel Nixon wrote to Ronald Wood's father in Headingley, Leeds to ascertain what the observer knew of Oswald's fate. Mr Wood could only inform him that Ronald, now hospitalised in the Osnabruck POW Camp in Germany, had been 'shot unconscious in the air and did not come around for two weeks', and so could be of no help. Ronald was exchanged into neutral Holland on 9 April 1918, finally making it back to Britain on 2 July 1918. He never could recall the circumstances of his encounter with Erwin Böhme.

Meanwhile, Oswald's mother had written to the War Office in heart-breaking tones: 'What can be done to ascertain what has happened, please, anything? He is our youngest and 20 only. Was he alone? I know the crowd of agonised hearts that fill your every moment with appeals but I cannot help writing and imploring that all possible may be done to trace him.' The RFC was hopeful that Oswald might still be alive – his name was about to be included on a list sent to German camps and hospitals (via the Embassy of the United States, still neutral at this point).

However, in fact Oswald's death had been instantaneous, such was the force of the impact of his crash. The Germans recovered Oswald's body from the mangled remains of his aeroplane, taking some macabre photographs of the wreckage in the process. Further searches in the German archives found pictures which appear to show the body of Nixon, badly burnt, prior to its removal from the wreckage. They removed the buttons and badges from Oswald's uniform and gave him a proper burial at Hervilly Churchyard, east of Peronne, with a cross which read 'Unknown British Officer – Aviator.' The War Office finally concluded in May 1917 that Oswald had died on 17 September 1916.

In 1929 Oswald's grave at Hervilly was opened, and his body identified using dental records. Sadly, both of his parents had died within weeks of each other in 1924, and so never knew that Oswald had not been missing at all but buried in a nameless German grave. He was laid to rest, with a proper headstone, at Serre Road Cemetery No. 2 on the Somme battlefield. His sisters presented Bloxham School with a silver cup for music to be presented in his memory - the cup is awarded to the winning house at the House Music Competition each year.

And what became of Erwin Böhme, the man who shot Oswald down? His victory over Oswald was the second of his career, and he would go on to record 24 victories, becoming one of Germany's greatest air aces. However, he was to encounter calamity a month after claiming Oswald Nixon's life when, in a fight with British DH2s of 24 Squadron, he collided with his commanding officer, Hauptmann Oswald Boelcke, then the greatest of all aces with 40 victories, while the latter was carrying out a complex mid-air manoeuvre. Böhme's Albatros smashed into Boelcke's upper wing, and to the horror of the other pilots of Jasta 2, their revered leader fell to his death. Böhme was devastated by the accident and had to be dissuaded by von Richthofen from suicide, but went on to claim a further 19 combat victories. He was awarded the prestigious Pour le Mérite ('the Blue Max') on 24 November 1917. The case containing the medal was still lying unopened on his desk back at the airfield when he was shot down in flames by a British Armstrong-Whitworth FK8 five days later; he was due to be awarded the Blue Max by the Kaiser later that day. Alongside the medal case on his desk was his last letter to his fiancée Annamarie Bruning.

We are fortunate that Oswald Nixon's story has been covered in two recent books, Alexandra Churchill's *Somme: 141 Days, 141 Lives*, which presents the story of one fatality for each day of the battle, and *Under the Guns of the Kaiser's Aces* by Norman Franks and Hal Gilbin, which sets out to identify and describe all the Allied airmen claimed by Böhme and three other German pilots of the Great War. Both provided important details about Nixon, though neither contained any of the information mentioned in the other one, and neither had anything about his school days.

Private Edward Boissier Board
12th Battalion, Middlesex Regiment
Pupil at Bloxham School 1888-1894
Killed in action 26 September 1916, aged 40
Commemorated on the Thiepval Memorial to the Missing, France
Panel 12.D

The 22 September 1916 marked the exact mid-point of the First World War. 37 of the 80 Bloxhamists to die in the war had perished by this date. The 38th was Edward Boissier Board, killed in action on the Somme four days later.

Edward was born on 17 July 1876 and was a pupil at Bloxham between 1888 and 1894. He was the son of Edmund Comer Board, a surgeon, of Hanbury Rd., Clifton, Bristol; his mother, Annie Louisa, was the sister of Frederick Scobell Boissier (Headmaster of Bloxham School 1886-1898) and also of Dr Arthur Boissier, the School's Medical Officer and founder of West Bar Surgery in Banbury. At the age of 18 he went to work for the National Provincial Bank of England in April 1894 as an apprentice at its Bristol Bedminster branch. In 1898 he moved to the Bournemouth branch as a clerk, moving again in 1900 to London and then in 1905 to the Hartlepool branch. His final move was to the bank's Bath branch in 1911; there he met Kathleen Garrod, whom he married in January 1916

Edward played rugby for Clifton Rugby Club. He joined the Artillery Volunteers in Bristol in 1914 and a year later the Athletes Volunteer Force in Bath. He was also a Special Constable. He enlisted in the 26th (Bankers') Battalion of the Royal Fusiliers on 24 March 1916 and was later transferred to the 12th Middlesex Regiment. He was killed on 26 September 1916 at the age of 40. Kathleen was informed that he was shot and killed instantly at the very outset of an attack which proved highly successful though very costly in officers and men. This is a reference to the fierce assault on Thiepval Ridge launched that day by the four divisions of Gough's Reserve Army, which finally succeeded in taking what was left of Mouquet Farm and the village of Thiepval, both of them first day objectives on 1 July. Some 148 men from the 12th Battalion of the Middlesex Regiment that day, of whom 108 have no known grave, which tells us something about the nature of the fighting for Thiepval. Edward was one of these, and he is commemorated on the Thiepval Memorial close to where he fell. He is also remembered on the Roll of Honour of the Royal Bank of Scotland, which took over NatWest, the successor bank to the National Provincial, where Edward had worked for twenty years. Edward is also commemorated, along with his brother John, on a plaque in St Andrew's Church in Burnham-on-Sea in Somerset, the Board family's home town. A Cambridge graduate, John had died in 1910 at the age of 28. Kathleen Board, widowed after eight months of marriage, survived Edward by half a century, continuing to live in the same house in Bath and dying in 1969.

In all, eight members of the Boissier family served in the Great War. One of them, William, was the son of the former Headmaster, Frederick Boissier, and died on the Western Front in 1917. William was born at Bloxham while his father was Headmaster but was not an Old Bloxhamist, having attended St John's, Leatherhead. His older brother Arthur Paul Boissier was a pupil at Bloxham before going on to St John's, Leatherhead and then Cambridge where he won a cricket Blue. He later played cricket for Derbyshire and ended his teaching career as Headmaster of Harrow. Members of the Boissier family attended Bloxham into the late fifties.

<h3 style="text-align:center">Second Lieutenant Ernest Victor Molson Orford
2nd Battalion, Essex Regiment
Pupil at Bloxham School 1908-1910
Killed in action 23 October 1916, aged 19
Commemorated on the Thiepval Memorial to the Missing, France
Panel 10.D</h3>

Ernest Orford was the son of Sydney Orford, of The Turn, Eardisley, Herefordshire, and the late Ellen Orford; Sydney was a banking cashier by profession. A pupil at Bloxham between January 1908 and July 1910, Ernest was only 13 when he left; *The Bloxhamist* later recorded that he had departed Bloxham while a little boy, 'for circumstances necessitated his removal to another school at an early age, although we were very unwilling to part with him.' The school magazine went on to report that 'he was already showing signs of developing into a man of fine character and ability.' He had made an early impression as a cricketer in Division IV – *The Bloxhamist* reported that 'in batting, Nixon came first, with Orford a very close second. Both these boys show good promise for the future. Higgins and Orford were both useful bowlers.' Ernest's affection for his old school is shown by his return to watch the Old Bloxhamists play cricket at Whitsun in 1912.

After a serious illness, 'when there seemed no hope of his life being saved', he made up his mind to enter the priesthood, and he matriculated at Leeds University and was entered as a student in the Theological College of the Community of the Resurrection at Mirfield near Leeds. These plans were to be abandoned due to the outbreak of the Great War.

He was commissioned as a 2nd Lieutenant in the 14th Battalion of the Essex Regiment in 1916 but was swiftly attached to the 2nd Battalion, and immediately went into the front line with them on the Somme in July 1916. In late October 1916, the regiment was in trenches near Trones Wood, when an attack was ordered on the German lines. Trones Wood, one of the five main woods on the Somme, had been the scene of especially heavy fighting between 8 and 14 July, and was of great strategic importance.

By October the Battle of the Somme had slowed to an attritional slog. The attack on 23 October was designed to drive the Germans out of the last area of the wood they still controlled. The start was pushed back from 10:00 a.m. to 2:00 p.m. owing to mist, and when the attack started, casualties were very severe owing to heavy machine gun fire. The battalion lost every officer and NCO during this action. The war diary mentions that Orford was wounded, but there is no description of his fate. He was initially reported to have been 'wounded, believed killed' as he was last seen walking back from the firing line, wounded. His file in the National Archives contains a number of letters from his father, with a final letter from the War Office in March 1917 confirming that for official purposes Orford was presumed dead on or around the 23 October 1916, and the March 1917 *Bloxhamist* duly stated that 'there can be no doubt that he was hit by a shell.' His body never having been identified; his name is commemorated on the Thiepval Memorial. He was 19 years old when he died.

Ernest is also commemorated in two churches in his native Grimsby. One is St James, the town's mother church, and the other the Church of St Augustine of Hippo, where he had been a server, on a beautiful carved wooden Station of the Cross depicting Jesus consoling the daughters of Jerusalem. It is the work of Sir Charles Nicholson, who had designed the church, which was consecrated in 1912.

Ernest's photograph was one of those lost when one of the four boards was destroyed in the vestry fire of 1985, and despite enquiries to his old regiment and Mirfield Theological College, no replacement could be found until SB recalled that Ernest had returned to the school at the end of May 1912, when the Old Bloxhamists had played cricket against the school, and that a photograph had been taken that day. Sure enough, there was Ernest Orford sitting at the front of the photograph which, unusually, contained the names of all those in it, though he was incorrectly listed as R.V. Orford. He is one of five Old Bloxhamists in the photograph who would not return from the coming war. Sitting behind him are two venerable Old Boys of the school: William Warriner, after whose family the state school built on their land in 1971 was named, and Charles Wilson, the first boarder at Bloxham, who in his capacity as Resident Secretary of the Old Bloxhamists painstakingly compiled the details of the lives and deaths of each of the 76 on the original war memorial, every one of them known personally to him.

Lieutenant Thomas Thomas
51st Machine Gun Corps
Pupil at Bloxham School 1908-1909
Killed in action 3 November 1916, aged 19
Buried in Guards' Cemetery, Lesbeufs, France
Grave X.I.5

'Thomas Thomas' might seem an odd name to us, but in Wales, from where his family hailed, it was not unusual to have the same first name and surname. He was the third son of David Robert Thomas and Margaret (Madge) Thomas (née Jenkins), who were cousins. They were both from Talybont, a village in Ceredigion (or Cardiganshire as it was known at the time) which lies mid-way between Aberystwyth and Machynlleth, an area with a reputation as a stronghold of the Welsh language. They had moved to Oxford by 1891 – David was a pharmacist and had a shop, Cousins, Thomas & Co., at 20 Magdalen Street. By the time of the 1901 census, the business had moved to 63 Banbury Road, which is occupied a century later by *Fabulous Flowers* in the area known as Park Town, in the north of the city.

Thomas had a younger sister, Margaret (born 1898) and two older brothers, David Robert (born 1894) and Jenkin (born 1895). He had a disjointed education, attending Oxford High School, where he overlapped with T.E. Lawrence, before arriving at Bloxham in 1908. He only stayed at the school for a year; according to his obituary in *The Bloxhamist*, Thomas 'was removed from Bloxham at an early age and sent to another school nearer home; but in spite of his short sojourn here he acquired a great affection for his first school and paid us visits from time to time, and also joined the Old Bloxhamist Society.'

After leaving Bloxham, he joined his brothers at Magdalen College School, Oxford as a day boy in September 1909. He won the Set V mathematics prize and the Form I and II classics prize at Easter 1910 and rowed for the Form I and II boat in the Form races in March 1911. In July of that year he won the Junior 300 yard race, leading all the way from start to finish. He left MCS that month but returned to play for the Old Boys XI at cricket on 19 June 1914, nine days before the fateful shooting of the Archduke Franz Ferdinand in Sarajevo.

Thomas had intended to go on to study at Jesus College, the Oxford college traditionally chosen by Welsh candidates, but when the war broke out he joined the 9th (Reserve) Battalion of the Oxford and Bucks LI 'quite early and was for some time in Oxford.' His brother Jenkin was in the same regiment and was wounded and taken prisoner by the Germans, while the oldest brother, David, was a member of the Welsh Regiment. Thomas became a Second

Lieutenant on 26 January 1915 at the age of 17. He landed in France in August 1916 but was then commissioned into the Machine Gun Corps as a temporary Lieutenant. He was posted to the 51st Company, MGC, which was part of 51 Brigade in the 17th (Northern) Division, serving on the Somme. The 51/MGC arrived at Delville Wood on the Somme on 4 August but was transferred to Gezaincourt on 16 August. There then followed a swift series of moves from Maison-Ponthieu to Gommecourt, Hébuterne and then Le Transloy, close to Bapaume as the corps alternated between spells, normally about a week, in the front line and similar periods in billets behind the lines. They relieved the 25/MGC in the front line at Le Transloy on 31 October and were there three days later when the Germans launched an infantry attack on the right of the line after a heavy artillery bombardment. The attack was defeated by effective machine gun fire, but Thomas Thomas was killed during the fighting.

His commanding officer, Colonel Maurice Pasteur of the Machine Gun Corps, wrote to Thomas' parents and was able to tell them how their son had died:

> I expect by now that you will have received news of your son's death. It was a great blow to us all to lose him, and although he had only been with us a short time we had got very fond of him. He always did his work well and cheerfully, and it was in carrying out his duty in taking up his section with ammunition to the front line that he met his death. I questioned the guide who was just behind him and who was blown a good distance by the same shell. He told me that after he recovered himself he ran to see what had happened to your son and found him badly hit in the head. He lived two or three minutes, as far as the guide could tell, but did not speak. I am sorry to say that it was impossible to have a burial service, owing to conditions which I know you will understand. We buried your son just outside our company headquarters at eight a.m. this morning, November 4th, and are having a cross made for his grave. My sincere sympathies are with you in your great loss. Your son died as every officer would wish to die; and although the loss be great you must feel as I do, proud of the way in which he met his death.

The Bloxhamist, in reporting his death, stated that Thomas had acquitted himself so well with the MGC that his commanding officer had recommended him for a permanent commission, in other words promotion to Lieutenant, despite his youth. *The Cambrian News* of 24 November 1916, printed in Aberystwyth, treated the story as a local one, observing that 'the many friends of Mr and Mrs D.R. Thomas, of Tanyrallt, Talybont, will be grieved to hear that they have lost their youngest son, Thomas, aged nineteen.' The newspaper also noted that his parents were 'so much esteemed in Oxford and in the district of Aberystwyth' and listed both of his Oxfordshire schools. Under the headline 'Rhydychen and Talybont Hero', *The Cambrian News* recounted how, 'with the courage of one of the old Cymric princes, he sacrificed his projected career at Jesus College, Oxford, and entered the army soon after war began, by a patriotic advance of his age and of his own free will.' In other words, he had lied about not being old enough to join up.

He lies in the Guards' Cemetery at Lesboeufs, having been reburied there in August 1919 as one of many graves brought in from surrounding battlefields and small cemeteries after the Armistice. His parents had the Welsh phrase 'Gwell Angau na Chywilydd' ('Death Rather Than Dishonour') inscribed on his gravestone. This was the motto of the Welsh Regiment. He is commemorated on the war memorials on both of his old schools, with the plaque at MCS listing him as a Second Lieutenant rather than the temporary rank of Lieutenant which appears on his gravestone. He is also listed on the war memorial inside the Memorial Hall in Talybont, opened in August 1924.

The search for a photograph of Thomas Thomas was one of the most protracted of all those soldiers whose images were lost in the vestry fire of 1985. There were no photographs of him in the school archives, unsurprising given his short time at the school and consequent lack of appearances in sports teams, the most plentiful source of images of the boys, and at the time we were unaware where he had gone after leaving Bloxham, but the reference in *The Bloxhamist* to 'another school nearer home' led SB in 2011 to contact the archivists of St Edward's, Radley and The Dragon, as well as Magdalen College School, Oxford, and the archivist of the latter school, Rebecca Rossef, was able to confirm that Thomas Thomas had been a pupil at MCS between 1909 and 1911 and was listed on their war memorial. This news was accompanied by the disappointment of learning that they did not have an image of him either. However, the centenary of the outbreak of the war in 2014 brought the publication of *Mister Brownrigg's Boys*, an excellent study by David Bebbington of the 50 MCS pupils who died in the Great War – Charles Brownrigg was the Master (Headmaster) of the school between 1910 and 1930. This supplied valuable biographical details of Thomas' life and, most important, a photograph, courtesy of Steven John, who has compiled a remarkable database of all those commemorated on the war memorials of West Wales. The original photograph came from *The Cambrian News* and its report on Thomas Thomas' death.

Private Arthur Walter Gepp
8th Battalion, Gloucestershire Regiment
Pupil at Bloxham School 1908-1911
Killed in action 18 November 1916, aged 22
Commemorated on the Thiepval Memorial to the Missing, France
Panel 5.A

Private Arthur Walter Gepp died in the last stages of the Battle of the Somme – indeed, the day he almost certainly died is the day on which the battle is generally agreed to have ended. He was declared missing on 18 November 1916, which is presumed to be the date of his death. He was 22 years of age.

He was the middle son of an Old Bloxhamist, Francis William Gepp, a pupil at the school between 1868 and 1872 who served on the Old Bloxhamist committee for some years. The family was originally from Chelmsford but had business interests in Rio de Janeiro, where Francis William was married. The family home was at Maybourne, Park Hill Road in Croydon. Naumann, Gepp & Co. was one of the two leading British coffee merchants in Brazil, with offices in London and Santos; this was at a time when Sao Paolo produced 12 million bags out of an estimated world output of 19-20 million bags for 1906. The firm, now Naumann Gepp Horcel, still ships Brazilian coffee.

Arthur had one older brother, Robert E. Gepp, and a younger one, Francis G. Gepp. He was a pupil at Bloxham between September 1908 and December 1911. He won the Form IVa Latin and French prizes in July 1909 and was moved up to Form V at the start of the next school year, in September 1909. Two years later he repeated the feat of winning the Latin and French prizes and was moved up to the Sixth Form for his final term at the school in September 1911.

He was one of the first boys to join the new OTC in 1910.

His greatest renown at school was as a footballer, though *The Bloxhamist*, often given to trenchant criticism of players in a manner unthinkable today, adjudged that, playing for the school's 2nd XI against Abingdon in 1910 'Gepp in goal was useless, and made little or no attempt to save the most ordinary shots.' The following season, still playing in goal, he clearly made progress. The school magazine now reported that he 'has tried hard. Fairly safe, but relies too much on kicking, and does not get the ball well away. Has on occasions saved well by rushing out at the right moment.' The reporter concluded that Arthur merited the award of his school colours 'for the pains he has taken in learning his art'. He was made a prefect at the start of his final term and passed his Cambridge Locals with 3rd Class Honours. He returned to school at Whitsun for the same Old Bloxhamist cricket match against the school attended by Ernest Orford.

By this time Arthur was working in the family coffee business. When war broke out he enlisted in the Royal West Kent Regiment, the Queen's Own, along with his younger brother. As with so many soldiers, he had a disjointed military career, joining the 20th Royal Fusiliers in May 1915 and going out to France in November of that year. At some point he transferred to the 8th (Service) Battalion Gloucestershire Regiment. The unit attacked the south-western outskirts of Grandcourt at 6:10 a.m. on 18 November. The first objective was reached and carried, but heavy losses were suffered among the supporting waves. Among the 295 casualties was Arthur Gepp, who was reported missing. *The Bloxhamist* for July 1917, which reported the deaths of five Old Bloxhamists in action, told its readers that 'no news of A. W. Gepp (1908-11) has yet arrived. He has been missing since November.' No trace of him was ever found and he is commemorated on the vast Thiepval Memorial to the Missing.

Arthur's brother Francis G. Gepp, who left Bloxham in 1913, also joined the 4th Queen's Royal West Kent Regiment. He was wounded at Ypres and was treated in Sheffield Infirmary. He was disabled for life but was able to work in the art department of an advertising agency in London. The eldest brother followed their father into the coffee business in Brazil.

Second Lieutenant Harold Bertram Rylands
16th Battalion, Lancashire Fusiliers (2nd Salford Pals)
Pupil at Bloxham School 1905-1909
Killed in action 23 November 1916, aged 21
Commemorated on the Thiepval Memorial to the Missing, France
Panel 3.C

Although 18 November was officially agreed to be the date on which the Battle of the Somme ended, we have chosen to count Harold Rylands as a casualty in the battle because he died at Beaumont Hamel on the Somme battlefield in an operation which proceeded directly from the battle. For his family, who had already lost one son the previous year at Gallipoli, such distinctions were doubtless irrelevant.

He was born on 18 April 1895 at Eccles in Lancashire, the second son of Richard Walter Rylands, a solicitor, and Mary Elizabeth (née Isherwood) Rylands of Ashburn Lodge, Worsley in Manchester. He was a pupil at Bloxham between September 1905 and July 1909. He was clearly musical, playing a duet with a member of staff, Mr Attwood, in the Christmas 1907 concert. He won an English form prize in 1908 and passed the Oxford Local examinations before leaving Bloxham in July 1909, when he was 14 years old. After Bloxham, Harold went on to another Woodard School, Lancing College, where he was in Olds House from September 1909, in News House from September 1910 and in Fields House from September to December 1912. He was a member of the Officers Training Corps for three years while he was at Lancing. *The Bloxhamist* for February 1910 recorded his gift of a book to his old school's library, adding: 'Old Boys please make a note of this excellent example!' Both Harold and his older brother Victor were active Old Bloxhamists, attending reunions, meetings and dinners.

On leaving school he went on to Manchester University, where he was a member of the University OTC. After university he joined Messrs. David Smith, Garnett & Co, chartered accountants, of Manchester but later followed his father and older brother into the law, being articled to Messrs. Bootle, Edgar, Grace and Rylands, solicitors of Manchester.

Before joining the army Harold was actively involved in the Swinton Boy Scouts and in the Swinton Home Defence Corps. When a second battalion of the Salford Pals – the 16th (Service) Battalion of the Lancashire Fusiliers – was raised in November 1914, many of the officers were drawn from the OTCs of Manchester Grammar School and Manchester University, and Harold was commissioned as a 2nd Lieutenant on 19 December 1914. He commanded No. 4 Platoon of A Company, composed of 67 men from Salford, Pendleton and Eccles. After training at

Conway, Catterick and Salisbury Plain, Harold Rylands embarked for France at Folkestone with his battalion on 22 November 1915, landing in Boulogne from where they made their way towards the Front, first by rail to Longpré and then by marching to the town of Albert on the Somme.

At this stage of the war, the Somme was seen as being a quiet sector, but this was soon to change. At 11:00 p.m. on 10 March 1916 the Germans raided the trenches of the 16th Battalion, causing a number of casualties, mostly from shellfire. The shelling lasted until 12:30 a.m. and an estimated 2,000 shells fell on or around their positions, causing 72 casualties among the officers and men. Harold Rylands was among the wounded and his parents received the following telegram from Lieutenant Colonel Abercrombie:

> I am sorry that your son was amongst the wounded on March 10th but hasten to tell you that his hurt is not serious …Your son was hit early in the action, but refused to go to the dressing station, and stayed at his post until the shelling ceased before he would consent to have his wound attended to. We cannot afford to lose such a cool and devoted officer as your son has shown himself to be.

His father received a further telegram dated 24 March: '2nd Lt H.B. Rylands Lancashire Fusiliers admitted 1 General Hospital Etaples March 22nd with slight influenza', and another one dated 3 April: 2nd Lt H.B. Rylands Lancashire Fusiliers discharged to duty March 19th after treatment for influenza.'

Harold survived the carnage of the opening day of the Battle of the Somme when his battalion attacked at Thiepval, suffering crippling casualties, and by November the battalion was involved in the closing stages of the battle, the Battle of the Ancre. On 18 November 1916, the day another Old Bloxhamist, Arthur Gepp, went missing presumed killed at nearby Grandcourt, an attack was launched by the 11th Battalion Border Regiment and the 16th Battalion Highland Light Infantry to the north of Beaumont Hamel on the German positions there. During the fighting about 120 men from both battalions became cut off in 'Frankfurt' Trench and were quickly surrounded but refused to surrender. For the next three days they fought on and four men came back through the lines to bring the news that they had a large number of wounded, that ammunition was running low and that there was an urgent need for a rescue mission.

On 23 November the Salford Pals were called on to launch an attack in an attempt to reach and relieve the beleaguered garrison of desperate men. In concert with a company of men from the 2nd Battalion Royal Inniskilling Fusiliers, and under the cover of a supporting barrage, they dashed across the shattered landscape and swept into Munich Trench. Fighting quickly became hand to hand and officer casualties were heavy. As a result, Harold Rylands was sent forward to take charge of the rescue attempt but was shot and killed almost immediately. Private Dai Davies saw him fall in the German lines but in a position where he could not be reached. After a fight lasting only 45 minutes the few survivors of the rescue party were forced to withdraw with casualties estimated at 60. On 25 November the men who had been cut off were forced to surrender, having had their number reduced to 15 effective soldiers and having been almost completely out of ammunition.

In a letter dated 24 November, 2nd Lieutenant M.J. Carew wrote to advise Harold's parents of the death of their son, adding that 'Personally I keenly regret his loss, having been associated with him in the Company for some six months, and during that time I found him to be a very true friend indeed.' Four days later, Lieutenant Colonel Abercrombie wrote:

> It is in deepest grief that I write to you about the loss of your son. Although I have made the most careful inquiries, it is still impossible to say whether we may still hope that he was wounded only and is now a prisoner. If this is so you will hear in due course from the War Office and your son will be restored to you at the end of the war. I sincerely trust this may be so. We were ordered to make an attack to rescue some men who had been cut off in an attack made five days previously, and who had held out in the German lines all that time. We captured the front line but the party that was to go forward did not affect the rescue. Your son was seen to fall beyond the German line, and so it was impossible to bring him in, and I can find no one amongst those who returned who were near him when he fell. I am deeply grieved at losing your son, one of the original officers who had become a great friend of everyone in the Battalion.

His parents also received a letter from Private Lancaster, who wrote that 'We were in trenches near Beaumont, when the Germans attacked us. Your son did us good and fought hard. I saw him near our trench and he looked like a confused person. I shouted his name and he turned to look at where I was when he was done by a German. The soldier was soon dead as well.'

Despite this apparently conclusive assertion, several statements were taken to determine Harold's fate, as he had been posted as missing. In addition, his father wrote to a number of members of his battalion. The extraordinary lengths the army went to in order to establish the fate of this one junior officer were not untypical and might make us question the image some would present of a callous and uncaring high command. His file in the National Archives contains statements and letters from 21 members of the battalion, which made it clear that there was no chance that Harold was still alive.

By now the High Command was questioning why the CO did not accept the overwhelming evidence that Rylands had fallen in action, probably from the effects of heavy machine gun fire, and Abercrombie finally wrote to the War Office on 6 June 1917 to concede: 'Reference attached and the fate of 2nd Lt. H.B. Rylands. I think that the death of this officer may be presumed on account of time which has elapsed since he was missing.' Seven months after the event his father was finally given official confirmation of his son's death.

Richard Rylands applied for his son's medals in March 1920; they are now in a private collection. In December 1923 he endowed scholarships in law at Manchester University to be awarded by the Manchester Law Society in memory of his two sons – Harold's older brother Captain Reginald Victor Rylands, 1/7th Battalion Manchester Regiment, had been killed in action on 29 May 1915 at Gallipoli.

Harold is commemorated on the Thiepval Memorial to the Missing, on the memorial at Bloxham and, along with his brother, on a plaque and a double stained-glass window in Holyrood Church, Swinton, Salford, Manchester. He is also commemorated on the memorial at Manchester University and in the beautiful memorial cloister at Lancing College, though there his second name is mistakenly written as Bertrand.

1917

The year 1917 dawned with the Allies once again licking their wounds on the Western Front, counting the cost of massive offensives which cost hundreds of thousands of lives for very little material gain. As Winter turned to Spring, Allied military planning was concerned with taking the offensive to the Germans again, this time in Flanders and the Champagne, in the hope of finally driving the Germans out of France once and for all.

Early January saw much fighting in Mesopotamia, one of the forgotten battlefields of the Great War, and three more Old Bloxhamists were to lose their lives in the fighting here. The campaign was being fought against Germany's ally Turkey, and the soldiers who served in this particular theatre of war had to put up with some of the worst conditions of anywhere during the whole war. A combination of heat, flies, disease and dogged Turkish resistance made this a truly terrible place to fight. The fighting in this sector lasted for the duration of the war, and losses on both sides totalled almost 500,000 men by the time the war ended.

In early 1917, the British, under the command of General Maude went on the offensive and advanced towards the city of Kut. In a stroke of tactical genius, Maude avoided a trap set by the Turks and moved his forces to the opposite bank of the Tigris river, and thus avoided a confrontation with the Turks. He was able to encircle Kut, which fell to the British in late January 1917. The advance continued and by early March 1917, Baghdad had fallen to the British, and reports from the city were that the Iraqi people viewed the British as liberators. There is of course a cruel irony that some ninety years later the British were back in Iraq under very different circumstances.

On the Western Front, the Germans were still completing their retreat to the Hindenburg Line, adopting a scorched earth policy (Operation Alberich) that destroyed everything in their path, that might have been of use to the Allies in the pursuit. At first the Allied advance was cautious, and they sought to take advantage of the high ground that surrounded the River Ancre. The British slowly followed the German retreat before their first encounter with the outer defences of the Hindenburg Line, where the British advance stalled.

By April 1917, the French were keen once again to take the offensive against the Germans and launched yet another offensive in Artois and in the Champagne region, in which the British were called on for support. In a master stroke of offensive action, the Canadian Corps successfully captured the Vimy Ridge on Easter Sunday, fighting their way through howling sleet to capture the heights that had been in German hands since 1914. While these initial successes were hugely encouraging, resolute German defensive actions caused the offensive, known as the Battle of Arras, to grind to a halt with a repeat of the stalemate and slaughter that came to typify the Western Front. The attacks dragged on until the final attacks against Bullecourt in May 1917, that proved terribly costly and caused thousands of casualties.

In the Champagne region, the so called Nivelle Offensive dragged on into the summer and after a series of costly attacks on the Chemin des Dames near Rheims, the French Army reached its breaking point and wide scale mutiny broke out. Soldiers threw down their rifles and refused to advance against the Germans. They demanded better pay, more leave, better food and above all a halt to the needless infantry attacks against heavily defended German lines. In the end, the situation was so bad that Nivelle was removed from his command and replaced by the 'Hero of Verdun', Philippe Petain. He managed through diplomacy and the promise of better conditions to stop the rot from within and prevented a wider mutiny taking place.

In Flanders, meanwhile, the British went on the offensive with the tactically brilliant and perfectly executed attack on the Messines Ridge. This feature which dominated the landscape to the south of Ypres, running from the village of Wytschaete to Messines, and had been in German hands since 1914. It was tactically and strategically important, and after the heaviest artillery bombardment of the War to date, nineteen enormous mines were detonated under the German lines. This was, until the atomic bomb some twenty-eight years later, the largest man-made explosion ever created. The blast was so loud that some claimed it could be heard in London, and swept the Germans off the Messines Ridge once and for all.

On 31 July 1917, the British got the chance for which they had been waiting almost three years, when they launched a massive offensive against the Germans in Flanders. The third Battle of Ypres or the Battle of Passchendaele as many, inaccurately, now refer to it, initially met with great success. However, 1917 was to see one of the wettest summers in Flanders' history, torrential rain fell on a battlefield whose fragile drainage system had been destroyed by shell fire, and the ground soon became a quagmire. The fighting dragged on through Summer and into Autumn, increasingly descending into a bitter attritional struggle. As casualties mounted on both sides, the advance descended to a snail's pace. When the Passchendaele ridge was finally taken by men of the Australian Army in November 1917, 300,000 men were dead, wounded or missing and an offensive that was supposed to have taken three days, lasted in fact for ninety-nine. Many Old Bloxhamists lost their lives in the mud of Flanders.

On 20 November 1917, the British went on the offensive again in France, this time in what was known as the Battle of Cambrai. This was a large-scale offensive using the first mass attack by tanks in the Great War (although they had previously been used at Flers on the Somme in September 1916). The attack at Cambrai was initially a huge success and massive holes were broken into the German lines, and a spectacular breakthrough looked to be possible. However, a spectacular rear-guard action fought by German reserves brought the advance to a halt, before a massive counterattack regained the vast majority of the land lost. While militarily the attacks at Cambrai were a failure, the tactics used and the lessons learned were employed by the British the following year during the fighting in the final 100 days of the war.

Lieutenant George Wilfred Harry Leslie Rawlings
6th Battalion, Hampshire Regiment
Pupil at Bloxham School 1906-1910
Killed in action 27 January 1917, aged 23
Commemorated on the Basra Memorial, Iraq
Panel 21

Of the next three Bloxhamists on the school war memorial, two died in the Middle East and the other in East Africa, a useful corrective to the notion that the fighting all took place on the Western Front and a reminder that this truly was a world war. George Rawlings was the only son of another Old Bloxhamist, Harry Rawlings, who was a coal merchant from Portsmouth, and his wife Emma. Harry Rawlings had been a star pupil at the school in the early eighties, Captain of Football, as was his younger brother Charles, and of Fives.

George was born on 3 November 1893 and was a pupil at the school between January 1906 and July 1910. He represented the school at cricket in 1908, playing for the 2nd XI as a useful bowler, but *The Bloxhamist* observed that he 'must remember that pitch comes before pace'. He took 8-73 in a dormitory match in July 1909. George was a prefect and became a member of the prestigious Committee of Games in September 1909. The Old Bloxhamists, short of two players, had to borrow him to play the school alongside his father in May 1910. In his final term he captained a 2nd XI which contained four other boys who would also perish in the war, Davy, Riddle, Sawyer and Bolton. This was truly the generation at the epicentre of the coming storm. He passed the Oxford Locals at end of his final term.

George passed the Prelims of the Institute of Chartered Accountants in 1912. He was commissioned as a 2nd Lieutenant into the 1/4 Battalion the Hampshire Regiment on 9 November 1914 – this was a Territorial Battalion (though he is listed in *The Bloxhamist* for December 1914 as being in the 6th Battalion) and was his local regiment as his parents lived in Southsea.

Lieutenant Rawlings was sent with his regiment to India in December 1914 and was stationed at Quetta for fifteen months. At the end of March 1916, he went to the Persian Gulf to join the 1/4th Hampshire Regiment serving in the stifling heat of Mesopotamia, where death from cholera, malaria and enteric fever was as much a threat as the Turkish enemy. According to his commanding officer, George 'appears to have borne the terrible heat of last summer. In addition to showing exceptional ability in his military duties, he won the high regard of his fellow-officers and men, his great musical talent adding much to his popularity among them.' This was something he shared with his father, a regular soloist on the piano at school concerts.

By the end of 1916 the Mesopotamia campaign was turning in favour of the British. Following the humiliating fall of Kut in April, they had replenished their supplies and, with a much larger and better equipped force, were now advancing methodically on the city under a new commander, General Maude. The Old Bloxhamist Brigadier General William Beach, a contemporary of George's father, acted as Maude's Head of Military Intelligence. By this time George had been transferred to the 6th Battalion (Duke of Connaught's Own) of the Hampshire Regiment.

We know little of his death on 27 January 1917 other than a letter which was sent to his father by a Captain F.H. Burnett which reads:

> I am writing to express to you and Mrs Rawlings my very great sympathy at the death of your son. As his CO for nearly two months, I saw a good deal of him, and was very soon captivated by his wonderful charm. The liking in which he was held by his brother officers was something more than mere popularity, and his sudden death at the hands of a Turkish sniper at a time when the Regiment was not actually engaged came as a terrible blow to every one of us. I was all the more sorry at the manner of his death because I had confidently looked to his distinguishing himself greatly on an early occasion by virtue of his courage and the power of leadership his personality gave him over the men. I feel that I have lost not only a friend of whom I hoped to see much after the war, but also a brave and reliable officer whose place it will be impossible adequately to fill. Owing to the fact that we were within 200 yards of the enemy we were forced to bury him just before dawn behind the trench, but the enemy have now been driven back and I was able a day or so back to recognise his grave and it has been tidied up and marked with a wooden cross.

Sadly this grave was later lost, unsurprisingly given the context of the British advance, and George is commemorated on the Memorial to the Missing at Basra, which lists 40,682 British Empire troops who died during the Mesopotamian Campaign and whose graves are not known.

Britain's intervention in Mesopotamia was of marginal strategic value but allowed her to shape the region's future once the war ended. As a direct result, Iraq, an entirely artificial state, was created in 1919, with all the consequences that have followed. British troops would be back in Basra in a later conflict, in 2003, and such has been the unsettled state of affairs in Iraq in recent years that the Commonwealth War Graves Commission advise against visiting the memorial. It has been in a sadly decaying state since the fall of Saddam Hussein and is only now being restored. George is also commemorated on a column next to the pulpit in St Margaret's Church, Southsea, which is where his parents were living by this time. The plaque records that George died 'doing his duty nobly till the end. This Pulpit was erected by his sorrowing parents.'

George's father continued to be an active Old Bloxhamist. He had donated £1 1s to the War Memorial Fund in 1916 little knowing that his son's name would eventually be added to it, and in 1922 he donated twice that amount to the school's Swimming Pool fund. He attended the Old Bloxhamist dinner, which celebrated the 60th anniversary of the school's founding, in January 1920.

Lieutenant Ralph Grenfell Hill DCM
1st Battalion, King's African Rifles
Pupil at Bloxham School 1904-1909
Killed in action 19 February 1917, aged 24
Buried in Iringa Cemetery, Tanzania
Grave IX.B.3

Ralph Hill was the eldest son of Charles Hill, a banker's clerk from Wood Green, North London and his wife Ella, and lived at 1, Earlham Grove in Wood Green. Ralph was a pupil at Bloxham for five years, making an impact on the cultural life of the school, which was a lot less well developed then than nowadays, and which often struggled to compete with games in terms both of the amount of time spent on it and coverage in the school magazine.

He was recorded as making his debut on stage in November 1906 in *A Scrap of Paper*, a comic drama by J. Palgrave Simpson which was an adaptation of Sardou's *Les Pattes de Mouche*. According to *The Bloxhamist*, 'in the small part of Pauline, R. Hill scored a great success; he brought down the house at every performance.' He once again played a female role in the play *Old Soldiers*, a comedy by H.J. Byron, presented on All Saints' Day in 1907, and was praised for the natural way in which he displayed 'feminine spitefulness and pique'.

Ralph was also a talented singer; at the annual supper and entertainment in November 1907, another pupil, Burbidge, was adjudged the success of the evening with 'The Zuyder Zee', but Hill ran him very close with 'Sailing in my Balloon'. After a concert the following year, at which Ralph himself sang 'The Zuyder Zee', *The Bloxhamist* opined that 'in a year or two, when his voice is a bit rounder, he will be able to sing this nicely.' His final vocal performance at the school came at a concert in April 1909, when he sang 'When Father put the Carpet on the Stairs', a comic gem from the Music Hall.

Ralph continued to tread the boards, playing the part of Joe in the play *On 'Change*, a farce by the German playwright Gustav von Moser in November 1908; 'he was really extremely good as a cheerful, boisterous, irrepressible optimist.' The following month he appeared in the one-act farce *A Silent System*; unusually, the production was taken on a short tour in aid of charity, being staged in Chipping Norton, Wigginton, and Adderbury.

Ralph was also involved in debating as Vice-President of the Debating Society. In February 1909 he proposed a motion supporting conscription. The motion was carried 17-4, reflecting the widespread concern among the British people about the growing prospect of war. He was less successful when he opposed a motion arguing that Mathematics formed a better training for the mind than Classics, arguing that 'the beautiful and interesting works of Virgil, Homer, and other great classical authors were bound to raise the enthusiasm of man or boy more than simply adding up strings of figures.'

By this time Ralph had gained his remove to the Sixth Form (in September 1907) and was made a prefect in May 1908. He gained Third Class Junior Honours in the Oxford Locals in 1908 and passed the senior version and won the Sixth Form Divinity and Latin prizes in his final year.

Ralph appears to have been less involved in sport, though it was virtually impossible to avoid spending a great deal of time on football and cricket at a school like Bloxham during this period. The closest he came to making an impact on Sports Day was in May 1907, when he reached the semi-finals of the junior 100 yards. He played in the forwards for the Second XI in a 4-1 win against MCS, Oxford in 1908, scoring the opening goal, but against Abingdon the following month, *The Bloxhamist* felt that he 'did a lot of useful work but is somewhat clumsy.' Four of the team that day would perish in the coming war – Cunliffe, Sawyer, Rawlings and Ralph Hill.

On leaving Bloxham in July 1909, Ralph emigrated to South Africa where he enlisted in the British South African Police as a corporal; according to *The Bloxhamist* following his death, 'he gained the admiration and respect of his comrades and popularity from the colonists and natives of his district.' At the outbreak of war he was commissioned in the 1st Battalion the Kings African Rifles, one of two Nyasaland battalions, and served with them throughout the East African campaign, being commissioned in the field.

The East African campaign, little remembered today, featured one of the most remarkable military leaders of the whole war. The German commander in the region, Oberstleutnant (later General) Paul von Lettow-Vorbeck, was tasked with using the small but resourceful German force in German East Africa to cause as much mischief to the British, Belgians and Portuguese as possible and divert forces from the Western Front. He was able to pin down large numbers of Allied troops, including South African, Indian and other colonial troops, for the whole of the war, only surrendering twelve days after the armistice in Europe. More than 40,000 Allied casualties were suffered, and over 16,000 German, most of them Askaris (native troops), as well as up to 300,000 civilians and porters on both sides, mostly from disease.

In a letter to his mother, published in *The Bloxhamist*, Ralph Hill described an attack he led against the Germans. The letter retains its original censorship:

> I am sorry I have not written before, but the Germans have kept us very busily engaged. They suddenly swarmed down upon us and completely invested our little column at _____ , cutting us off from the outer world for eight days. We had to live in trenches in this terrible country —the heat awful and we only 500 feet above sea level. It was rather rotten, and food getting low on the eighth day. We decided to move out before dawn in two parties and try to disperse the Huns, who seemed to be on every rise. It was completely successful. I was with forty men of A company. We charged a German position with fixed bayonets at 5:30 a.m. We captured two machine guns, killed four whites and twenty Askaris and took another twenty prisoners; the rest fled for their lives. The position was held by fifteen whites, 150 Askaris, and three machine guns, and we were 44! I however lost my greatest friend and fellow-scout Judson. He was the

best and bravest man I knew, and we were always together. The poor fellow died two minutes after he was hit, as I was trying to bandage him in a rifle-pit. It will take me a long time to get over this, as we were such close friends and understood each other so well.

The letter, which went on to describe night patrols behind enemy lines, shows Ralph to have been a thoughtful and sensitive young man. His final paragraph reveals that he was unsure what to do in the long term:

This war is going to last a long time; the country is too big, and the Germans mean to stick it out. My colonel has recommended me for a commission in the King's African Rifles, after the campaign here. I do not know whether to accept it or not, because (1) the commission is probably only for three years; (2) German East Africa is only healthy in spots, though not bad on the whole; (3) I am very fond of Rhodesia and the BSAP. However, most people advise me to take it, and at present I have not time to think it over properly.

Ralph was awarded the DCM, the oldest British award for gallantry, for his part in this action, the London Gazette recording on 17 April 1917 that it was awarded 'for conspicuous gallantry and devotion to duty in carrying out dangerous reconnaissance; on one occasion, accompanied by another man he penetrated the enemy's position and captured an outpost, obtaining most valuable information which enabled a successful attack to be made.' He was also twice mentioned in despatches (25 September 1917, 7 March 1918) for his deeds during the campaign, including for the action in which he lost his life.

On 19 February 1917, Hill's company, commanded by Captain A.C. Masters, was in action a few miles south of Tandala in western Tanganyika, defending a position in the hills from an attack by German troops under the command of Captain Max Wintgens, who was advancing from the border of Northern Rhodesia towards British East Africa with a force of 524 Askaris, 13 machine guns and three field guns, as well as hundreds of porters. In the early morning darkness, Hill's outpost came under heavy attack from the Germans. When daylight came Wintgens deployed two companies of infantry and several machine guns, assisted by shell fire from a field gun. The main German assault fell on the two British machine guns, posted on a small hill covering the right flank of Masters' position. By mid-afternoon the hill had been overrun following a bayonet charge. Half the KAR had become casualties, but they had delayed the German assault and Corporal Stima and Private Saidi, the only men to survive from their detachment, had managed to disable the machine guns before they were forced to withdraw. According to the KAR report on the action, 'Masters then extracted his force, having lost two officers and seven other ranks, 18 wounded and 8 missing.' Hill was one of the two officers. He appears to have died in the early morning of 20 February (the date recorded in *The Bloxhamist*), but the Commonwealth War Graves Commission records his death as taking place on 19 February, and this is the date we have taken as official.

General Northey paid ample tribute to the role played by Ralph Hill 'fighting one against ten for twelve hours' in his dispatch following the combat: 'I wish to draw your attention to the splendid defence of Lieutenants Hill and Angell and Sergeants Ashton-Smith and Weissenberg and Askari machine gunners, of whom Lance Corporal Stima was the sole unwounded survivor.'

The delay imposed on the Germans by the KAR at Tandala proved to be of crucial importance. The arrival of the rest of the 1st Battalion over the next two days forced Wintgens to withdraw to the northwest and ultimately to abandon his advance, though his force would not finally be surrounded and forced to surrender until early October 1917. Von Lettow-Vorbeck eluded the Allied forces, led by the South African Major General Jacob van Deventer, by crossing into Portuguese East Africa in November 1917 and carried on his campaign by living off Portuguese supplies for the next year.

Ralph Hill is buried in Iringa Cemetery, Tanzania, in a collective grave with three comrades. His friend Jack Judson of the BSAP, who was killed in action on 30 October 1916, lies in the same cemetery. The parish magazine of Christ Church, Southgate for April 1917 contained the following notice (the parish included the family home – by now Charles and Ella Hill had moved to 61 Old Park Road, Palmers Green – as well as Barnet and Southgate):

> Far away on the battlefield of East Africa, among the noble lives laid down in the Great Cause, Ralph Grenfell Hill has died. He enlisted in that fine force, the BSA Police, and for distinguished service he had won his commission as Lieutenant. We have no particulars, but we feel sure he made a worthy and glorious end and so passed to a higher 'mansion of the Father's House'.

It was to Iringa Cemetery that the furthest pilgrimage was made by MD to take a picture of Hill's headstone. The cemetery itself is several hundred miles from the nearest large town but it is still cared for with the same high standards as all others by the Commonwealth War Graves Commission. While taking the picture of the headstone, MD found that a monkey was removing his lunch and water from his bag before running off up a nearby tree with said articles.

Captain Herbert Cooper Keith Bidlake
9th Battalion, Worcestershire Regiment
Pupil at Bloxham School 1912-1914
Killed in action 25 February 1917, aged 20
Commemorated on the Basra Memorial, Iraq
Panel 13

Herbert Cooper Keith Bidlake was the eldest son of Mr. Herbert Howard Bidlake, an estate agent and later a chemist, and Mrs Charlotte Isabel Bidlake née Apperly. He was born on 21 October 1896 in Southport, Lancashire and baptised at North Meols, Birkdale, on 21 March 1897. He had two sisters, Margaret and Dorothy, and three brothers, Howard, Douglas and John. Howard was also a Bloxhamist and left school at the same time as his older brother, even though he was only sixteen. Ultimately Howard gained a commission in the Duke of Wellington's (West Riding Regiment) in August 1917 and saw action in France. He survived the war to become a rubber planter in Malaya.

By 1905 the Bidlakes had moved down to Reigate in Surrey. Herbert Bidlake senior was a Director of a company called Malt Products Ltd. and the family lived in a house called 'Ivyhurst' on Ringley Park Road in Reigate. Keith – he was always known by his third Christian name – attended Reigate Grammar School between 1905 and 1912, boarding with one of the teachers, Mr Samuel Eade. He then transferred to Bloxham as a pupil between September 1912 and

July 1914, though when the summer term ended the intention was for him to go back for his final year. Events over the summer holidays, notably Germany's invasion of Belgium and Britain's declaration of war, meant a change of plan.

Keith was a good, though apparently not outstanding, sportsman, playing for the school's 2nd XI in both cricket and football in his first year at Bloxham. He played football against Abingdon School in October 1912, playing in midfield. Abingdon won 3-2, scoring the winning goal with eight minutes to go. *The Bloxhamist*, outspoken as ever, praised the goalkeeper, Hugh Bonnewell, but observed that 'Bidlake was weak, and could not hold his wingman.' The full back came in for even harsher treatment – 'Drewe's kicking at times being very erratic—one of the goals against us came from a weak clearance by him.' The following June Keith was playing cricket for the school, again against Abingdon who won by two wickets. Playing in the same team as Kingsley Fradd and Arthur Stevens, he was out for 10 and did not bowl. When Bloxham won the return fixture later in the season, he opened the batting and was top scorer in both innings.

By now he had progressed to the 1st XI in both sports. Against Magdalen College School, Brackley, where Bloxham squandered a 4-1 lead to draw 4 all, it was reported that 'Bidlake was fair and kicked neatly, but he allowed the small outside left to cut rings round him towards the end.' Six of the team were awarded 1st XI colours at the end of term, but Bidlake had to make do with his 2nd XI colours. The December 1913 *Bloxhamist* reported of him as follows: 'Bidlake (centre half) shows promise of becoming quite a good half. Traps the ball nicely and kicks accurately with either foot. Is as yet slow.' In the first match of the 1914 cricket season, on 16 May against MCS, Oxford, he opened the batting and was out for 12 as Bloxham, chasing 89 to win, collapsed to 57 for 7. Excellent batting on the part of Coleman and Anderson took the score up to 86 before they were parted with three runs still required to win. The last two batsmen managed only two runs between them, Coleman was left stranded and the game ended in a tie.

Not all of Keith's time was spent playing sport. He was a cadet in the school's OTC, enrolling in December 1912 and attending two camps. In the 1913 Oxford Local Examinations, when Bloxham recorded its best ever results and finished ahead of all the other Woodard schools, a point of some pride to the school, Bidlake's name appeared some way down the list, well below Fradd, Harvey and Stevens, with the single word 'Pass' next to it.

The original intention seems to have been that Keith would go on to the University of Leeds when he left Bloxham, where he would follow in his father's footsteps and study Chemistry. At the outbreak of war, however, he applied for a commission but was rejected on account of his age, as he was only 17. He first joined the Army Service Corps, before he finally gained his commission in the 9th (Service) Battalion of the Worcestershire Regiment, part of Kitchener's New Army, in March 1915. One of his fellow officers was the sculptor Charles Jagger, who drew a pencil sketch of the young subaltern in barracks over Easter 1915; Jagger was invalided to Malta from Gallipoli and would survive the war to achieve fame for his war memorials, notably the extraordinary Royal Artillery Memorial at Hyde Park Corner and the GWR Memorial in Paddington Station. The sketch and some family photographs were designed to enable Jagger to draw Keith's portrait; a typed letter (dated 4 October 1919) from him to Keith's parents expressed his sincere regrets for their tragic loss and reassured them that his brother David would be sending them the completed portrait from London. Sadly, the whereabouts of the portrait are unknown.

Keith arrived on active service in Mesopotamia on 10 August 1916 where the British were fighting the Ottoman Empire in one of the 'sideshows' which made the war truly a global one. The battalion had been there since February 1916, following evacuation from Gallipoli, where 13th (Western) Division, of which it was part, had suffered over 6,000 casualties from its original strength of 10,500. The battalion's primary mission after it was moved to Mesopotamia was to assist in the relief of the besieged garrison at Kut al Amara, but by the time of Bidlake's arrival the garrison had surrendered. Following this humiliating defeat, the British spent the next six months preparing to advance on Baghdad from their base at Basra, while General Maude attended to his logistical arrangements and trained and organised his army. By the middle of December, the British were ready to launch their offensive.

Keith was wounded in fighting as part of this offensive on 15 December 1916, when, according to the adjutant of his regiment, Captain Holmden, he 'showed the greatest gallantry, taking into action a Lewis gun and firing same in face of an entrenched position until both he and his gun were put out of action. He remained at duty for two days, although he had a bullet in his arm, and I know he remained at hospital for as short a time as possible.' He was singled out for early promotion, and on rejoining his battalion the following month, he was advanced to acting captain with command of a company on 25 January. He wrote home on 7 February to thank the family for their regular letters and to apologise for not writing more frequently:

I wish I could write you all more longer letters but I am afraid it is improbable just now. As you know I have got a company now as we are very short of officers there is a tremendous amount of work to be done in the trenches. Also I am feeling very tired as I have had very little sleep for the last week, and so when I get a little time off I am making the best of it for sleeping. I am feeling awfully well though enjoying it all thoroughly.

In a very human touch, he reassured his mother that she did not need to worry about the fact that he had spent his first Christmas away from home without a stocking to hang up; he and another officer had hung up a sandbag between their beds, and the nurses had filled it up.

After his death, the family received letters from Keith's commanding officer, Colonel William Duff Gibbon, and from the adjutant, Captain Trevor Holmden, and excerpts from both were reprinted in The Times' report of his death as well as The Bloxhamist. Colonel Gibbon wrote that 'I can truthfully say he was my best company commander. He had an opportunity of showing his worth in an attack on a strong point about a fortnight ago and did his work so thoroughly that the Brigadier General's attention was drawn to his work. If he had lived his name would have been submitted for reward.' As it was, Keith was to be mentioned in despatches by General Maude in August 1917. The adjutant added that Keith was 'a brave soldier, a good officer, and a charming friend. Your son was a fine type of manhood. In action he showed the utmost contempt of danger.'

There was a third letter, from Major Cyril Sladden, who was with Keith at the moment of his death, and there was no mention of this in *The Times*, perhaps unsurprisingly given its contents. While Sladden showed the usual determination to reassure grieving parents through insisting that their son had not suffered in his final moments, the letter is surprisingly graphic in its details.

Sladden had gone forward to order Bidlake to halt so his company did not get ahead of the advance, and the two men were sitting and talking in a shallow trench which the Turks had dug during the previous year's siege operations. From time to time they had to lift their heads to see what was going on around them:

> It was while doing this that he was hit. The bullet entered close to the ear and passed out in the neck on the other side, cutting the artery. He fell without a sound right across my feet as I sat there. From the first moment I knew he could not possibly live but attempted to apply a field dressing which was powerless to check the bleeding. Death was very quick, and I am sure completely painless. There was no look of pain even upon his face, which was quite peaceful.

The Bidlakes received one further letter, from Lieutenant Arthur Alford of the 9th Worcestershires, who wrote from hospital on 28 March, having been wounded in January:

> I have only just received the sad news about the death of dear old Keith and I feel I must write a hasty line to say how very deeply and sincerely I sympathise with you all in your irreparable loss. As I had a brother killed in France last September I fully realise the most awful blank that is left when a loved one is taken away never to return. Keith had a very high sense of duty which carried him through his army career, and which showed him to be a man in the true sense of the word. He was greatly liked by all who came into contact with him, and especially the men who served under him. I myself know that in Keith I have lost one of my greatest friends, a man for whom I had the greatest admiration and respect. I feel that your loss is my loss too. May God comfort you in your sorrow.

Keith's body was never found and he was commemorated on the Basra Memorial along with George Rawlings, killed the previous month. He is also listed on the war memorials of Reigate Grammar School and St Mary's, Reigate. Mrs Bidlake contributed 5 shillings to Bloxham School's war memorial in July 1917.

Sapper Arthur Charles Victor Bigwood
2nd Royal Engineers
Pupil at Bloxham School 1902-1904
Killed in action 11 March 1917, aged 29
Buried in Faubourg d'Amiens Cemetery, France
Grave XI.F.7

Arthur Bigwood was the only son of Theodore Charles Bigwood and his wife Mary; the family lived at 23, Compton Road in Wolverhampton, and Theodore ran a metal-working firm, founded in 1879 by Arthur's great-uncle. Joshua Bigwood & Sons was an engineering company based in Wednesfield Road, Wolverhampton, which produced a wide range of machinery and heating equipment. Arthur was a pupil at Bloxham between April 1902 and July 1904 but made little impression on the school in his short time there, scarcely surprising given that he was only 16 when he left.

The pages of the school magazine at the time were dominated by sport, and the only mention he received is a handful of performances in Division III cricket. The standard was not high – *The Bloxhamist* opined of Bigwood and his companions that 'Not for some years, and probably never, has the fielding of a division been so bad. Not only were balls not stopped and catches dropped with most annoying regularity, but the throwing in was often pitiable to see.' Lest his readers be misled, the curmudgeonly writer went on to observe that 'Though perhaps at first sight the batting of this division seems encouraging, such is not the case.' Although their averages were higher than the previous season's, 'the batting is of an incomparably lower standard, and the high averages are entirely due to poor bowling and wretched fielding.'

Arthur joined the Old Bloxhamist Society on leaving school but was not an active Old Boy; *The Bloxhamist* would later record that he was 'one of the many Old Bloxhamists of whom we hear little and see nothing after they leave the school', though he was recorded as having sent a telegram of congratulation on the school's Jubilee in 1910.

On leaving school, Arthur was employed as an Assistant Engineer at his father's metal working business in Smethwick. He joined the Royal Engineers at the start of the War, as Sapper 40301 and he served initially at home, before arriving in France on 12 May 1915. He served with the Regiment throughout and his athleticism saw him take up a position as a battalion runner as a member of 64th Field Company, Royal Engineers.

This was an extremely dangerous role which involved taking messages on foot between the battalion and HQ or behind the lines - it often involved crossing terrain that was swept with machine gun fire or artillery bombardment. Bigwood fulfilled this role with distinction throughout the hell of the Somme, and his devotion to duty and success was noted by senior officers, who stated that 'he was selected as a runner on account of his intelligence and keenness.'

On the morning of 11 March 1917, Arthur Bigwood was taking a message by bicycle while the battalion was in trenches near Arras, when he stopped to perform maintenance or clean his bicycle. He was hit in the back by shrapnel from artillery fire and died instantly, his spine being severed. His commanding officer wrote to Arthur's parents in the following terms:

> I regret to have to inform you that Sapper Bigwood was killed in action on the 11th of March. He was hit by a piece of shell in the back while he was cleaning his bicycle and died almost immediately. I am glad to say that he did not suffer to any great extent. As his officer commanding at the present time I feel it my duty to let you know what sort of a soldier he was, and how much we miss him, and I hope that what I have to say will tend to relieve your sorrow, so that when you think of him the pain will be mingled with pride for a brave man fallen.

He went on to assure Mr and Mrs Bigwood that Arthur had distinguished himself by his fearlessness in taking messages through the barrage: 'Never once did he fail to take or deliver information given to him either verbally or in writing. He is dead—but his example lives, as does that of many another brave soldier, to help us all daily to do our duty as it should be done. This spirit of devotion to duty can never die and is the mainstay of the race.'

Arthur Bigwood was buried in Faubourg d'Amiens Cemetery at Arras. It was at his grave that the pupils gathered to read out the names of the Bloxhamists to perish in the Great War at the conclusion of the school's 2015 Western Front trip. His father contributed 10 shillings and sixpence to the school's War Memorial Fund in July 1917, his subscription being marked 'in mem. ACVB'.

Private Richard Frank Bolton
8th Battalion, Canadian Infantry
Pupil at Bloxham School 1907-10
Killed in action 2 April 1917, aged 22
Buried in Villers Station Cemetery, France
Grave VII.G.33

The next of the names on the school's war memorial is that of Richard Frank Bolton. He was the son of Richard Hardy and Emily Gertrude Bolton of Braunston, Rugby and he was born on 15 July 1894. He was a pupil at the school between April 1907 and December 1910.

At Bloxham, Frank played cricket for the 2nd XI and was a midfielder in football, playing for the 1st XI in his final year; *The Bloxhamist* adjudged that he was 'a hard-working half. Quite good with his head. Should be quicker on the ball and make more use of his left foot. Rather inclined to take his man to the neglect of the ball.' He entered the Sixth Form and won the Bernard Ashworth Prize in 1910. This was awarded in memory of a Bloxham pupil who had died from a heart condition, aged 17, in June 1904. It was awarded annually for a project whose subject matter was left entirely to the pupil; thus the winners between 1910 and 1914 included a model aeroplane, photographic prints and an essay on 'Engineering of Today'.

On leaving the school in December 1910 Frank, like so many Old Bloxhamists, emigrated to Canada where he pursued a career in farming, living in Ontario. He was reported as visiting the school in March 1914, but returned to Canada. On 19 March 1916 he enlisted in Winnipeg, joining the 8th Battalion the Canadian Infantry (the Manitoba Regiment) as a private soldier, with service number 830680. He was recorded on the attestation paper as being unmarried and 5 foot and 10 inches in height, with blue eyes and auburn hair. He remained in the ranks throughout his service with the Manitoba Regiment. According to *The Bloxhamist*, he arrived in France in March 1917 and was killed about a fortnight later, when he was attached temporarily to an entrenching battalion, whose commanding officer reported the circumstances of his death.

In April 1917, Bolton was working on the construction of a railway line which ran behind Vimy Ridge, in preparation for the Canadian assault on the ridge scheduled for Easter Sunday, 9 April. It was during this process that he was killed by shell fire, and he is buried in Villers Station Cemetery, 11 km north-west of Arras. Many of the graves there are Canadian and date from April 1917 and the attack on Vimy Ridge. He is also commemorated on the cenotaph in the cemetery at Rodney, Ontario. He was 22 years old when he died, not 23 as recorded on his headstone and in *The Bloxhamist*.

Lieutenant Thomas Alfred Turner
50th Brigade, Royal Field Artillery
Pupil at Bloxham School 1891-1893
Killed in action 19 April 1917, aged 38
Buried in Ste. Catherine British Cemetery, France
Grave K.15

Thomas Turner was born on 18 August 1878 and was the son of Mr and Mrs A.W. Turner of Milestone Cottage, Wickford in Essex; the name of their house came from the 18th century milestone that can still be found on the corner of the Nevendon and London roads. He was a pupil at Bloxham between January 1891 and April 1893 but made little or no impression in his time at the school; indeed, the first mention of him in the school magazine is the information that he had arrived as a new pupil in Form IV in January 1891 and the second in May 1893 that he had left, having progressed by that time to Form III.

From Bloxham he went onto Whitgift Grammar School in Croydon, as a pupil in the Pre-House between 1893 and 1896. He is known to have won the Cadet Race while at Whitgift, but little else besides. He served in the South African War in the City of London Engineers,

and when war came in 1914 he re-enlisted, this time into the Royal Horse Artillery, on 18 September (service number 152166); at the time of his enlistment he was living with his wife Evelyn at Summerhill Cottage, Basildon, and he was a lay preacher and Churchwarden at St Peter's Church, Nevendon, close to his parents' home. He was commissioned as a 2nd Lieutenant in the 50th Brigade, RFA on 16 August 1915. On 4 February 1916, less than a month after arriving in France with D Battery, 50th Brigade, he wrote a letter to the Rev. A.W. Hands for inclusion in the parish magazine. It offers his fellow parishioners a fascinating insight into life in the trenches:

What a strange mixture of civilisation and brutality war as waged in this campaign is. It seems almost incredible that so short a time ago as Christmas I was with you all. And here I am now at the Front, most of you have friends and dear ones here as well, so my attempt to give you in a few brief lines some idea of the life we lead may be of interest.

Our 'home' where I write this, consists of a little hut built of trees and bags filled with earth, and is in a large wood, which no doubt may be quite a nice place in the summer, when the Boches do not send us any compliments in way of shells, but just now it is little more than a lake of mud. From here a walk of about a mile over shell-torn desolate country takes one into the fire trenches. You must not imagine them as resembling any you may have seen in your neighbourhood.

Try to imagine what a rabbit warren would look like if it were left undisturbed for months, only substitute men for the rabbits, and it may give you some idea of the life that we lead. Holes burrowed into the earth provide kitchens, bedrooms and parlours, whilst here and there a gramaphone [sic] can be heard reeling off some well-known popular refrain.

During the day things are usually more or less quiet, but when dusk comes activity on all sides is noticeable. Huns are by no means the only creatures to be killed, for rats then come out in their hundreds. A sergeant of a certain famous regiment proudly showed me yesterday a bag of twenty which he had made with the help of a little terrier he possesses. I wish it were as easy to kill our larger enemy, but of course one has to be careful that he does not kill you first.

Another interesting excavation is the TP, or Trench Post Office, carefully protected by hundreds of sandbags, here letters and parcels are sorted, and then distributed to the eager recipients. Life would be indeed dull without these messages of home to cheer the men in their monotonous vigil. I will now say goodbye.
Always yours, Thos. A. Turner

Thomas Turner fought at the second Battle of Ypres and on the Somme, and was killed in the so-called Battle of Arleux, part of the Arras offensive (9 April to 16 May 1917), which was designed to secure the south-eastern flank of Vimy Ridge, taken by the Canadian Corps a few days before, on Easter Sunday in driving sleet and snow. The Canadians succeeded in capturing Arleux on 28 April but the British made slower progress in attempting to take the neighbouring village of Gavrelle. They did so early on the evening of 28 April but the Germans counterattacked and pushed the British back before reinforcements finally managed to secure the village. The Germans attacked once more the next day, 29 April, and it would appear that Turner was killed in one of these attacks. The Whitgift Book of Remembrance provides 26 April as the date, but the War Office telegram, which stipulates the 29th, seems conclusive proof otherwise.

Thomas' wife Evelyn was informed of his death on 4 May, and *The Bloxhamist* for July 1917 contained news of his death, though 'up to the time of going to press we have received no information about his military career.' He is buried at Ste. Catherine British Cemetery, on the outskirts of Arras, and is commemorated on a choir stall in his parish church at Nevendon as well as on Bloxham's war memorial, the fund for which received a contribution of two guineas from Thomas Turner's widow. The inscription on his headstone reads 'He is risen'.

Driver Maurice Alwyn Adams
5th New Zealand Artillery
Pupil at Bloxham School 1898-1900
Killed in action 28 May 1917, aged 33
Buried in Dranoutre Military Cemetery, Belgium
Grave I.J.17

Maurice Alwyn (Bill) Adams was born on 20 January 1884 and was the son of a priest of the Church of Ireland. According to the 1901 census, Maurice lived at the rectory in Kill in County Kildare, now known as 'Kill House', along with his parents and four sisters, Amy Maud (20), Edith Marie (18), Blanche Eileen (13) and Alice Ruth, as well as a niece, a female visitor, and two servants. The Reverend Canon James Moore Adams, who had been born in Martland in New South Wales, was the Rector of Kill and Rathmore and Precentor of Kildare Cathedral. He was 57 in 1901. His wife Frances Maud Johnston had been born in Monkstown, County Dublin, and was six years younger. They had been married in Rathdown, Dublin in 1878.

James Adams had been the Rector of Kill since 1881 and was a well-known figure in the area; he was also Rural Dean of Naas and was conferred as Precentor of Kildare Cathedral in July

1898. According to *The Kildare Observer* of 9 July 1898 Mr. Adams had been working in the diocese for more than twenty years and had raised a large amount of money for restoring and beautifying the churches under his care as well as being an active member of the committee which organised the restoration of Kildare Cathedral. He occupied a large number of official positions as a Representative of the Diocese on the General Synod, the Diocese Council, the Joint Finance Committee, the Board of Education, and the Temperance Society. He was also a leading light in the County Kildare Archaeological Society, in which capacity he was a close associate of Lord and Lady Mayo.

Maurice was a pupil at Bloxham between September 1898 and December 1900. He played football in the 2nd XI during the 1899-1900 season but as with so many players of the time, he was the object of trenchant criticism from *The Bloxhamist*: 'Plays a very fair game at left-back and has improved a lot this term; tackles well and uses his weight but is handicapped considerably through not being able to use his right foot.' However, whereas he had previously been dismissed as 'slow. Very frequently loses the ball through delaying to kick', in his last year at Bloxham he finally became a key member of the 1st XI: 'He has shown a wonderful improvement and is now a very good player. Is fast, and a splendid tackler, passes well, though, perhaps, a little inclined to kick the ball too far up the field. Is a good shot, and places corners well. He and his partners in the half-back line have shown wonderful consistency and have been the mainstay of the team.' He was also a cricketer, noted for being 'a very fair bowler' but 'no bat'.

After leaving school he went out to New Zealand, and by the time war broke out he was living in Wellington at 34 Adelaide Road, Wellington, with his wife Lily, whom he married at Gisbourne in 1914. Bill, as he was now known, enlisted at Tokomaru Bay in the Military District of Wellington, his service number being 2/2350. He started his army career as a gunner in 5th Battery, New Zealand Field Artillery; his last rank was as a driver. Bill sailed from Wellington on 13 Nov 1915 with the 8th Reinforcements, New Zealand Field Artillery. They were heading for the European and Middle East war zones, on board two transports, the *Willochra* and *Tofua*. They stopped en route at Suez in Egypt, on 18 December 1915. After a period of training and assigning to units the reinforcements proceeded to England and then to the Western Front, where the New Zealand Division formed part of the Second Army. In the spring of 1917 the Second Army began preparations for the assault on Messines Ridge. Wire-cutting and artillery bombardments began on 21 May as troops, tanks and artillery massed for the offensive, which was scheduled to begin on 4 June.

Bill Adams never lived to see the main attack; he was killed on 28 May 1917, probably by German counter battery fire on the New Zealand positions. In the middle of June, the news reached his home in Ireland that their son had been 'killed in action' in France (in fact, in Belgium). Maurice Alwyn Adams was buried in Dranoutre Military Cemetery in Flanders.

Three years later, on 17 May 1920, a service conducted by his father, by now the Venerable Archdeacon Adams, was held at St. John's Church, Kill, for the purpose of unveiling a memorial tablet, placed in the church by the parishioners, in memory of those who died during the Great War. The tablet contained seven names including that of his son Maurice, and was unveiled by Lady Mayo, who then addressed the congregation:

> I have been asked by my old friend and rector of this parish, to say a few words. We have subscribed for and placed this tablet in our parish church in memory of those gallant men who went forth to fight for home and country against the German hordes.

These young men went to the war full of hope and ambition, and, no doubt, when in France looked to coming home again to our little village of Kill and the green pastures of Kildare. Alas, they fell. They made the great sacrifice. The grass grows over their graves in France, but their memory remains green in our hearts. As long as the walls of our parish church stand, so long will this memorial be there to remind you, your children, and children's children of what these men performed, how they suffered and fell. This marble tablet is a tribute to their memory 'Lest we forget.'

On retiring as Rector of Kill, James Adams moved to York Road, Kingstown, Dublin. In January 1928 Rev. Adams officiated at the funeral of his old friend Lord Mayo. Frances Adams died in 1923, aged seventy-three, and was buried in Deansgrange Cemetery. The Rev. James Adams must have died at some point in late 1939 or early in 1940, as it was mentioned at the County Kildare Archaeological Society meeting, of 11 March 1940 that he had passed away since they had last met.

In the 1990s the FAS Leinster Leader projects in Athy and Naas compiled records of all known County Kildare casualties, but Maurice Adams appeared in the 'Unaccountable and spurious connections' list. It was not until 2012, when the Kildare Collections and Research Services decided to update the list and confirmed Maurice's identity, that the link between the Old Bloxhamist who emigrated to New Zealand and a war memorial in rural Ireland was established. As well as the memorial in Kill, Bill Adams is commemorated on those at Gisborne, where he was married, and Tokomaru Bay, where he lived.

Private Charles Roy Munckton Morris
9th Battalion, Royal Fusiliers
Pupil at Bloxham School 1905-1912
Killed in action 4 July 1917, aged 21
Buried in Monchy British Cemetery, France
Grave I.G.24

Charles Morris was born on 22 September 1895 and was the second son of Henry William George (Will) Morris, a chemist and druggist from Charlbury, and his New Zealand born wife Anna, known as 'Nan', whom he married in Dorset in 1889. Charles had a brother, Cyril, who was three years older than him and who also attended Bloxham School. The family moved around a good deal with Will's work; at the time of Charles' birth the young couple were living in Thame, but by the time of the 1901 census they were in 55 Market Street, Charlbury with two young sons. They are later recorded as living at 18 High Street in Chipping Norton, which is where they were when the two boys were at Bloxham. When Will retired in 1913 the family moved to Creake House in Abingdon.

Charles was a pupil at the school from 1905 to 1912, leaving two years after his brother. Cyril was a notable cricketer, earning his colours in 1908 when only fifteen years of age, and heading the bowling averages in his final season (1910). Charles – listed in school records as R. Morris to distinguish him from his older brother – was quickly noticed for his cricketing prowess, along with another boy who would perish in the Great War – 'R. Morris and Davy are most promising, the former for his size doing wonders.' This early promise did not lead to later success at the game, and he never emulated his brother's feats for the Bloxham 1st XI. Instead

he made some impression in art, winning the Bernard Ashworth Prize in July 1911 for a set of six drawings. Charles left school in July 1912 and *The Bloxhamist* made no mention of him for the next five years.

In early 1916, whilst he was working in the Godalming branch of Capital & Counties Bank (now Lloyds Bank), Charles enlisted in the 30th Battalion Royal Fusiliers (City of London Regiment). This was a reserve battalion for the 23/24 Sportsman's Battalions – hence his service number SPTS/4826, but by 1917 he was serving with the 9th Battalion of the Royal Fusiliers.

In July 1917 the Battalion was in trenches at Monchy-le-Preux, near Arras. The battle of Arras had ended two months before, and so the sector was relatively quiet, but the troops were still kept busy with 'cleaning up and improving trenches'. There was still a good deal of shelling going on, and on 4 July 1917 Charles Morris was killed by a stray shell. *The Bloxhamist* recounted the circumstances of his death: 'He was hit by a shell and killed instantaneously shortly after midnight on 4 July. In short letters to his mother, his platoon and section commanders both speak very highly of him. He was wounded a few months ago and had not long returned to the front.'

Charles Morris was aged 21 when he was killed, and is commemorated on the Bloxham School war memorial, the appeal for which his mother contributed 10 shillings ('in memoriam C.R.M.M.'). He is buried in Monchy British Cemetery. The inscription on his headstone reads 'Peace, perfect peace.' The words come from a popular hymn written in 1875 by Edward Henry Bickersteth, later Bishop of Exeter. Charles' brother Cyril was a Captain in the 8th Royal Berkshires and was twice wounded, but survived the war, becoming a chartered accountant.

Second Lieutenant John Henry Stuart Simons
1st Battalion, Northamptonshire Regiment
Pupil at Bloxham School 1908-1909
Killed in action 10 July 1917, aged 21
Commemorated on the Nieuport Memorial, Belgium
Panel 7

The memorial website page *Every Man Remembered* for John Simons, a young man from Dunstable in Bedfordshire, indicates that he was educated at Bloxham School before going onto Dunstable Grammar School, and this sole reference is what led to his being identified in 2017 as missing from the Bloxham memorial. He is also missing from the school's Roll of Honour, listing those Old Bloxhamists who served during the Great War, hardly surprising given that he left Bloxham at the age of only 13. Clearly the school lost touch with him completely, and was wholly unaware at the time, and since, that he had fought and died in the Great War. The website *Ashton at War*, an impressive piece of work drawn up by Ashton Church of England

Middle School in Dunstable, makes no mention of John's time at Bloxham. However, recourse to his school record card confirms that he was – briefly - a pupil at Bloxham School. He has the same three names as the man listed in the Commonwealth War Graves Commission's records, and the same date of birth, and his father's name and address are the same. So he was clearly another Old Bloxhamist who died in the Great War and needed to be added to the war memorial. This has now been done.

John Henry Stuart Simons was born on 26 June 1896, at High Street, Markyate, the son of Henry Edgar Simons, a farmer, and Agnes Louisa Simons (née Jones). By the time of their son's death, they had moved to Turner's Hall, off Annables Lane in Kinsbourne Green, Luton. According to their relative, Dorothy Hemmings, 'John's father was, to coin a phrase, a bit of a rogue, and frequented the Assizes on a fairly regular basis.' Agnes lived to a good age, but her life was sadly plagued with terrible health problems including tuberculosis; she died shortly after the Second World War.

John was only at Bloxham very briefly, from September 1908 to July 1909, one school year. He had an older brother, Gerald (born in February 1895), who arrived and left at the same time as him. The only reference in *The Bloxhamist* to John is to his cricket; he and his brother both played in Division III. In those days, the school put all its efforts into the 1st XI, so there were no opportunities for the younger boys to play in matches against other schools. Whether in Division II, III or IV, they therefore had to make do with a regular diet of internal matches. Playing alongside his brother and a number of boys who would perish like him in the coming war – Peecock, Gepp, Rylands, Barrow – John is recorded as having mustered a meagre eight runs in five matches in the summer term of 1909. That is the sum total of his recorded impact at the school, and he sadly does not appear in any school photographs from his one year here.

John went on to Dunstable Grammar School, which had been founded in 1888 by its first headmaster Lionel Thring, a member of the same family as Edward Thring, founder of Uppingham School and creator of the Headmasters' Conference. The school had approximately 60 boarders and 100 dayboys when John arrived there in September 1909. John was a contemporary of Frank Cooper, a young American pupil who would one day become the highest paid film star in Hollywood after returning to the United States in 1912 and changing his first name to Gary. Frank's brother Arthur was a year older than John so would have been the member of the Cooper family he knew best. The school closed in 1971 with the onset of comprehensive education, and after 1973 the buildings were used by Ashton Middle School. Among the 62 names on the war memorial in the school library was that of John Simons, as well as that of Ashton Edward Thring, the only son of the school's founder.

On leaving school in 1912 John went to work on the family farm. When war came two years later, he enlisted as a corporal in the Bedfordshire Yeomanry on 11 September 1914, with the service number 1238 30364. He was subsequently commissioned into the 3rd Officer

Cadet Battalion before joining the 1st Battalion, Northamptonshire Regiment on 4 November 1916. He was commissioned on 27 March 1917. According to *Ashton at War*, in early 1917 he transferred to the Labour Corps, which tended to be manned by officers and other ranks who had been medically rated below the 'A1' condition needed for front line service. Many were men who had returned to the front after recovering from wounds. These units were frequently engaged, often for long periods, in work within range of the enemy guns. The Corps always suffered from its treatment as something of a second class organisation: for example, the men who died are commemorated under their original regiment, with the Corps being secondary, which makes it difficult to research men of the Labour Corps. In addition, few records remain of the daily activities and locations of Corps units. This issue of John's time in the Labour Corps requires further research in the archives if possible to make sense of what precisely his role was.

On 20 June 1917 the British XV Corps took over the French sector on the Belgian coast at the very end of the Allied trench system, prompting the Germans to begin planning *Unternehmen Strandfest* (Operation Beach Party), a pre-emptive strike to eliminate the Yser bridgehead. At 5:30 a.m. on 10 July the massed German artillery, including three 24cm naval guns in shore batteries and 58 artillery batteries, opened up on the British positions in the bridgehead where mustard gas was used for the first time. All but one of the bridges over the Yser River were demolished, isolating the 1st Northants on the extreme left flank. Telephone communication was also cut.

The German bombardment continued throughout the day. The British artillery attempted a counter barrage but several guns were knocked out and the German infantry were well protected. At 8:00 p.m. the Germans launched their infantry assault, by which time the two British battalions had suffered 70-80% casualties. The Germans attacked down the coast, outflanking the British and followed up with waves of German Marines, supported by flamethrower teams to mop up dugouts. The British battalions were overwhelmed – only 4 officers and 64 other ranks managed to reach the west bank of the Yser.

Captain Hayes of the RAMC later reported 'Simons was killed, we found a man on the way who was in the dugout when Simons was hit by a bomb.' John's body was never recovered, and he is commemorated on the Nieuport Memorial in the town of Nieuwpoort on the Belgian coast. Of the 566 names of Commonwealth officers and men on the memorial, over 260 were killed or mortally wounded in the fighting on 10 July 1917. It is indicative of the scale of the losses suffered by the 1st Northants that another Old Bloxhamist in the battalion, Lt. Arthur White, immediately wrote to his family to reassure them that he had not been involved, in case they read press reports of the 'Dunes Disaster'.

John Simons is also commemorated on a memorial in St. Nicholas' Church, Harpenden, Hertfordshire, and at long last his name has been added to the Bloxham School War Memorial as the 80th name on the list. Most of the information on John's life after Bloxham is courtesy of Robin Marriott, who wrote the page on *Every Man Remembered* which sparked the school's discovery. We were able to track down Mrs Dorothy Hemmings, whose mother's cousin Sarah (always known as Bunty) was married to one of John's paternal uncles. It was Dorothy who supplied information on the Simons family and who provided the only photograph which shows John. This photograph was taken in 1909, when John would have been 12 or 13 years of age.

Second Lieutenant John Constantine Nuthall
14th Company, Machine Gun Corps
Master at Bloxham School 1912-1915
Killed in action 14 July 1917, aged 28
Buried in Coxyde Cemetery, Belgium
Grave I.A.2

John Nuthall was one of four members of the Bloxham teaching staff to perish in the Great War. He was born on 12 November 1888 at Dibrugarh in Assam, known as India's tea capital; his father Arthur Frederick Nuthall was a tea planter, and married to Constance Mary Pritchard, the daughter of the Rector of South Luffenham in Rutland. The Nuthalls had strong connections with India; Arthur was born there, as was his brother, John's uncle, Lieutenant Colonel Henry John Nuthall, a veteran of the Rebellion of 1857 who was made a Companion of the Order of the Bath in 1907.

John was educated at Clifton College, where he was a couple of years below A.E.J. Collins, who earned cricketing immortality by scoring 628* in a house match at the school in June 1899, the highest ever score until broken by an Indian schoolboy in 2016. Collins, born in India like Nuthall, would be killed in action during the First Battle of Ypres in November 1914. From Clifton (also the alma mater of the commander of the BEF, Sir Douglas Haig), John went on in 1909 to Durham University, where he studied Classics at University College. His scholastic career proceeded smoothly: He passed his finals in *Litteris Antiquis* in 1911 and, in the first division, in Theology a year later. He was granted his BA in Classics in 1912 and then his MA in 1914.

Meantime, John showed every sign of being an outstanding all-round sportsman. He represented the university in tennis and played hockey for the Durham Colleges division of the university. As well as gaining his county colours in hockey, he played football and rugby for his college. His best sport, though, appears to have been cricket. He captained the university XI and was recorded in *The Sphinx,* the student magazine, as achieving a batting average of 21.5 and a bowling average of 5.62 for the 1912 season.

John was appointed as an assistant master at Bloxham in 1912, and for the next two years busied himself with teaching Classics and taking charge of games. He coached the 1st XI at all three of the major games, cricket, football and hockey. The latter was a relatively recent development at Bloxham, the first match against Magdalen College, Oxford having only been played as recently as February 1910, but John was keen to raise the profile of the sport. On the eve of the Great War, masters could still turn out in matches against college and club sides, though not when playing other schools, such as MCS, Dean Close and St Edward's. Nuthall quickly made a name for himself as a centre forward, scoring a goal in the school's 4-0 win over Exeter College, Oxford in November 1913. Playing alongside his young colleague James Pastfield, John scored a remarkable eight goals in a 14-0 victory against C.A. Fletcher's XI, a scratch team drawn from various Oxford colleges, in February 1914.

His impact was equally great in cricket, where he was one half of a formidable bowling attack with John Champneys, who would perish in June 1918 while piloting a Sopwith Camel; opening the bowling for the school in the first match of the 1913 season, against St Catherine's, Oxford, John took 3 for 26, and later 4 for 91 against Bloxham Cricket Club. In the return match against St Catherine's he hit 68 runs.

The following season, his last at the school, John took 6-58 against the Old Bloxhamists in May 1914 and hit 88 against the village on 20 June. A week later, he hit 46* against Chipping Norton. That match took place the day before the assassination of the Archduke Franz Ferdinand in Sarajevo, and the rest of the season was played against the backdrop of the developing crisis which would lead to war, not that any of the Bloxham cricketers would have been aware of the diplomatic manoeuvrings which would have such fateful consequences for many of them. On 14 July, the day on which Austria-Hungary decided to send its ultimatum to Serbia, John was in great form once more against the village side, taking 5 for 41 and top scoring with 71, though the village managed to win by 11 runs. Against Chipping Norton on 18 July, John scored 77*, with no one else reaching double figures in a total of 117, and in his final game of cricket at the school, on 25 July against Adderbury, he took 5-33 with Champneys also taking five wickets. On that day Austria-Hungary broke off relations with Serbia and both countries ordered mobilisation, but it is unlikely that John Nuthall saw any connection between events in the Balkans and his own, apparently carefree, life in north Oxfordshire.

By the time the school returned at the start of September after the long summer holidays, things had changed drastically. What had started as a Balkan dispute had widened to include Germany, France and Russia, and Britain had joined the war to protect Belgium. The first, heavy losses had been suffered at Mons and Le Cateau, and John's colleague, James Pastfield, had decided to join up rather than return to Bloxham. At the end of the Michaelmas Term, *The Bloxhamist* reported that 'we hear a rumour that Mr Nuthall is leaving', and sure enough he departed before the start of the Lent Term, by which time James Pastfield had been killed in action.

It might be expected that John had left to enlist, but events contradict any easy assumption that every likely young man joined up as soon as the war started. In fact he had left Bloxham in order to get married – his wife to be, Clara Evelyn Ormond, the third daughter of Richard Ormond, a merchant and silk dealer from Pembroke, where he was the Secretary of the Farmers' Club. They were married in Cheriton Church, near Pembroke, on 30 July 1915, and John then took up a post as a Master at a prep school near East Grinstead in Surrey. Having served in the OTC at university, he enlisted in 1916 into the Inns of Court Officers Training Corps and was gazetted as a Second Lieutenant in the Machine Gun Corps on 5 September 1916. The Military Service Act, passed by Parliament in January 1916, had introduced conscription for all single men other than the medically unfit, clergymen and teachers as well as certain classes of industrial worker. John was doubly exempt as a teacher and married man, but he clearly saw as it as his duty finally to join up.

John progressed into service with the 14th Company Machine Gun Corps in 1917, arriving in Belgium on 23 April, and it was while serving with them in July 1917 that he was part of a ration party, tasked to bring food up into the trenches from the relatively safe coastal town of Nieuwpoort (also known as Nieuport, the French spelling). He was struck by shrapnel and, despite the best efforts of medical staff, died in an ambulance en route to a field hospital. According to the letter from Lieutenant Owen Bentley of the MGC to John's parents, 'he was struck by shrapnel as he left the town. Though alive when we picked him up, he died a few minutes later, with apparently no suffering.' After these conventional words of reassurance, Bentley closed with another familiar phrase, stating that 'though he had been with us but a short while, he was liked by all.'

The Bloxhamist reported John Nuthall's death in its November 1917 edition, recording all the salient details but getting the date of death wrong, stating 23 July. John had been the magazine's editor four years before as well as running the school's sport, and his old magazine now paid tribute to the way he had exercised both roles 'in an altogether admirable way. His own powers as a cricketer and footballer were considerable, and to these he united an unfailing courtesy and tact which endeared him to everyone.' It concluded, 'He will be remembered not only as a painstaking and capable sportsman and schoolmaster but also as a lovable man and a typical English gentleman.'

He is buried in Coxyde Military Cemetery, and its location on the Belgian coast makes it an obvious first stopping point on a visit to Ypres; this was the first Old Bloxhamist grave SB ever visited. Also buried there is Lieutenant William Boissier, who was the son of Frederick Boissier, Headmaster of Bloxham between 1886 and 1898. It should be noted that John Nuthall's gravestone gives 13 July as the date of death, but we have chosen to go with 14 July as in the Battalion war diary. There was often a discrepancy over dates between different sources, especially when deaths occurred at night-time.

John Nuthall is commemorated in St Stephen's Church in Cheltenham as well as on the Durham University Roll of Honour. He left behind him his widow, Clara, of Melbourne House in Pembroke, a fine late Georgian town house which still stands on Main Street in the Ormonds' home town. She lived until 1975.

Private Geoffrey William Whitmore Marshall
4th Battalion, Oxfordshire and Buckinghamshire Light Infantry
Pupil at Bloxham School 1906-1909
Died 2 August 1917, aged 23
Buried in Shenington Churchyard, England

Geoffrey Marshall enlisted in his local regiment, the Oxford and Bucks LI on 1 September 1914. He served in France between March 1915 and May 1917 but was discharged as medically unfit on 16 June 1917. He died on 2 August 1917. Until July 2017 it was thought that he was commemorated on the Arras Memorial and that his body was lost, but we now know that he lies a lot closer to home.

Geoffrey William Whitmore Marshall was the only son of William Edward Marshall and Annie Caroline Marshall, and he was born on 24 July 1894. His father was a prosperous farmer

and miller who owned the Manor House in Barcheston in Warwickshire, a large family home judging by the fact that there were 19 people living there with the Marshalls at the time of the 1911 Census. Geoffrey was a pupil at Bloxham between 1906 and 1909, making an impression as an athlete – he was the junior champion on Sports Day in 1909 – but on leaving school he moved away from the family home, living with Joseph and Mary Lawson at 70 Manor Road in Rugby and working as a bookseller's apprentice.

At the start of the war, Geoffrey enlisted in the Oxford and Bucks LI, finally arriving in France on 29 March 1915. He managed to survive unscathed for the next two years but was then invalided out of the army due to 'sickness'. He was admitted to hospital in Rouen where he was diagnosed with malignant stomach cancer and was discharged from the army under King's Regulations Paragraph 392 section XVI. He was transferred to England on 18 May and his discharge was served in Warwick on 16 June 1917. He received radium treatment at Middlesex Hospital, but the fact that he only survived his discharge by two months suggests that the disease was already far advanced when it was detected.

Discharge from the army could be due to a number of causes, including poison gas, disease or shell shock. In the case of those discharged due to enemy action, the patient's papers would be marked with a W and he would be entitled to wear, on the arm of his uniform, a 'wound stripe', but in Geoffrey's case his papers were labelled S for sickness, meaning that he was entitled to neither the wound stripe nor a war pension. He was, however, awarded the 'Silver War Badge', along with the usual campaign medals. This was given to soldiers honourably discharged from the forces due to wounds or sickness. The badge, to be worn on the right breast of civilian clothes, was designed to indicate previous service and to deter the attentions of those ladies who chose to present white feathers to men of military age whom they encountered not wearing uniform. These badges were carefully regulated and individually numbered; Geoffrey's badge was number 200198.

White feathers were frequently handed out in the towns and cities, but it is unlikely that Geoffrey would have been at risk in his home village of Shenington, where he returned in June 1917. In any case, he did not have long to ponder the matter, as he died on 2 August 1917 in Senendone House, which still stands just behind the chestnut tree on Shenington Green. He was buried in Shenington churchyard on 6 August and is commemorated on the memorial in Holy Trinity Church.

For a long time there was considerable confusion about the circumstances of Geoffrey Marshall's death. It did not help that he was listed in the school records as George rather than

Geoffrey, as he is in the school's Roll of Honour and the list of the fallen in the handwriting of the chaplain, Hugh Willimott. He did not receive an obituary in *The Bloxhamist* at the time, but he was included on the school war memorial and his photograph was presented to the school and placed with all the others. When the school's Western Front trip visited Arras in October 1915, it was still thought that Geoffrey (or George as he was then thought to be) was commemorated on the Arras Memorial, and William Brodey, the pupil who played him in the school play '79', paid his respects there.

Recently this identification has been shown to be incorrect, as he had been confused with another Private G. Marshall (George Marshall) of the Oxford and Bucks LI who died in April 1917. Thanks to dogged detective work by the authors, confirmed by the researches of Alistair Cook, who has written on the war dead of the villages of Alkerton and Shenington, we now know of Geoffrey Marshall's fate. As he was no longer on active service when he died, does not appear on the CWGC database, and died from disease rather than wounds, a case might be made for Geoffrey's removal from the school's war memorial, but this would be entirely wrong given his lengthy war service, not to mention the intention behind the memorial in the first place.

Major Cyprian Edward Borton
Malay States Guides
Pupil at Bloxham School 1890-1894
Killed in action 2 August 1917, aged 37
Buried in Maala Cemetery, Yemen
Special Plot 3.1

Nothing emphasises the global nature of the Great War more than the deaths on the same day, 2 August 1917 of two very different Old Bloxhamists on two very different fronts. Geoffrey Marshall was a young Private from North Oxfordshire who enlisted in his local regiment and died at home a few miles from Bloxham, while Cyprian Borton was a career soldier, an officer with an impeccable background in Britain's empire who was killed in action in a far-flung imperial outpost, Aden, in the Persian Gulf.

Cyprian Borton was born in South Africa, the elder son of the Rev. Neville Borton, a clergyman who had gone out to the Northern Cape in the aftermath of the first major diamond rush, in 1870. Cyprian's mother Annie Louisa was the daughter of another clergyman, the Rev. Edward Heale, of All Saints, Jersey. Neville Arthur Blachley Borton, MA, served as the second rector of St Cyprian's Church in Kimberley, having been brought to the Diocese of Bloemfontein in 1876 by Bishop Allan Becher Webb and sent to the diamond fields. Neville ran a small church school at St Mary's Barkly West, but when he and his wife lost all their possessions in a fire in 1878, an opening was found for him in Bloemfontein, when he was appointed principal of St Andrew's, College, a considerable promotion in the educational world. It was at this point that Cyprian was born on 15 August 1879 and named after his father's first church in Kimberley. It is said that large numbers of worshippers were attracted to St Andrew's due to Neville's reputation in the diamond fields. Bishop Webb's high regard for him was confirmed when he was made a Canon of Bloemfontein Cathedral in 1882. He subsequently returned to England as Vicar of Burwell, Cambridgeshire, where he served until 1920.

Cyprian was a pupil at Bloxham School between September 1890 and July 1894. He made few appearances in the school magazine in his time at Bloxham, winning the Divinity Prize two years in succession and triumphing in the under twelve 25-yard race at the July 1892 Aquatic Sports. After leaving Bloxham when he was nearly fifteen years of age, he went onto Felsted and then to Selwyn College, Cambridge, where he was still studying when the Boer War broke out. Eager to return to the land of his birth, Cyprian was successful in obtaining one of the army commissions offered to the university.

Gazetted 2nd Lieutenant in the Worcestershire Regiment on 23rd May 1900, he went to South Africa in August 1900 where he saw action, gaining the Queen's Medal with three clasps, visible in his photograph. He was promoted Lieutenant on 3 August 1901, and proceeded to India in March 1902, when for a time he was attached to the Suffolk Regiment, but in May 1903 he decided to join the Indian Army, serving in the 129th Duke of Connaught's Own Baluchis. He served at Karachi, Hong Kong and Ferozepore and was promoted Captain on 23 May 1909. *The Bloxhamist* continued to report intermittently on the progress of his career, for example following a visit to the school in May 1906 when home on leave.

There was clearly something in Cyprian's character which made him restless for new challenges, and with no wife or family to worry about, he underwent another change of direction; after a decade in the Indian Army, he was seconded to the Malay States Guides for three years, going to the Malay Peninsula with the local rank of Major. This was a force mostly recruited in India, made up of 584 Sikhs but also including 200 Pathans and 102 Punjabi Muslims, with 11 European and 16 Indian officers. It had been set up for internal defence duties in the new federation of the Malay States, which had been created by the states of Perak, Pahang, Selangor and Negri Sembilan in 1895. When the Guides joined the Aden Field Force, two Regiments, comprising Pathans and Punjabi Muslims, almost revolted when asked to fight against the Turkish caliphate, which had declared a jihad (holy war) against the British and their allies.

Cyprian Borton was a keen sportsman, a term which would have been used by contemporaries to include his love of big game hunting – it was reported that he sent home many heads and skins from his forays in India and South China. He had been 'an ardent oarsman' while at Cambridge and was a member of the Penang Cricket Club. He was in command at Penang when the harbour was attacked by the German light cruiser *Emden* in October 1914; she succeeded in sinking the Russian cruiser *Zhemchug* and the French destroyer *Mousquet* and continued to play havoc with merchant shipping in the Indian Ocean for the first three months of the war.

The Malay States Guides were sent to Aden in October 1915 with the brigade of Major General George Younghusband, who swiftly departed for Egypt, handing over command to Brigadier-General C.H.U. Price, CB, DSO. Price's force settled down to pursue a policy of 'active defence' that employed 'moveable columns' deployed for very limited periods to deter further Turkish advances and smaller 'flying columns' that could be put into the field more rapidly. The British could match the Turks for infantry and cavalry but were inferior in artillery and so had to be careful in their tactics. This was a punishing theatre of war, where dysentery was a constant danger. Fighting was almost impossible in the summer months, and the decisive factor all year around in any operation was water, as the Turks controlled the desert wells, while the British relied on their camel convoys to supply sufficient water for men, horses, mules and camels.

If the Arab Revolt was, in the words of T.E. Lawrence, 'a sideshow of a sideshow', how should one describe the Aden theatre? Aden was a small British outpost on the south-western tip of the Arabian peninsula, annexed by Britain in 1839. It was a vital point for traffic through the Suez Canal, as well as being an important trading post for trade with Arabia and East Africa. A garrison consisting of a brigade of Indian Army troops resisted a Turkish offensive in November 1914 and, reinforced by a second Indian Army brigade in 1915, continued to hold onto Aden against the 14,000 men of Ali Sa'id Pasha's 7th Army Corps which advanced and captured Sheikh Othman in July 1916, from where the Ottoman guns could shell Aden Harbour. The Arab Revolt left Ali Sai'd isolated in a theatre the Ottoman Empire could no longer afford to reinforce, but his troops continued to launch small raids against Aden's perimeter defences, making effective use of local tribesmen, and he did not surrender until January 1919. It was in this obscure backwater that Cyprian Borton met his death.

Cyprian was second in command of the MSG contingent, and took charge of field firing practice, while other British officers trained the men in desert entrenching and wiring. They were engaged in the defence of a sector of the Sheikh Othman defence line, and it was there that Cyprian died having been shot by a stray bullet when in command of raid about 100 yards from the enemy on Thursday 2 August 1917. There is precious little information about the action in which he lost his life, but according to the Turkish official history the British launched an attack on 28 July to seize the town of Elvaht, which covers the approach to the neck of land connecting Aden to the mainland. The fighting lasted through 29 July. Imad, where Cyprian Borton died, is about seven km north-east of Sheikh Othman, and though the Turkish history makes no mention of any fighting on 2 August, it seems that Major Borton was killed while leading a raid on Ottoman positions near Hatum. He was 37 years of age. His commanding officer, Lieutenant Colonel Charles Lees of the 53rd Sikhs wrote to Cyprian's parents:

> I cannot tell you what his loss means to the regiment, and to me personally. He was one of the finest soldiers that I have ever met, with a fund of energy that I never got to the end of, and he was just my right hand as regards this regiment; to me he is irreplaceable. He was also my one pal here, and my opinion of him professionally was as great as my affection for him personally. I never heard him say, I never saw him do, a mean or unworthy thing; he was a clean living, clean minded, thorough English gentleman, with all that that term implies, and we all mourn his loss very deeply indeed.

Cyprian's body was recovered and was buried in Sheikh Othman Cemetery, but it was one of 14 bodies exhumed and reburied in nearby Maala Cemetery, located on the southern side of Aden Harbour, in January 1982. He was commemorated along with two brother officers, Captain Leslie and Lieutenant Maclean, on a brass plaque in All-Saints Church, in Taiping, the MSG's base in Malaya. He is also commemorated on the war memorial at Ipoh and was listed on the memorial in the pavilion at the Penang Cricket Club, sadly destroyed during the Second World War. Finally, his name appears on the war memorial at Burwell, where his father was the parish priest at the time of Cyprian's death.

The caption for his photograph in the school's collection indicates that Cyprian Borton had been awarded the DSO, but there is no evidence that this is correct. It may be that confusion was caused by the initials DCO, denoting his Indian Army regiment, the Duke of Connaught's Own.

Major Derrick le Poer Trench DSO, MC
Royal Artillery
Pupil at Bloxham School 1893-1898
Killed in action 27 August 1917, aged 35
Buried in Noeux-les-Mines Communal Cemetery, France
Grave I.X.1

Derrick le Poer Trench was the son of Colonel and Mrs. Stewart Trench, of 21, Hans Mansions, Sloane Square, London. He was born on 25 May 1882. He had two older brothers, Alfred (born 1878) and Stewart (born 1879), both Bloxhamists, and a much younger sister (Violette, born 1893) and brother (Rupert, born 1896). Violette would go on to marry a Russian Prince, Konstantine Lobanov-Rostovsky, scion of a notable family which had provided generals and ministers for the Tsars over the centuries.

The Trench family was itself a distinguished one, and Derrick was well-connected on both sides; through his father he was related to William le Poer Trench, fifth Earl of Clancarty, who famously fell out with his family after marrying the music hall singer Belle Bilton. The first Earl had had nineteen children, and the Trench family had many branches. Another cousin was Baron Ashtown, of Woodlawn House in County Galway. Derrick's maternal grandfather was Sir Alfred Hickman, an industrialist who was President of the Wolverhampton Chamber of Commerce and Chairman of the Staffordshire Railways Association. In 1906 he became Chairman of the newly formed Tarmac Limited, a company which used large quantities of the waste slag from his colliery in Tipton. Elected Conservative MP for the new seat of West Wolverhampton in 1885, he lost it in 1886 but regained it in 1892 and held it until the Liberal landslide of 1906. He was knighted in 1891 and became a baronet in 1903. Derek's father was a colonel in the Duke of Wellington's Regiment who died a month before his third son, in July 1917.

Derrick arrived at Bloxham along with his older brothers in April 1893 for the start of the summer term. It is not immediately obvious why a distinguished military family chose Bloxham for their sons' education, but in most such cases the main attractions to parents seem to have been either the relatively low fees or the school's well-known strain of High Church Anglicanism. Alfred swiftly made his mark as a sportsman, playing regularly for the football XI, and was appointed a sub-prefect in 1894. Derrick and Stewart made less impact but proceeded with the familiar procession of class promotions in the ensuing years.

The results of the 1895 Cambridge Locals show Derrick to have significantly outperformed Stewart in the classroom. He was awarded the Latin Prize at the end of the summer term in 1894. This prize was donated to the school by Mr and Mrs Hinde, the son in law and daughter of Bloxham's Founder Philip Reginald Egerton. Stewart's departure in July 1897 left Derrick as the only Trench brother still at the school. In the same month, he was awarded a prize for his performance in the Cambridge Locals – significantly in terms of his future career, his choice of book was Malleson's *Indian Mutiny,* and he also won a Mathematics prize, choosing a worthy textbook, Ganot's *Treatise on Physics,* as his prize. He left at the end of the summer term in 1898, so never had the chance to make his mark as a senior pupil at the school. Instead, he entered the Royal Military Academy at Woolwich – the time between leaving school and going to Woolwich in 1899 was probably spent being prepared for the entrance examination by a 'crammer', as unlike bigger and more prestigious schools, Bloxham did not possess an army class to do the job.

Derrick was commissioned in the Royal Field Artillery and remained a Gunner for the rest of his life. He returned to the school for Bloxham's Jubilee celebrations in July 1910 and visited again in June 1914, on the very eve of war, with his brother Stewart. The Roll of Honour in the October 1914 *Bloxhamist* recorded Derrick as serving as a Lieutenant in the Royal Artillery, but in fact he had already been promoted to Captain in December 1912. He went out to France at the start of the war, serving with the Guards Division Artillery and going through all the early battles. Derrick was wounded in September 1914, though not seriously, and news only reached his old school of his wound in April the following year, the same year he was promoted to Major.

Derrick would go on to become the most highly decorated of all the Bloxham war dead. He was mentioned in despatches on no fewer than four occasions, on 22 June 1915, 1 January and 15 June 1916, and 11 December 1917, and was awarded the MC on the first of those dates. He was made a Companion of the Distinguished Service Order in 1917. This award was gazetted in the Birthday Honours list of 4 June 1917, and so there was no citation as it would have been for general good service. The DSO was the highest award an officer could earn other than the Victoria Cross, and the practice of awarding them for meritorious service rather than a specific act of gallantry led to some resentment, with some cynics claiming that the initials stood for 'Didn't Shoot Once'. In Trench's case, however, his MC and four MIDs suggest that it was well deserved.

Derrick le Poer Trench progressed steadily up the ladder on the Western Front, serving as Adjutant to 42nd Brigade, Brigade-Major to Divisional Artillery, and finally being appointed DAAG in February 1917. The rather misleading job title obscures the importance of this senior staff appointment, which paired him with Brigadier General Malcolm Peake, a highly respected officer who had spent the early part of the war at the War Office, where he was in charge of all matters of artillery personnel – he it was who had selected another Old Bloxhamist, Wilfred Ellershaw, for the mission to Russia. In April 1916 Peake was sent to command 29th Division's Artillery, which he did throughout the Battle of the Somme, afterwards being promoted to BGRA for 1st Corps in December 1916.

Peake and Trench were on reconnaissance at Hill 70, near Loos, on 27 August 1917 when they were hit by an enemy shell which killed them both. Peake was one of 78 British generals who were killed in action, died of wounds or as a result of active service in the Great War, which shows just how grossly inaccurate and unjust is the popular image of senior commanders skulking miles behind the front line. Derrick le Poer Trench is buried in the grave next to Malcolm Peake in Noeux-les-Mines Communal Cemetery, near to where they died. Derrick's headstone reads: 'Faithful unto death'.

Second Lieutenant John Newbery
1st South African Infantry
Pupil at Bloxham 1894-1897
Killed in action 20 September 1917, aged 38
Commemorated on the Menin Gate, Belgium
Panel 16.A

This was another puzzle that took some unravelling, as the school recorded his name as John Newbery (formerly Boschetti), but the only Great War casualty with that surname was Lieutenant Laurence William Newbery Boschetti, a merchant seaman who was given Naval Reserve rank and commanded HMS Albacore, a B class destroyer, and was then given command of P32, a coastal patrol vessel of 600 tons. He died of pneumonia aged 34 on 26 October 1918 and is buried in Cookham Cemetery. But this is not our man and is probably his cousin. The John Newbery who is on the school's war memorial was known when at Bloxham as John Boschetti – the record card written for him by Charles Wilson clearly states, 'John Newbery Boschetti, later known as John Newbery, ward of Miss Boschetti of Eccles, Lancashire'.

John Boschetti was born on 10 April 1879 and was a pupil at the school between January 1894 and July 1897. He was a good cricketer, being a member of the school's 1st XI for two years and earning his colours at the end of the 1896 season. The highlight of his cricketing career was probably his 7-52 against Wroxton Abbey in a 36-run victory in June 1897. *The Bloxhamist* judged that he was 'a most successful bowler, with a puzzling action; good length and break. Awkward and stiff batsman, with no wrist action.' He also played goalkeeper for the 1st XI in the football term.

After leaving Bloxham John went out to South Africa to find his fortune. Little is known about him between then and the start of the war in 1914, except that he served with the British South Africa Police. When war broke out he enlisted at Potchefstroom as a Trooper in 7 Squadron 2nd Imperial Light Horse. By now he was known as John Newbery. He went through the German South-West Africa campaign with the Imperial Light Horse. He then joined the infantry for overseas service as a Private and went to Egypt with the South Africans and then to France. John was wounded in Delville Wood on the Somme in July 1916, with a gunshot wound to the buttock, which was more serious and decidedly less comical than it might sound, as he was hospitalised in Britain.

However, he was back with his unit in France by 14 December 1916. He rose rapidly through the ranks and won his commission as a Second Lieutenant in the 3rd Regiment, 1st Brigade South African Infantry on 29 April 1917 for services in the field, for the way he led and handled his platoon when there was no officer to lead them at Arras. In September 1917 the SAI were fighting close to Bellewaarde Ridge in the Ypres Salient. On the date in question, 20 September, they lost 126 men to a German artillery attack and flamethrowers. This would tie in with John Newbery being on the Menin Gate, indicating that he died in this fighting but that his body could not be found or identified. He was 38 years of age when he died. His name is spelled incorrectly, with a double r, on the Menin Gate.

Lawrence Newbery Boschetti adopted the name Newbery after the death of his father, according to the Cookham Researchers. We presume that John did the same but he went a step further and dropped the Boschetti. The person who gave the school all the information on John was his brother, who is described as Harry Newbery, not Harry Newbery Boschetti. On John's enlistment papers, Harry's address, as next of kin, was given as the Knight Central Mine, Germiston, Transvaal, and as John's occupation in the same document is given as 'clerk', it is possible that he too may have worked at the mine, in a clerical capacity.

The Boschetti family were originally from Gibraltar. The oddly named John Maria Boschetti Newbery Boschetti, who was born in Gibraltar in 1801, moved to Eccles in the 1830s and is shown in the 1871 census as a retired merchant living there with his wife Agnes and four daughters. Our John Newbery Boschetti was born eight years after that and appears to have been his grandson. When he died in 1880 J.M.B.N. Boschetti left £140,000 in his will, so had clearly done well for himself. One of his daughters, Isabel, married Sir Francis Arthur Stanley ffolkes in 1893; he was Chaplain-in-Ordinary to all four Kings between Edward VII and George VI.

Private Wilfred Entwisle Bury
1st Battalion, Canadian Mounted Rifles
Pupil at Bloxham School 1892-1900
Died of wounds 15 November 1917, aged 36
Buried in Lijssenthoek Military Cemetery in Belgium
Grave XXII.D.3

Some of the 80 names on the school war memorial are of boys who only attended Bloxham briefly, in several cases for just a year or two. Wilfred ('Bill') Bury, on the other hand, was a

Bloxham pupil for fully eight years, arriving at the start of the summer term in May 1892 and only leaving in July 1900. He was born in Geneva on 21 August 1881 to Edward Alexander and Augusta Marie Bury, the fifth child of a family of seven. One of his sisters married Arthur Peel, a contemporary at Bloxham and School Captain in 1898.

Being only ten years of age on arrival, it is unsurprising that there is little record of his school career in his early years beyond his gradual progress up the form ladder as he got older. It was not until June 1896 that Wilfred received a mention beyond the barest details in *The Bloxhamist*, when it was reported that he 'showed very promising form' as a batsman.

When he returned to school in September, Wilfred made a greater impact than before as a member of the senior football division and made his first appearance for the 2nd XI in November. He was forced to wait a long time until he could force his way into the 1st XI, the reason being made plain in *The Bloxhamist*, which commented in December 1898 that he was 'a most hard-working half, who, but for his size and lack of weight, would have easily gained a place in the first eleven'; elsewhere, the magazine observed that 'Bury, Read, and Spence may make half-backs in time and with more experience', and lamented the shortage of 2nd XI fixtures.

While it was in the sporting arena that Wilfred made his biggest impact on school life, he also found time for plenty of other pursuits. An interest in ornithology is suggested by the report in June 1896 that the Curator of the school's Natural History Society had gratefully received a gift from Wilfred of a handsome purple coot and three other stuffed birds. He was also one of those congratulated for his part in the decorations erected to celebrate Queen Victoria's Diamond Jubilee in 1897, which included 'a large tri-coloured shield, 9 ft. x 8 ft. of red, white, and blue, bearing on its face the monogram VRI in gold, surmounted by a most elaborate royal crown in gold'.

In the summer term of 1898, Wilfred was elected to the editorial staff of *The Bloxhamist* as its most junior member, as well as joining the Camera Club, of which he was elected captain in his final term at the school. He also played the role of Lydia in the farce 'My Turn Next', and the *Banbury Advertiser* judged that he 'made excellent use of the opportunities afforded him for providing fun in his feminine character'.

His stature in the school was recognized by his election early in 1899 as Secretary of the Committee of Games, which ran the school's sport and which was mostly made up of pupils. The following month, Wilfred finally made his debut for the 1st XI, against Abingdon, and was commended for playing well in a losing cause, with Abingdon winning 9-2. He played right half for the remainder of the season, and earned praise from *The Bloxhamist*, which adjudged that he 'tackles splendidly and feeds his forwards well, his only fault is lack of speed, which he compensates to a large extent by seldom letting a man pass him easily.' At the end of the 1899-1900 season, his second in the 1st XI, he was complimented on his passing to his forwards and his tackling. He and the Courtney brothers were said to be 'a trio that takes some getting past.' Wilfred was universally praised for his hard work and good judgement on the football field. His cricket made less progress, with his batting in his final season, in 1900, generally agreed to have been a disappointment, though he was awarded his cricket colours to go with those he earned in football.

As well as his sporting ability, Wilfred was clearly blessed with a good voice, singing a football song at the concert held to celebrate the relief of Ladysmith in February 1900, when he was one of six senior boys who were said to have strengthened the choir by deciding to join it, somewhat late in his school career. At another concert in March 1900 he contributed 'Forty Years On'. He performed the song again as an encore in a third concert the following month, following his advertised performance of 'The British Grenadier'. When he left Bloxham at the end of the summer term, it was remarked that the loss of his tenor voice was a severe blow to the school choir.

On leaving Bloxham, Wilfred, or Bill as his family knew him, moved onto Keble College, Oxford to study Biology. He was a student at Keble from Michaelmas 1900 and was a member of the college's football team between 1901 and 1903, captaining them during the 1902-03 season. He was also a member of the Oxford University Volunteers. He obtained his degree in 1904 and went as an Assistant Master to Michaelhouse School in Natal, South Africa early in 1906 – *The St Michael's Chronicle* for May of that year offered a hearty welcome to him and mentioned his prowess at football. *The Natal Mercury* reported a match in November 1906 as follows (clearly members of the teaching staff were still allowed to play in matches against other schools at this point):

'The Michaelhouse eleven were considerably the heavier side, and included several soccer "experts", but they deserve every credit for making such a good display in a code which is not their own. The High School continued to press, but the defence was too good, especially in the case of Mr. Bury, who played a very fine game throughout.' The final mention of him at Michaelhouse comes in June 1907, when a rugby match was played between Mr Lawrence's team and the school, which resulted in a win for the former by 5 points to 3, with Wilfred scoring the try for the invitation team.

Wilfred must have been back in England by June 1908, as he visited his old school then to play cricket for the Old Bloxhamists. He emigrated to Canada in 1909 with other members of his family and purchased a farm north-east of the town of Vermilion in Alberta. In January 1915 he enlisted in the 1st Canadian Mounted Rifles, alongside a friend from Vermilion, Ernest Mosley Taylor. Ernest had emigrated to Alberta from Derbyshire with his brother Raymond in 1905, and Raymond had married Bill's sister Elisabeth in 1914. In January 1915, just prior to going overseas with his regiment, Bill married Sarah Kay ('Sadie') Lord of Vermilion, Alberta.

The unit's horses were shipped to England where the men had to attend to them before the British Army took the horses away and issued the soldiers with infantry equipment. Bill came over to Britain in May 1915 and trained until September 1915, when he crossed over with his unit to France. Thanks to the remarkable Canadian Letters & Images project, we have several letters written by Bill and sent to members of his family between March 1916 and July 1917.

One of these, to his sister Elisabeth, whom he addresses as 'Dear old Fatty', her childhood nickname, gives a real flavour of life in the front line as they prepared for the 'Big Push' which would clinch victory, though Bill insisted that 'I don't see how the war can actually finish for years.'

From these letters we learn that he was wounded twice in 1916. Writing from a convalescent camp in Boulogne in June 1916, he mentions his finger healing, while in one from October of that year, he writes from Southwark Military Hospital in London to his sister Grace, 'Gre', and observes, 'I am very lucky, aren't I? Just a splinter of shell through the left wrist. It must have been very small for I don't think it's smashed any bones.' The fact that he was still in hospital a month later suggests that the wound was perhaps more serious than he was letting on. We learn in a letter from Ernest Taylor that Bill was in the thick of the action when their trench received a two-hour bombardment in early December 1915 – 'Bill was knocked senseless while extricating a man from the debris, but mercifully is not damaged.'

Bill's most poignant letter was written to his sister's mother-in-law Mrs Taylor, the mother of Ernest, who was killed at Hooge on 7 May 1916. Writing on the same day that Ernest was shot by a sniper while on sentry duty, Wilfred reassures her that her son was killed instantly without suffering, and goes on to conclude that 'I saw a quotation in a story the other day which I think Ernest would whisper to you if he could, "Dulce et decorum est pro patria mori".' Ernest is buried in the Menin Road South Cemetery.

Upon his second recovery Bill was shipped back to the front, once again finding himself in the Ypres Sector. Wilfred Bury died on 15 November 1917, of wounds received in action at the battle of Passchendaele, in which the Canadians were very heavily involved. The details contained in his Circumstances of Death Registry Card show the horrors routinely hidden by bland phrases such as 'died of wounds'. In this case, these included a shrapnel wound to his right knee, which was fractured, as well as wounds to his head, hand, abdomen and right arm, which was amputated.

He is buried in Lijssenthoek Military Cemetery in Belgium. This village was on the main communication line between the Allied military bases in the rear and the Ypres battlefields. Most of the 9,901 burials there are of soldiers who died in one of the nearby CCSs, which were set up there as it was out of the extreme range of most German field artillery. It is one of the cemeteries on the Western Front that the authors would strongly recommend visiting, as it is an unusual one for containing 883 war graves of other nationalities, mostly French and German but also American and Belgian, as well as those of British nurses and 35 workers of the Chinese Labour Corps. King George V, who lost several members of his family in the war, visited the cemetery in 1922. Wilfred's grave was the very first one visited on Bloxham School's Western Front trips in October 2015 and March 2019, when a cross was placed on his grave by pupils from his old school.

Second Lieutenant Alick Mayson Sawyer
59th Battalion, Machine Gun Corps
Pupil at Bloxham School 1906-1910
Died of wounds 12 December 1917, aged 23
Buried in Mont Huon Military Cemetery, Le Tréport, France
Grave VI.D.7

Of all the stories of the 80 Bloxhamists to perish in the Great War, that of Alick Sawyer must be one of the most poignant, if only for the circumstances of his last days in a military hospital at Tréport.

Alick Mayson Sawyer was the son of Charles Montague Sawyer, a cotton merchant from Birkdale in Lancashire. He and his wife Margaret had three other children, all older than Alick, a son Charles and two daughters, Constance and Alice. Alick was born on 21 April 1894. At the time of the 1901 census the family was living at 20 Trafalgar Street in Birkdale, but by the time he started at Bloxham they had moved a few streets away to a house called The Wrekin in Lancaster Street, in an area of smart Victorian and Edwardian detached houses in a prosperous Merseyside suburb – the renowned Royal Birkdale Golf Club was only a few minutes' walk away.

Alick was a pupil at the school between April 1906 and July 1910 and made his first impression through his athletic abilities, though his third place in the Junior Long Jump on Sports Day in May 1907 was perhaps not the achievement it might at first glance appear; *The Bloxhamist* opined that 'anyone who had taken the trouble to practise beforehand sufficiently must have won'; the following year, in a more competitive event, he was beaten by a margin of 3 ½ inches by Robert Cunliffe, who would perish at Aubers in 1915. He also finished third in the High Jump. Meanwhile his cricket was also improving, but with no school team for the junior boys, a constant diet of internal matches had to suffice; *The Bloxhamist*'s report in the 1908 season stated that 'Sawyer and Foxwell should have had more opportunities.'

In football, he was on the winning side in the 1908 dormitory match, a title retained by Dormitories II and V for the next two years, and progressed to the school team in October 1908, making his 1st XI debut in a 6-3 victory against Magdalen College School, Brackley. The following month, however, he was playing for the 2nd XI against another Magdalen College School, that in Oxford. Five of the Bloxham side that day would perish in the coming war. Playing against Abingdon for the 2nd XI, Alick was adjudged to be 'not quite safe in his kicking', but after Christmas managed to secure a permanent place in the 1st XI, playing half back rather than full back as before.

The 1909 Sports Day took place on Easter Tuesday, April 13th. The day was marred by heavy rain throughout the proceedings. Alick once again finished second in the Long Jump, this time in the senior competition. The following term saw him playing for the 2nd XI at cricket, though making little impact as a number 10 batsman who did not bowl. He topped the averages, apparently showing good hitting powers, but was said to be 'lacking in defence'.

For his final year at the school, Alick was elected to the Committee of Games, a prestigious post in a school whose daily life was dominated by sport. He was a leading light for the 1st XI in his final football season, gaining a reputation for long-range attempts on goal – including one from the half-way line against Jesus College, Oxford – and being singled out for praise in a draw against a club side, Chipping Norton Swifts. At the annual Gymnastic display, Alick and John Whiting put on a three-round boxing contest. While no winner was declared, Whiting was said to be quicker on his feet in both attack and defence, while Alick, though slow in defence, showed decided ability in 'ducking'.

By this stage in the school's history Hockey was being played for the first time, and he earned his colours in the sport in March 1910, one of four in the side to do so, following excellent performances against Banbury HC and Exeter College, Oxford. The comments of *The Bloxhamist* on his hockey read similarly to his football – 'On his day a fine defensive half. Inclined to tire too soon. Does not follow up sufficiently to be of real use in attack.'

At his final Sports Day Alick finally reached the summit of Bloxham sporting excellence, winning the High Jump jointly with Frank Riddle, the day's 'Victor Ludorum', while also finishing third in the Long Jump, Shot Put and the 100 Yards as well as coming second in the 'throwing the cricket ball' event. Alick left at the end of the summer term in 1910 having made a name for himself as a games player, though earning less distinction as an academic – he never rose above Form IVa.

When he left school at the age of 16, it was in order to study agriculture with the intention of moving to the Colonies. His service record paints a picture of a young man, well over six feet tall, who would have been well suited to the tough outdoor life. In the event he never did go into farming. He had served two and a half years as a Private in a territorial regiment, the Denbighshire Hussars, and he enlisted with his old regiment on 5 August 1914, the day after war broke out. He went out to Egypt with them and the other Welsh Yeomanry regiments in 1916. By the time they arrived in Egypt, the main part of the campaign was already ending. With the Turks adopting a low profile after their failed attack on the Suez Canal in February 1915, the Denbighshire Hussars and the rest of the Welsh Horse found themselves employed in guard duty in oases in the desert.

It seems that Alick was frustrated at ending up in a quiet backwater, and he returned home after 18 months to join the Machine Gun Corps and seek a commission. After initially serving as a Private, he was commissioned as a 2nd Lieutenant into the 59th Machine Gun Corps. A photograph taken in the Summer of 1917 in the back garden of the family home shows clearly the strain of military service, especially when compared with the fresh-faced young man in the photograph taken after he was commissioned.

Shortly after arriving at the front, he was horrifically wounded in November 1917 whilst serving near Pilckem Ridge in Belgium. In the grim description supplied by *The Bloxhamist*, having 'had part of his spine shot away' and having become 'armless', he was transferred to the base hospital at Tréport on the coast. His service records contain the ensuing correspondence between his mother and the War Office, which reveals a sorry tale of bureaucratic intransigence. Mrs Sawyer received a telegram from the War Office informing her that her son had been severely wounded on 28 November 1917. She immediately telegrammed requesting a travel warrant to visit France with Sawyer's younger sister instead of her husband. As Alick's father was still alive at the time (dying in 1921) it must be assumed that he was in ill health or the couple were separated. The War Office responded that travel warrants could only be provided for the parents of a wounded man, therefore the application would have to be re-submitted. Mrs Sawyer then returned the necessary forms, only for the War Office to send them back, requesting a further signature that had been missed from the original form.

The form was duly returned to the War Office who once again sent it back as the money order sent by Mrs Sawyer was 1 penny short. The War Office finally telegrammed back on 11 December to say that the travel warrant would be dispatched. A final telegram arrived on the 13th instructing the family that the travel warrant would not be issued, as their son had died the previous day. The exchange of telegrams provided one of the most dramatically effective scenes in the school's play 79, in which Alick's mother was portrayed exchanging messages with an unseen military voice, culminating in the last shattering telegram. Given the rapid pace at which the exchange happened – surprising perhaps to those who have grown up in the age of emails – it is unlikely that the delays prevented Mrs Sawyer from reaching Alick while he was still alive, but it must have been an agonising experience for the family.

The Bloxhamist magazine for June 1918 reported that Alick 'passed away...very peacefully in the presence of the chaplain'. The use of the word 'armless' is an arresting one but would appear to mean exactly what it says. By 1917 the military medical system had become extremely proficient at casualty evacuation and kept people alive who would otherwise have died. The amount of practice army surgeons received in damage limitation meant that any upper limb wounds were treated surgically, and because of the spinal damage and possible circulatory impairment, these wounds failed to heal, so more surgery was done, infection set in and so on in the most vicious of circles until the patient's physiology could no longer stand it. As so often in military medicine, doctors had become more efficient and perhaps focused on what could be done rather than what should be done, leaving the ethics to catch up much later, if at all. The only consolation in Alick's case would have been that the presence of a chaplain implies that he had been moved to what was called a moribund ward, where there were plentiful supplies of analgesia so that his pain could be managed, and experienced palliative care nurses to stand by him and ensure that he was not alone in his final moments.

The Bloxhamist offered its sympathy to Mr and Mrs Sawyer and recorded that their other son had already died in the war. We were interested to see if we could trace this brother, and recourse to the CWGC identified him as Captain Charles Quinton Sawyer of the East Yorkshire Regiment, who commanded a trench mortar battery and was killed on 14 July 1916 on the Somme. We tracked him down to Sedbergh School, where he was a pupil between 1905 and 1908. Charles was born in 1891, so was three years older than Alick, and spent five years farming in Canada after leaving school, and Alick was clearly planning to follow in his footsteps until the outbreak of war changed his plans.

Charles' connection to Alick was clear from the address given in The Sedberghian for 1905 – 20 Trafalgar Road, Birkdale, the same address as Alick was living at in 1901. This discovery led to the further revelation that Alick's father, Charles Montague Sawyer, was a distinguished sportsman, who played cricket for Lancashire as a right-handed batsman and rugby union for Broughton RUFC and Lancashire, as well as representing England in two internationals, against Scotland in 1879-80 and against Ireland in 1880-81, when he scored a try playing as a three quarter. He also played in the first rugby match ever to be played under floodlights, when Broughton took on Swinton in Salford on 22 October 1878. The match was comprehensively won by Broughton by two goals, three tries, and three touchdowns to Swinton's none, with Charles kicking one of the goals and his brother James scoring a fine try. It would appear that Alick inherited his sporting ability from his father.

Alick was buried at Mont Huon Cemetery, Le Tréport, France. He was 23 when he died. Researching Alick Sawyer's story has not been made easy by a number of errors and confusions in official records over names, details and dates, probably greater than for any of the 80. His name itself presents difficulties, with the correct Alick sometimes replaced in records by Aleck (as in *The Bloxhamist's* report on his death). *The London Gazette* for 3 October 1917, which announced his commission, listed him as Alick Hayson (rather than Mayson) Sawyer, and the Graves Registration Form for Mont Huon Military Cemetery gives his surname as Sawer. It also manages to get his unit wrong (50th Company MGC rather than 59th) and gives his date of death as 13 December, though this error was fortunately not perpetuated on his headstone. The final telegram sent to Mrs Sawyer (on 13 December) clearly states 'died of wounds December twelfth', the same date as on the school's Roll of Honour. There was also some confusion over the Sawyers' address. The CWGC gives his address as 23 Manchester Road, Southport, but the War Office's telegrams were addressed to 18 Lancaster Road, Southport. Just to make things even harder, the address is sometimes given as being Southport, at other times Birkdale, the latter being an area of the former.

Rifleman Harold Frank Corn
2/21st London Regiment (First Surrey Rifles)
Pupil at Bloxham School 1908-1912
Killed in action 13 December 1917, aged 22
Buried in Jerusalem War Cemetery, Israel and Palestine
Grave P.86

Harold Frank Corn was born on 4 June 1895 in Stoke Newington, the only surviving child of Frank William and Maria Corn. His father, aged 28, had married Maria Buswell, who was five years his senior, in September 1894 in All Saints at Cuddesdon in Oxfordshire. Harold was privately baptised on 7 June 1895 at St. Mary's Church in Haringey. By the time of the 1901 census, the family had moved from 'Newland', Carysfort Road in Haringey to 'Fairlight', London Road in Ewell, Surrey. Harold's father worked as a clerk in the Steward's Office in Lincoln's Inn. They employed one domestic servant. According to the census, they had had two children, but one had died.

Harold arrived at Bloxham in September 1908 and was one of 22 boys confirmed in the school chapel by the Bishop of Reading in March 1910. He moved up to Form IVB in September 1911 and left Bloxham in July 1912 without having made the impact on the sports field or in the classroom that many of the others on the war memorial did, hence our lack of information on his school career. He was, however, an active Old Boy, joining the Old Bloxhamist Society on leaving school and returning to Bloxham for the annual Festival at All Saints in November

1912. He also subscribed to the memorial fund for the school's beloved former Matron, Miss Mallinson in 1914.

Harold enlisted on 15 November 1915 into the London Rifle Brigade as a Private in the 5th City of London Rifles with service number 3147, and he served with them until June 1916 when in preparation for the Somme offensive he was transferred into the 2/21st London Regiment, The First Surrey Rifles. The Battalion was in the 181st Brigade as part of 60th Division. Harold's service number with the First Surrey Rifles was originally 5951, but when the Territorial forces were renumbered with six digits in March 1917 his number was changed to 652738. He survived the Somme and in December 1916, he was sent to the oft-forgotten theatre of the war at Salonika, where an allied force under the French General Maurice Sarrail was tied down by the Bulgarian army. In April 1917 he was serving in Egypt before being sent to Palestine in the continuing fight against another of Germany's allies, the Turks.

On 8-9 December 1917 the 60th Division, including the 2/21st Surrey Rifles, took part in the capture of Jerusalem from the Turkish Army, an event whose symbolic importance far outweighed its strategic value for a British public brought up from an early age on stories from the Bible. Harold was killed in action on 13 December, the only man from his battalion to be killed in action that day. According to *The Bloxhamist* he was shot through the chest and died instantaneously, and so without prolonged suffering, though those familiar with such formulations know that this may disguise a more brutal truth. There was a romantic element to the fighting in the Holy Land for the British, and *The Bloxhamist* informed its readers that 'the scene of the fight was Tower Hill, immediately north of Jerusalem, and east of the Mount of Olives, and a little to the north of Bethany. He is buried at the foot of the hill', a somewhat confusing description as anyone trying to trace these places on a map will discover. According to the Battalion war diary,

> We did a lot of firing and our Infantry advanced. Moved off and camped just outside Jerusalem in evening. Elements of the 2nd/21st (the First Surrey Rifles) and 2nd/22nd (the Queen's) advanced their front when they launched a surprise attack and captured Ras-el-Karrabeh, near Anata. In the process they took 43 prisoners and two machine guns. Two soldiers, one from each Battalion, Harold Corn from the First Surrey Rifles and Robert Jones from The Queen's died during the days fighting.

Harold Corn is buried in Jerusalem War Cemetery, almost the furthest extent of MD's travels in his pursuit of the Old Bloxhamists' resting places. His father chose the brief inscription 'Jesu, mercy' for his headstone. The *Epsom Advertiser* for 18 January 1918 reported that the Council had resolved to send a letter of sympathy to his father, Frank Corn, who was granted probate of his effects valued at £307 16s. 5d. Harold's mother Maria died on 23 March 1934; Frank remained at their home in Ewell until his death on 28 March 1952. Harold is remembered on the memorial at St Mary's, Cuddington in Surrey as well as his old school's war memorial.

Private Horace Charles Kruger
1st/5th Battalion, Northumberland Fusiliers
Pupil at Bloxham School 1903-1908
Killed in action 19 December 1917, aged 25
Commemorated on the Tyne Cot Memorial to the Missing, Belgium
Panel 19

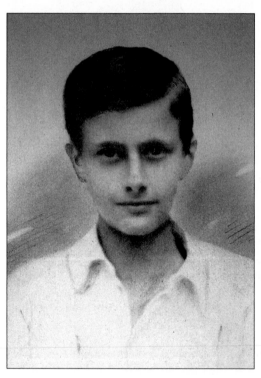

Photographs have been sourced for every one of the 80 Bloxhamists to perish in the Great War. In some cases these are images of them when they were pupils, typically from a sports team photograph, to replace those lost in the fire of 1985. In the case of Horace Charles Kruger, the school clearly could not find an adult photograph of him at the time, hence their use of an image of him in cricket whites, which makes for a very haunting impression, with Horace forever frozen in youth.

Horace Charles Kruger was born on 14 April 1892 in Las Palmas in the Canary Islands, the son of John Kruger. There is a question mark over his forenames, as his service record has him as Charles Horace, as does the CWGC, and he is listed on the Tyne Cot memorial as C.H. Kruger. However, genealogical research suggests that the names should be the other way around, as they were in the school records. As Horace is what he was known as at Bloxham, that is what we have chosen to go with. Despite the German sounding surname, we have been unable to establish any German ancestry, though his father and grandfather shared the middle name Plessen, which is a town near Dortmund. They were originally from Southport in Lancashire.

Horace's mother, Edith Mary Quiney, was the sister of another Old Bloxhamist, Charles Quiney, who died of wounds received in the Ypres sector in September 1915. The Krugers lived on Gran Canaria like the Quineys, who were hoteliers. Horace had two older sisters, Florence and Ethel (a third, Constance, had died as a baby). He was a pupil at Bloxham School between May 1903 and 1908, winning the Senior Drawing Prize in 1907 and playing cricket for the 1st XI and football for the school 2nd XI. It was said of him at the end of the 1908 cricket season that 'he bats in remarkably nice style, and with perseverance, should develop into quite a good bat, as he has a good forward stroke and plenty of wrist. Shows some promise as a bowler. A fair field, but slow.' From the sound of it, he might have developed into a useful cricketer with two more years in the school, but like so many Bloxhamists at the time, Horace left when he was only 16 years of age.

Nothing more would be heard of Horace at his old school until the report in the school magazine for June 1918 that he was missing in action. We know that after school he had sailed to Chile and was working as a motor mechanic in Valparaiso when the war broke out. He sailed back from Chile on the SS *Orita*, sailing via the Falkland Islands and landing in Liverpool in December 1914.

Horace's military career was to be a dispiriting series of personal setbacks, all because of his severe stammer, which repeatedly frustrated his quest for a commission. He first applied for a commission into the Royal Naval Air Service but was turned down because of the stammer, so he instead joined the Royal Navy and sailed on board HMS *President* to the Dardanelles, where he took part in the Gallipoli campaign as part of the Royal Naval Division. He served until June 1916 as a Petty Officer in the Naval Armoured Car Division. He left the service and applied once again for a commission, this time with King Edward's Horse, a former Yeomanry Regiment known officially as The King's Overseas Dominions Regiment. Once again, his stammering let him down, and he was forced to serve in the ranks, first in Ireland and then in France. At this point he was actually recommended for a commission into the Royal Flying Corps, but yet again his speech impediment got in the way, and he was refused. He transferred into the 1st/5th Northumberland Fusiliers and volunteered to serve overseas.

In December 1917 he was in the Ypres Salient, near the shell-shattered village of Zonnebeke, when his company lost touch with the company on its left. Kruger offered to go and find them, and was never seen again. The Battalion War Diary notes heavy shelling with gas shells on the afternoon of the 19th, and mentions that one OR was missing, presumed killed - probably Horace Kruger. Confirmation that he had been killed did not reach his widowed mother in the Canary Islands for another year.

He is commemorated on the Tyne Cot Memorial to the Missing, along with 35,000 other British and New Zealand troops who have no known grave.

John George Clifford
5th Battalion, Oxfordshire and Buckinghamshire Light Infantry
Pupil at Bloxham 1910-1912
Died of wounds 20 December 1917, aged 20
Buried in Ypres Reservoir Cemetery, Belgium
Grave IV.B.11

John George Clifford was the son of Arthur John and Elizabeth Clifford of Manor Farm, Wootton. John was a pupil at the school between 1910 and 1912, at which time the family were living in Hordley, which lay a mile south-east of Wootton on the River Glyme. This tiny hamlet contained a large range of brick and stone farm buildings erected by the Blenheim estate in

1883, and two cottages for farm workers on the old turnpike road.

On arrival at Bloxham John moved slowly up the school, being promoted to form II in October 1910. He won the Form II French prize in 1911, choosing as his prize book *South Africa*, and was then promoted to Form III. He was confirmed by the Bishop of Reading in the school chapel in March 1912. This was followed less than a week later by the minor triumph of winning the sack race on Sports Day ahead of Mitcalfe, another of the 80. John is recorded as passing his Preliminary Oxford Examinations in 1912, one of 28 passes, which enabled Bloxham to finish ahead of all the other Woodard Schools except for Hurstpierpoint. He played his first football match for the school on October 1912, making a big impression for the 2nd XI in a 3-0 win against Abingdon School's 2nds – *The Bloxhamist* reported that 'Clifford did much damage at half and had quite a day out.' John's last mention as a Bloxham pupil came for winning the Junior OTC Shooting cup; he easily beat ten other junior cadets from the new Officers Training Corps and received his prize from Mrs Hinde, daughter of the school's Founder, on All Saints Day 1912. He left the school at the age of 14 at the end of the Michaelmas Term, probably to work on the family farm.

John joined the Old Bloxhamist Society on leaving school and was an active member; he is recorded as visiting his *alma mater* during the Lent Term 1914 and in May 1915 and played football for the Old Boys against the school in November 1913. The Old Bloxhamists won the game 3-2 despite being one player short (not an unheard-of occurrence a century later) but John was on the losing side in the following term's hockey fixture against the school. He is also recorded among the names of subscribers to the stained-glass window placed in the school chapel in May 1914 in memory of the old school matron, Miss Mallinson.

John joined the Oxfordshire Yeomanry (Queen's Own Oxfordshire Hussars rather cruelly referred to as Queer Objects On Horseback), with Army no. 2786, in 1915, before transferring two years later to the 5th Battalion, the Oxford & Bucks LI, with Army no. 235049. This was a battalion of Kitchener's New Army, which had been raised at Oxford in August 1914. He was serving as a lance corporal when he died on 20 December 1917 of the wounds he received at Passchendaele. Sadly, and unusually, *The Bloxhamist* contains no record of his death, but he has an entry in the school's Roll of Honour and a photograph was submitted to the school by his family.

John Clifford, who was 20 years of age when he died, is buried in Ypres Reservoir Cemetery and is commemorated on a plaque in the Church of St Mary the Virgin, Wootton. The church also contains his grave cross. As has been observed by Samantha Fryer, who surveyed the church for the *Returned from the Front* project, one gets a strong feeling from the eight grave markers and the numerous plaques that this was a village which felt its losses very deeply and was keen to ensure that these men were not forgotten. The inscription on his headstone reinforces this impression: 'Of Hordley Woodstock, Oxfordshire "Till The Dawn Breaks"'.

1918

The final year of the War began with the Allies having made small gains in France and Flanders, but still the Germans held on. The capitulation of the Russians on the Eastern Front freed up almost a million German soldiers who were transferred to the Western Front. On 21 March 1918, the Germans launched their largest offensive of the war, codenamed Operation Michael, or the *Kaiserschlacht* (Kaiser's Battle). The mass offensive against the British Fifth and Third armies inflicted enormous casualties (including several Bloxhamists) and pushed the Allies back several miles along a wide front.

On 28 March the second phase of the German operation (Operation Mars) was launched against Arras, but through dogged resistance the Allies managed to halt the Germans before the strategically important city of Amiens fell. A change of command was agreed, with the French General Foch appointed as Supreme Commander of Allied Forces. As many reserves as possible were found and thrown into the fighting, where they managed to resist the German advance for long enough to allow the Allies to commit every available soldier on the Western Front into action.

On 9 April, the Germans went on the offensive against the Allies in Flanders and managed to push the Allies back to within two miles of Ypres. Their objective of capturing key road and rail junctions and then opening the route to the Channel ports was close to being a success, but once again dogged resistance held up the German advance long enough for it to be checked, and the city of Ypres remained in Allied hands.

In one of the lesser-known actions of the Great War, nine exhausted divisions of British soldiers were sent to a 'quiet' sector in the Champagne at the end of May 1918, to allow large numbers of French troops to be sent to the Artois and Picardy regions. This movement coincided with another massive German offensive (Operation Blucher), and the almost total annihilation of the British troops in the Champagne.

By this stage in the fighting tens of thousands of American troops had begun arriving in France to support the British and French (one German officer estimated that for every 100 Americans killed, there were at least 1000 more in reserve), with their almost unlimited supplies of both men and equipment.

On 20 July a huge Anglo-French offensive (Third Battle of the Marne) was launched which pushed the Germans off the River Marne and opened the way to the final series of successful Allied offensives that would see the war over by Christmas. By August 1918, momentum was swinging firmly in the Allies' favour and another offensive near Amiens on the Somme, pushed the Germans back several miles. 8 August was described by the German General Ludendorff as 'the black day of the German Army'. Of the 27,000 casualties suffered by the Germans that day, a remarkable 12,000 surrendered and it became very apparent to German high command that the writing was on the wall for the Germans, and defeat was inevitable.

With momentum swinging firmly in the Allies' favour, a series of massive offensives took place against the Germans, first of all against the Drocourt– Queant line in August 1918, before attention finally turned to the most challenging objective of all, the attack on the Hindenburg Line. The assaults on this line began in September and were a dramatic success, with the line finally being broken in early October. The actions of the First, Third and Fourth British armies in breaking the Hindenburg Line are to this day regarded by military historians as being one of the finest examples of offensive action and tactical planning ever seen.

By now the Allied advance was unstoppable and the Germans were in full retreat. A combined Anglo-Belgian offensive in Flanders pushed the Germans out of the Ypres salient for the first time since 1914 and eventually back towards Mons, where the fighting had begun some four years previously.

Despite the progress, men were still being killed in their hundreds and the final Old Bloxhamist to be killed in combat died just seven days before the Armistice having served in France and Flanders for four years. His mother received the telegram informing her of his death as the bells rang out to celebrate the end of the war.

By 11 November, the Germans had been pushed back to Mons where the fighting first began in 1914, and as the Armistice began at 11am, an outpost of the Canadian infantry found themselves less than 100 metres from where the first shot had been fired in the War in August 1914. Four years and almost a million dead from Britain and her Empire, and the protagonists were back where they started.

Lieutenant Edmund Percy Roberts
11th Battalion, Essex Regiment
Pupil at Bloxham School 1907-1909
Killed in action 21 March 1918, aged 24
Commemorated on the Arras Memorial, France
Panel 7

By the spring of 1918, there had been no Bloxhamist deaths in the Great War for three months, the longest spell without a Bloxham fatality in the entire war, and this was in part due to both sides attempting little on the Western Front in the winter months, with the Germans making preparations for a massive offensive to take advantage of a numerical superiority in the west for the first time since 1914, thanks to Russia's withdrawal from the war. The German commander Ludendorff knew that he had to launch a decisive attack before American troops started to arrive in France in significant numbers, and he assembled large numbers of shock troops – mobile, well-trained and heavily armed – to spearhead the attack, which was preceded by the heaviest bombardment of the war, a five-hour pounding by more than 6,000 guns. Among those British troops in the path of the 65 German divisions assaulting a 60-mile British front around St Quentin on 21 March was Edmund Roberts.

Lieutenant Edmund Percy Roberts was the son of Mr and Mrs George E. and Elizabeth A. Roberts, and he was born on 21 December 1893. In the 1901 census, their address was given as 291 Seven Sisters Road, Stoke Newington, London, but by the time of the war the family home was Ivy Farm in West Mersea, Essex.

Percy, as he was known by the family, was a pupil at Bloxham between April 1907 and July 1909. There is not much record of his school career, not all that surprising as he was only 15 when he left. He is recorded as competing in the School Sports (at the 100 yards) in May

1907 and having been confirmed by the Bishop of Reading in March 1908. Six of the 23 candidates that day would perish in the coming war.

After he left Bloxham in July 1909, Percy went on to Aspatria Agricultural College in Cumbria, and on leaving there in 1913 he took up farming on his family's land at Ivy Farm. Shortly after the outbreak of war Percy gave up his farm and enlisted at the Albert Hall in Colchester on 10 September 1914 as a trooper in the 11th Hussars along with his friend Harry Pearl Cross from Waldegraves Farm. The following month Percy requested a commission and his commanding officer Lieutenant Colonel Ronald Brooke recommended him for one in the infantry, although Percy's application showed that he would have preferred to have remained with Harry in the 11th Hussars. In November 1914 Percy was commissioned as a 2nd Lieutenant with the 11th Battalion Essex Regiment. He was billeted in Brighton while training proceeded at Shoreham. Harry would himself become a Lieutenant in the Guards Machine Gun Regiment and would survive the war.

January 1915 brought a setback to Percy's military career, when he was declared unfit for service thanks to an unerupted upper wisdom tooth, but the following month he rejoined his battalion for training. It was not until 21 August 1915, by which time the battalion was practising trench warfare on Chobham Common, that news was received that it would be ordered to France within a week.

Percy headed over to France on 28 August with the advance party, the main body of men landing at Boulogne two days later. They moved to Ostrohove rest camp before marching to the front line near Béthune on 21 September, where they were intended to be employed in the offensive which would be known as the Battle of Loos, which was to start on 25 September.

Following the debacle of Loos, the battalion was transferred to the Ypres Salient. Here Percy encountered another setback, when he was taken ill and diagnosed as having tonsillitis and jaundice, the latter thought to have been caused by contaminated needles, as he had an injection prior to the appearance of the jaundice. He was evacuated from the salient and admitted to the St John Hospital at Etaples before being sent home to West Mersea to recover.

It was not until 11 March 1916 that Percy was fit to report for duty with the 12th (Reserve) Battalion, Essex Regiment at Harwich, and early June before he rejoined his old battalion in the Ypres Salient. At the end of July he went for retraining with the Royal Flying Corps, either as a pilot or an observer. There is some confusion over this period of his service, and in November he returned to Britain once more, suffering the effects of shell shock. The available evidence suggests that he was gassed.

In March 1917 the Army Medical Board decided that he was permanently unfit to serve as a pilot or observer, and Percy was ordered to join the 3rd Battalion, Essex Regiment at Felixstowe for a further period of service on the Home Front while he recovered fully. In August he embarked for France and once more rejoined the 11th Battalion which was again in action in the Loos area. On 11 November he was promoted to the rank of Lieutenant and took part in the Battle of Cambrai.

The Bloxhamist suggests that he was mentioned in despatches after his return to the front. In January Percy took command of 'A' company, and it was as an acting Captain that he and his unit faced the Germans' spring offensive, code named 'Michael' but widely known as the Ludendorff Offensive. The 11th battalion, at Bapaume on the Somme, took the brunt of the first day of the offensive, and it was in this fighting that Percy is assumed to have been killed on 21 March 1918; his body was never recovered. It was not until 2 April that his family in West Mersea were informed by telegram that Percy had been killed.

His colonel wrote 'Your son's sad death will cause a sad gap in the battalion. He was a capable, hardworking officer, and much beloved by his men, with whom he was always closely in touch. He died gallantly, as an officer should, leading his men, and gave his life for his country and our dear ones at home.'

Percy is commemorated on Bay 7 of the Arras Memorial, one of 35,000 names on the Memorial. His name is also on the West Mersea War Memorial, as well as appearing on the family grave in the West Mersea Cemetery, Barfield Road. Percy had a younger brother, Edgar, who joined the Honourable Artillery Company at the outbreak of war and went to Egypt with them in April 1915. The following year he transferred to the Royal Flying Corps as a Second Lieutenant, passing his Flying Certificate at the Military School, Ruislip, where he trained on Maurice Farman biplanes, before moving on to BE2s. While at Ruislip Edgar flew and trained with his faithful fox terrier Mick. He was sent to 205 Squadron of the newly formed Royal Air Force in 1918 and flew DH9s in bombing missions against the German Army during the final, victorious campaign of the war, the Hundred Days.

In February 1988, nine-year old Leon Butterfield from Colchester was playing on the beach, where he found an old jar at the tide's edge. The jar was still sealed, and when opened was found to contain a 1919 penny, a yellowing envelope and letter, along with a faded photograph, signed Edgar George Roberts, Ivy Farm, East Mersea, 22 February 1927. The jar turned out to be from the grave of Edgar's dog Mick, along the cliff-edge in the bluebell wood at Ivy Farm. Distraught at the loss of his old flying companion, Edgar had placed a final letter in the jar, which ended with the following words: 'Friends, if you have ever loved a dog, leave his earthly remains in peace. I trust his spirit will have joined his master in the other world.' By his master, Edgar meant his brother Percy, whose dog Mick had originally been. We are grateful to Mersea author Veronique Eckstein, who has written a children's book based on the story of Edgar and Percy, for details of their lives.

Major Robert Peter Villar
18th Battalion, Liverpool Regiment
Pupil at Bloxham School 1902-1904
Killed in action 22 March 1918, aged 30
Commemorated on the Pozières Memorial, Pozières, France
Panel 21

Robert Villar was the son of an auctioneer and estate agent, William James Villar and his wife Annie Elizabeth Villar, of Tauntfield House, Taunton, which is where Robert was born on 16 June 1887. He was a pupil at Bloxham from January 1902 to July 1904 but left little impression in his brief time at the school. It is clear, however, that he was a bright boy, rapidly earning promotion from Form IV to Form V in April 1902 and then to the Sixth Form in September of that year. He is recorded as having been successful at the Oxford Local Examinations in July and was awarded the Mathematics prize in December 1902. The following year he passed the Oxford Locals, this time at Senior level. He played cricket in the second division, and seems to have been a reasonable, if unadventurous, batsman; *The Bloxhamist* asserted that 'Villar has plenty of patience but should hit more.'

On leaving school he went up to Pembroke College, Cambridge at the start of the Michaelmas Term in 1904, taking an honours degree in law. He then read for the Bar and joined the Inner Temple but wanted a more active life and joined the Royal Irish Constabulary, finishing 4th in Competitive Examination; he is listed as a cadet in July 1911. The RIC was at that time finding its hands full with keeping order in Ireland during the Home Rule crisis.

When the war came, Robert was keen to join up and 'do his bit', but thanks to the importance of his work with the RIC, he was not allowed to join the Army until 1916. It was reported by the RIC from Dongloe in County Donegal that he had been transferred to Fermoy in County Cork, having in his six months in the North 'proved himself an efficient and capable officer.' He was said to be awaiting a commission in the Army: 'He is a plucky officer, and the District Force and the County in general wish him success and fame on the fair fields of France and Belgium.' When the call finally came, Robert was seconded to the Lancashire Hussars, a Yeomanry regiment which was dismounted and dispatched for training as infantry in July 1917; in September they were redesignated the 18th (Lancashire Hussars Yeomanry) Battalion, the King's (Liverpool) Regiment. Robert Villar was sent to France and subsequently obtained the rank of Major, serving as second in command of his Battalion, though at the time of his death he was commanding as his colonel was away on leave.

On 22 March, the second day of the Germans' Ludendorff Offensive, his company was in trenches near Vaux, just west of St Quentin, when they were ordered to provide carrying parties to take supplies to the 2nd Battalion of the Bedfordshire Regiment. As this was happening, the Germans attacked and smashed through the British lines. Reinforcements were urgently called for and Robert rushed forward with his men to defend an isolated point in the line held by the Bedfords called Stevens Redoubt. At some point that day he was killed and was never seen again. He is remembered on Panel 21 of the Pozières Memorial. He was 30 years of age when he died.

Second Lieutenant Godfrey Burnside Hudson
1st Battalion, The Gloucestershire Regiment
Pupil at Bloxham School 1910-1911
Killed in action 18 April 1918, aged 20
Buried in Gorre British and Indian Cemetery, France
Grave V.A.27

By the close of March 1918, the German offensive between Arras and La Fere had begun to run out of momentum. A deep salient some 60 km deep had been carved into the Allied line, but the Germans had started to outrun their supplies and the Allies' appointment of a single commander in chief, Ferdinand Foch, signalled a new determination to fight together to prevent defeat. On 9 April Ludendorff's second thrust, code-named 'Georgette', struck further north, against the British in Flanders, with Ypres and the Channel ports the target. Godfrey Hudson was one of those caught in the path of this massive offensive in the Givenchy sector.

Godfrey Burnside Hudson was the second son of the Reverend Arthur Reginald Hudson and his wife Mary Frances Birch, who had been born in Jamaica. The Rev. Hudson was the vicar of Huntsham, a small village about five miles north-east of Tiverton in Devon. The Hudsons married in Toxteth, Liverpool, in 1887 and proceeded to have six children, Stella (born 1888), Cuthbert (1889), Francis (1890), Frances (1891), Margaret (1895), and the baby of the family, Godfrey, who was born in Tiverton on 16 April 1898.

Godfrey was a pupil at the school between January 1910 and July 1911, making little impact in his short time at the school beyond an appearance on sports day in the junior long jump competition and some cricket in the lowliest group in the school, Division IV, where according to *The Bloxhamist*, 'unhampered by any strict adherence to hard and binding rules, the play was always fast and furious.' His end of season batting average of 3.91 does not suggest a major talent in the making. At the end of the summer term in 1911 he then progressed to St Edward's School in Oxford, where he was a pupil until December 1915.

Godfrey enlisted into the 3rd Battalion of the Gloucestershire Regiment in February 1916, despite noting on his attestation papers that he suffered from extremely poor eyesight. It is not known what service he saw during the next two years, but we know that on 18 April 1918, he was attached to the 1st Battalion near the small French village of Festubert, holding a 'keep', that is to say a strongpoint in the line (also commonly referred to as a redoubt). Like the two previous Bloxhamists who died in 1918, the Gloucesters stood in the way of three German armies trampling the Allies out of their way in a last desperate attempt to break the front and finally win the war. They captured a German sergeant major on the afternoon of 17 April and he provided vital information about the German plans.

At 4:15 a.m. on the morning of the 18th, the Germans unleashed hell on the British. The shell fire was incessant, with thousands of high explosive, gas and incendiary shells dropping all over the front line. The keep at Festubert East where Hudson was posted was atomised, but miraculously he survived the bombardment, one of only eight from a company-strength detachment (approximately 250 men) to do so. As the Germans repeatedly made suicidal attacks throughout the day, including using field guns at near point-blank range, a massive hole suddenly appeared in the British line. The Germans poured through and massacred the beleaguered defenders, including Godfrey Hudson, killed two days after his twentieth birthday. In the summer of 2019, the authors managed to locate the site of the keep on a blisteringly hot day in Artois. While the site is little more than a field behind the church, it was still emotional to be standing on the site knowing that one of the 80 had been there over a century before. He is buried in the lovely Gorre British and Indian cemetery near Richebourg L'Avoué in France. His headstone was one of five vandalised in 2010, but thankfully it was swiftly repaired. In addition, Godfrey is commemorated on the war memorial in Huntsham, his father's old parish, which also bears the name of his brother Francis, a Captain in the RAF, killed in a flying accident on 21 March 1918, three weeks before his brother. At the time of his death Godfrey's mother had passed away, but his father was still alive, and living in Teignmouth in Devon.

It should be noted that there is some confusion about Godfrey's rank at the time of his death. Bloxham's Roll of Honour lists him as a Lieutenant, as do that of St Edward's, Oxford and the Huntsham war memorial, but the Commonwealth War Graves Commission has him as a Second Lieutenant, and we have followed their lead. His father chose a simple two-word inscription for his son's headstone: 'In peace'.

Second Lieutenant Geoffrey Owen Thomas
19th Battalion, Lancashire Fusiliers (3rd Salford Pals)
Pupil at Bloxham School 1893-1894
Killed in action 25 April 1917, aged 33
Commemorated on the Tyne Cot Memorial to the Missing
Panel 43

Geoffrey Owen Thomas was born on 18 October 1883, the son of the late Mr. and Mrs. Samuel James Thomas, of 61 Chepstow Place, Bayswater. Later the family moved to Barnet. Geoffrey was the husband of Ethel Mabel Thomas, of Evanston, Churchfields, Woodford in Essex.

Little is known of his school career, other than that he was a pupil at Bloxham School between May 1893 and August 1894, and that he joined the youngest class, Division IV, on his arrival at Bloxham and was promoted to Division III at the end of the year. It is not known where he went after leaving Bloxham at the age of ten. Eventually he progressed to the University of London where he was a member of the OTC. In 1910 he was a member of the London Stock Exchange.

Geoffrey joined the ranks in October 1914, enlisting as a private in the 22nd Royal Fusiliers. He went out to France in November 1915 as a corporal, serving in the infantry and in the attached Trench Mortar Battery. He is believed to have been recommended for a gallantry award on at least one occasion. In December 1916, Geoffrey was recommended for a commission by his battalion, and went back to England for several weeks of officer training at a cadet school. He returned to France in June 1917 as a Second Lieutenant attached to the 19th Lancashire Fusiliers (3rd Salford Pals), becoming Assistant Adjutant in February 1918.

The battalion was in trenches near Kemmel Hill in the Ypres Salient, and it was there that he was killed on 25 April 1918. At 2:30 a.m. the battalion was hit by an intense bombardment from gas and high explosive shells, the precursor to a large-scale German assault which broke through the British lines. According to French troops at HQ, the bombardment was 'far worse than anything ever experienced at Verdun'. By morning, about 400 officers and men were casualties. Geoffrey was reported missing, but it was not until after the war ended that his colonel, who had been taken prisoner in the action and was only now able to return to Britain, could disclose what had happened to him.

He reported that he had had no runners available to carry a message forward from battalion headquarters, and Thomas, seeing the urgency of the situation, volunteered to take the message. He arrived safely but was last seen fighting the advancing enemy. His colonel went on to tell Geoffrey's widow, Edith, that in my opinion he died like the soldier he was, he gave the last ounce for his battalion of which he was so proud. I should like to add that he was always perfectly cool and collected under fire or not and most energetic in all his duties. He had become quite a welcome addition to the HQ mess since his appointment as Assistant Adjutant.'

One of his men wrote: 'He undoubtedly was one of the most popular officers in the battalion. He always inspired one with confidence by his great unconcern under the worst of conditions.' Another added: 'He was a real fine man and as straight as a die. When he was in command of his platoon his men almost worshipped him. A real true British gentleman and one whom everyone misses.'

Geoffrey Owen Thomas was 33 years of age when he was killed in action, and is remembered on the Tyne Cot Memorial, one of 34,959 names of soldiers with no known grave on the memorial in addition to the 11,956 graves in the cemetery. SB visited the spot where Geoffrey Thomas' name is listed on the occasion of the official commemoration of the 3rd Battle of Ypres on 31 July 2017, attended by the British Prime Minister and the King and Queen of the Belgians.

Geoffrey Thomas was a man of strong religious faith, though of a non-conformist stamp different from the High Church Anglicanism he would have encountered at Bloxham – his colonel recorded that 'he carried his little Testament, and I often remarked to myself that he read some little each morning before commencing the day' – and he was a member of the Union Church in Woodford. After merging in 1946 with Woodford Congregational Church, which had been wrecked by a flying bomb in June 1944, the Union Church was renamed Woodford Green United Free Church. Geoffrey Owen Thomas' name is recorded on the memorial tablet inside the church to the right of the altar.

The Kemmelberg, where Geoffrey Thomas died, is one of the most famous cobbled hill climbs in Belgian cycling and the route is tackled by the professionals during the Gent-Wevelgem cycle race which covers many of the battlefields of the Great War. The race was being run on the day in 2019 when the authors attended a ceremony at St George's Church in Ypres, when the plaque to Bloxham's war dead was unveiled.

Captain Harry Godfrey Massy Miles MC
Royal Army Medical Corps
Pupil at Bloxham School 1900-1903
Died of wounds 26 April 1918, aged 32
Buried in St Sever Cemetery, France
Grave II.B.12

Captain Harry Godfrey Massy Miles MC was born on 19 February 1886 in Dublin. He was the son of Revd. Joseph Henry Miles, Rector of Pangbourne in Berkshire, and Adelaide Mary Louisa Massy. Known at this stage in his life simply by the surname Miles, he was educated at Bloxham School from April 1900 to July 1903, starting in Form III and being swiftly promoted to Form IV in October of that year. He was noted in the headmaster's address at Speech Day as having done especially well in Divinity, which would no doubt have pleased his father. He also won the form prizes for Divinity and English, choosing for the latter Creasey's *Fifteen Decisive Battles*.

Harry went on to enjoy a busy and fruitful school career, making important contributions to the school's drama, music and games as well as excelling academically. In November 1900

he appeared in a play, *Our Lottie*, playing the part of the villainous Mr Zeberdy Benjamin Catterpole, a gentleman described as 'a semi-clerical, smooth, sleek sort of person'. It was reported of his performance in *The Bloxhamist* that Miles 'acted and looked his part splendidly. He was exactly what they call 'slim' in South Africa, and his 'slimness' was only concealed for a time by a large amount of what we sometimes call 'oiliness' in England.' The following year he came in for lavish praise in *The Jacobite,* a production which some returning Old Boys judged the best they had seen at the school. Playing the comic role of John Duck, he was 'undoubtedly the attraction of the day, his action being natural and free throughout, and his acting excellent at times.'

A year later, in his third and final performance in the school play which then traditionally closed the Michaelmas Term, Harry played one of two brothers, one (his role, Benjamin) a philanthropist and the other (Gregory) a misanthrope, in a play then well-known but now long forgotten, *A Pair of Spectacles.* He was adjudged to have given 'an excellent and forcible interpretation of the character.' He was also a keen singer, judging by his regular solo contributions to the school's concerts, whether performing *Simon the Cellarer, St Patrick was Gentleman* or *Soldiers Three.*

Harry was reported in March 1901 as having finished second in the competition for a paper on Sir Walter Scott's *Ivanhoe.* The first prize, given by the school's Founder Egerton, went to the future journalist William Barr, who would die on the Western Front a few months after Massy Miles. Harry was successful in the junior section of the Oxford Local Examinations, and with his father sitting (presumably proudly) in the audience, Miles was again singled out by the Headmaster for praise at Speech Day in July: 'Miles did some excellent papers in Divinity, English and French.' Once more he picked up a number of prizes, for Divinity, the Form IV prize and the Reading prize. He was therefore promoted straight to the Sixth Form at the start of the new school year in September 1901.

Harry's appointment as a Prefect in January 1902 confirmed his status as one of the school's senior pupils. When a Debating Society restarted after a lapse of several years, he was, inevitably, an active member. At its first meeting, with a motion supporting conscription being debated, Miles, described in view of his Irish background as the Honourable Member for Dublin, was said to have given a characteristically humorous and genial speech. He argued that the current volunteer system was inadequate and commended the benefits to be derived from the habits of punctuality and discipline taught in the army. Something of his personality can be gauged from the sardonic comment in *The Bloxhamist* that 'to those who knew the Hon. Member's practice in regard to the former virtue, this argument was absolutely convincing.'

In a school culture which worshipped the cult of the athlete, Harry Miles was unusual for achieving greater prominence in the classroom than on the sports field. He did play for the football XI but never made it beyond the second team in cricket. He showed more ability in athletics, winning the Senior 100 yards in 1903 in a time of 12.2 seconds and the quarter mile in 61.2 seconds as well as finishing second in the hurdles and high jump. Both his winning times were considerably slower than those of the previous year, and *The Bloxhamist* was unimpressed with the general standard on show: 'The racing cannot be said to have reached a high standard. With a few praiseworthy exceptions, little interest was taken in training.'

He left Bloxham in July 1903 and then went on to study medicine at the Royal College of Physicians of Ireland, where he received his diplomas, LRCSI, LRCP and LM in 1909. He was appointed Maternity Assistant to the Rotunda Hospital in Dublin that year.

Harry was married on 3 July 1911 at Zion Church, Rathgar, Dublin to Charlotte Elizabeth Josephine Ingle, eldest daughter of A. F. Ingle (Superintendent of Indian Post Offices), and Mrs. Ingle of 24 Grosvenor Place, Rathmines, Dublin. The new couple's address is shown as Meath Convalescent Home in Bray, Co. Wicklow. By now Harry was known as Massy Miles. He was an active Old Bloxhamist and contributed to the fund for the stained-glass window in memory of Miss Mallinson, the much-loved school matron for thirteen years, who died in January 1914; the window cost £44 16s., and 118 subscribers are listed in *The Bloxhamist*; to many Bloxhamists of the pre-war generation, Miss Mallinson had been a second mother – twenty of the 80 Bloxhamists to perish in the Great War were included in the list. Dr Massy Miles visited his old school whenever he could, coming with his wife when on leave in 1917.

Following the outbreak of war, he was assigned to the Royal Army Medical Corps and appointed a temporary Lieutenant on 21 December 1914. He was then assigned to the 2nd/ 8th London Regiment Post Office Rifles, part of 58th (London) Division.

On 21 March 1918 the battalion was in the thick of the action at the start of the Ludendorff Offensive. The battalion suffered heavy casualties, including thirteen officers and over 300 other ranks. It was recorded that as Medical Officer, Captain Massy Miles was conspicuous in the aftermath of this devastating blow. He was awarded the Military Cross for his actions at this critical time. According to *The British Medical Journal* of 17 August 1918, he kept in close touch with the battalion during several days of severe fighting, working unceasingly without rest during the whole period, dressing the wounded including French troops. He showed great initiative in establishing forward regimental aid posts, reconnoitring their sites beforehand under heavy hostile shell fire, thus greatly assisting the rapid evacuation of casualties. His courage and cheerfulness throughout a period of great strain were beyond praise.

The action in which Massy Miles lost his life was part of the Battle of the Lys (7-29 April 1918), launched against the British lines in front of Amiens in an attempt to maintain the momentum of the Ludendorff Offensive. He was at his Regimental Aid Post when he heard that a gas shell had burst on the Battalion H.Q. at Villers-Bretonneux, had pierced the roof, and penetrated into the cellar. He at once went to attend to the wounded and, when he had finished, returned to his post. Later, he complained of feeling ill and lay down. On getting worse, he was removed to the 8th General Hospital at Rouen where he died on 26 April 1918. His colonel wrote to Harry's old school:

Captain Massy Miles was with this division for a long time and was one of my ablest and most gallant officers. He did splendid work during the retirement in March and was awarded the Military Cross for his gallant work. We all deplore his loss deeply, and I lose a valued friend and trusty officer.'

The regimental history recorded that

> Captain Massey (sic) Miles, MC, one of the whitest and most gallant Battalion Medical Officers in France, died of gas poisoning after an heroic attempt to succour others similarly poisoned, removing his gas-mask in order to do so, and thus courting an inevitable and agonising death. Three Medical Officers were sent in quick succession in one day, two of whom became casualties, one killed and one wounded.'

He is buried in the St Sever Cemetery, Rouen. His mother chose as the inscription for his headstone 'Beloved son, husband, brother with Christ, which is far better'. A prize in the field of Obstetrics and Gynaecology was established in his memory by his widow at the Royal College of Physicians of Ireland and continues to be awarded to this day. His half-brother Corporal Martin Hugh Miles of the 2nd Battalion Gloucestershire Regiment landed on Gold Beach on D Day and was killed in action aged 32 (the same age as Harry at his death) at Tilly-sur-Seulles on 11 June 1944.

Rifleman Edgar Percy Mitcalfe
2/17th Battalion, London Regiment
Pupil at Bloxham School 1908-1914
Killed in action 2 May 1918, aged 20
Commemorated on the Jerusalem Memorial, Israel and Palestine
Panels 45-52

Edgar Percy Mitcalfe was the only son of Conrad Mitcalfe and his wife Minna Gregor Mitcalfe. His father was an agricultural engineer and the family lived at 10 Calthorpe Road in Banbury, though by 1911 their address was listed as Cornhill Mansion, Banbury (for those that know Banbury, Cornhill is the area between the Castle Quay Shopping Centre and the multi-storey car park).

Edgar arrived at Bloxham School in May 1908 and was promoted to Form III the following year. Promotion to Form IVa ensued in September 1910. Here he seemed to get stuck, only earning promotion to Form V four years later. He was a regular, though unsuccessful, competitor in running events on Sports Day each year. finished second in the sack race on Sports Day, beaten by John Clifford, in April 1912. He passed the Oxford Local Examinations at the preliminary level that year, repeating the feat, this time at junior level, the following year. These were the best years yet for Bloxham's examination results, as in 1913 the school outperformed all the other Woodard schools, while in 1912 one of Edgar's classmates, J.S. Hughes, finished first in Arithmetic out of more than 3,000 candidates in the whole country. Edgar won the form prize in Latin that year, but made no further academic progress before leaving the school in 1914.

He enlisted into the 17th Battalion of the London Regiment on 13 March 1917; the 17th was known as the Poplar and Stepney Rifles. He remained in Britain training until June 1917 when he progressed overseas with his battalion. He went with the Londons to Palestine, where the war against the Turks was still raging. The battalion took part in the Third Battle of Gaza and the capture of Jerusalem (December 1917) and would go on to participate in the capture of Jericho and the attack on Amman. With the focus on the Western Front, progress after the capture of Jerusalem was slow. Edmund was killed in action on the morning of 2 May 1918 near Jerusalem. His body was never found, and he is commemorated on the Jerusalem Memorial. When the school's war memorial was unveiled in chapel on All Saints' Day in November 1920, Mr Mitcalfe was one of those parents present.

Second Lieutenant John Amyan Ludford Champneys
Royal Air Force
Pupil at Bloxham School 1914-1915
Killed in an accident 17 June 1918, aged 19
Buried in Marissel National Cemetery, France
Grave 664

John Amyan Champneys was born on 19 April 1899 to Edward Hugh Stanley Champneys and his wife Magdalene Frances A. Champneys (née Mason). The Champneys were an old Kent family, having come over with William the Conqueror in 1066. Amyan Champneys was a knight at Henry II's court, while Sir John Champneys was Lord Mayor of London in 1534. William Champneys (1699-1772) served as Usher of the Black Rod and Commissioner of Revenue for Ireland while the family was also connected to the Earls of Derby (after whom the race is named) and the Astley baronets. John's father, Edward was a landowner and veterinary surgeon, and the family lived at Otterpool Manor, Sellindge in Kent, where the Champneys family still lives and farms. The current occupant is called John like so many of his ancestors.

Edward and Magdalene married in Skerton in Lancashire in 1891 and had seven children, of whom Amyan (as he was known in the family, and so the name by which we will call him) was the fourth child and second son. An elder brother, Edward Geoffrey (born August 1897), also briefly attended Bloxham (1913-1914), there was another brother Hugh (born March 1903) and four sisters, Magdalen (born March 1894), Violet (born June 1896), who married the Liberal MP Sir Eric Macfadyen, Kathleen (born December 1900) and Gertrude (born June 1905).

Amyan was a pupil at the school between September 1914 and December 1915, arriving the term after his brother Geoffrey left. Geoffrey had been one of the school's leading sportsmen, gaining colours in both football and cricket, and John emulated him on the football pitch, playing for the 2nd XI in his first term before getting into the first team in his final term. *The Bloxhamist* described Amyan as 'a fair back but a poor kick' and judged that 'he played hard but was not always very successful.' He arrived as a member of Form V and was still there when he left at Christmas 1915, by which time the war had been going on for over a year.

Amyan had been a member of the school's OTC and applied for a commission in the Royal Flying Corps on 19 May 1917, when he was serving with the Territorial Rifle Brigade. According to *The Bloxhamist*, he gained his commission in December 1917 and his wings in April 1918. He served in 73 Squadron. At 3:10 p.m. on 17 June 1918, only three days after the squadron had moved from Fouquerolles to Planques, Amyan Champneys was on a training flight and was coming in to land when his Sopwith Camel C8289 suddenly flipped over in the air and nose-dived into the ground, killing Champneys instantly. Amyan was originally buried in an extension to the communal cemetery at Beauvais, but in February 1922 he and twelve other officers and men were removed and reburied at Marissel French National Cemetery.

Amyan Champneys is remembered on the school war memorial, to which he had donated 2s and 6d in July 1917, as had his brother Geoffrey. A treble bell which hangs in the church of St Stephen's, Lympne was given in memory of Amyan and of his parents in 1948 - Edward died in 1940 and Magdalene in 1942. There was also a stained-glass window in Amyan's memory in the same church which was destroyed in a bombing raid in 1944.

Second Lieutenant John Otto Boole
Royal Air Force
Died of wounds 9 July 1918, aged 26
Buried in Penarth Cemetery, Wales
Grave C.494

John Boole was from a family of engineers; both his father and grandfather were mining engineers, and John followed them into the profession as well as serving in the Royal Engineers for the first half of the war. In his childhood home, John would have seen the portrait proudly displayed of his illustrious great uncle. This was George Boole, Professor of mathematics at University College, Cork, who was responsible for Boolean logic, which is used to analyse digital gates and circuits. Because of its importance for computer science, he is widely credited with laying the foundations for the computer age.

John was the second son of Kate Eliza Boole and lived with her in Penarth, a prosperous seaside resort about four miles outside Cardiff; at the time of his childhood, Cardiff was undergoing an extraordinary expansion thanks to the growth of the coal industry and the trade which flowed through the city's docks. John was born on 23 September 1891 in Rainford in Lancashire, where his father George Boole was the manager of the colliery. In 1865, George's

father Charles had been appointed to manage the new pit opened by the Rainford Coal Company.

Charles put his surplus earnings into buying shares in the colliery, and by 1881 he was a part-owner of the mine and able to retire to Croydon with his wife. He left an employee, Thomas Greene, to manage the colliery until George could take on the post. George was a student at King's College, London, before studying mining engineering in Merthyr Tydfil, at the heart of the world's greatest coalfield, and became a mining engineer at Treharris Mine in Monmouthshire in 1881. While there, he courted Kate Eliza Thomas, the daughter of a prosperous Cardiff brewer. They married in Cardiff on 9 July 1881 and went to Ilfracombe for their honeymoon. George was still working at Treharris Mine when their first child was born the following year, a girl whom they named Dorothy Gwenllian. Eventually they had five children, of whom John was the youngest.

By the time John was born, Charles had moved with his family to Rainford on taking over as Mining Engineer in 1884. Tragically, in 1898, when John was only six, George died of bronchial pneumonia at the age of 39, leaving his wife to look after their five children alone. Kate left Lancashire and moved to Penarth to be close to her relatives. The decision was taken to send John, the baby of the family, off to boarding school in England.

John arrived at Bloxham in April 1905 and was only a pupil at the school for just over two years, leaving in July 1907, but packed a great deal of activity into his time there. On the cricket field, he swiftly made an impression through his wicket-keeping and defensive skills as a batsman and represented the school 2nd XI at football against Abingdon in September 1905, earning praise for his defending despite Bloxham going down to a 7-0 drubbing. He was still in the 2nd XI in November when the side was defeated 3-0 by MCS, Oxford. A return fixture against Abingdon resulted in another 3-0 defeat.

By March 1906 John had forced himself into the 1st XI, and he was elected a member of the influential Games Committee in May 1906, always a sign that a boy had 'arrived' as a senior pupil. In June, he played in a 21-run victory against Abingdon, the 2nd XI's first victory of any sort in three years. *The Bloxhamist* was of the opinion that 'Boole has improved considerably, and shows very promising form, and should easily get in the first eleven next year.'

For the 1906-07 football season, John played left back all season; *The Bloxhamist* commented that he was much improved since the previous campaign: 'Always tries hard and can tackle and kick well, but like some others, does not keep his arms down when tackling.' He was made a prefect in April 1907 for his final term. He had a good cricket season, though missing several games due to illness, and finished third in the final of the 220 yards on Sports Day. He left having gained colours in football, cricket and gymnasium. There is little record of his activities other than in sport, which loomed large in the Bloxham curriculum, but he did do the scene shifting for the school play *A Scrap of Paper* in November 1906.

The Bloxhamist reported that on leaving the school he travelled abroad, but we know that he was back at the school for Whitsuntide 1908 and was still in Britain at the time of the 1911 census, being recorded as an engineering apprentice living at 75 Plymouth Road, Penarth with his mother, who had now remarried and become Mrs Window. At some point he went overseas to work as a marine engineer. His name is recorded in the nominal roll of the Egyptian division of inland waterways for the P&O line, suggesting that he may have worked on steam ships on the Nile. After the outbreak of war he returned to Britain and enlisted as a signaller in the Royal Engineers in July 1915. According to *The Bloxhamist*, he was promoted to Serjeant and appointed Serjeant Instructor, going out to France in the 38th Division in November 1915, and took part in the battle of the Somme, serving at Mametz Wood. He also saw service in the Ypres sector. He was given a commission in the newly-formed Royal Air Force and was undergoing his training with the RAF at the Central Flight School located in Brecon when he met with a fatal accident, something all too common in those early days of aviation.

On the afternoon of Tuesday 9 July 1918, Boole was flying SE 5a D8063 when he was in a mid-air collision with SE 5a C1775 flown by Second Lieutenant Richard Carter Pellow, above the Brecon Beacons. Both men were killed in the resulting crash. Richard Pellow was a 21-year-old from Par, in Cornwall, who had worked as an apprentice fitter in the Great Western Railway's locomotive and carriage works at St Blazey before enlisting. Intriguingly, the GWR's records suggest that the accident took place at Upavon in Wiltshire rather than the Brecon Beacons.

John Otto Boole was buried in Penarth Cemetery, and he is commemorated on a plaque in the club house of Penarth Yacht Club on the Esplanade, one of seven names listed there. He is also commemorated on the Roll of Honour in St Michael's, Croydon, where his grandparents had been active members of the church. His mother's letter of condolence from King George V expressed sympathy that her son had been 'accidentally killed whilst in the service of his country.'

John had two older brothers, Philip (born 1884), who served as a Lieutenant in the Royal Garrison Artillery and Llewellyn (born 1885), known as Leo, who was unfortunate enough to have been visiting a German cousin, Enid Marschall, in Cologne when war broke out. As a result, he was interned for the duration of hostilities and spent the war teaching French, Latin and Greek in a prison camp. According to *The Penarth Times*, all three of the brothers were members of Penarth Lawn Tennis Club. Philip's son, Robert Hugh Philip Boole, born in September 1912, was a pupil at Bloxham between September 1927 and March 1929 and was ordained in 1948. There were also two sisters, Dorothy Gwenllian (born 1882) and Rosemary (born 1886), who would become a nun in 1907, teaching in a convent run by the 'Sisters of the Church'.

Private Edward James Harvey
28th Battalion, London Regiment (Artists' Rifles)
Pupil at Bloxham School 1906-13
Killed in action 22 August 1918, aged 22
Commemorated on the Vis-en-Artois Memorial, Arras, France
Panel 10

Edward James Harvey was the only son of James and Ada Harvey and lived at Spring Grove, Frome in Somerset. His father was 31 years older than his mother, having been born on Christmas Eve 1821, and so was 73 when Edward was born on 12 November 1895. In the 1901 census, when he was 79 years of age, James was shown as living off private means. He died aged 84 on 26 April 1906, leaving his widow and son comfortably off – at his own death in 1918, Edward left an estate of over £66,000, a substantial amount of money in those days.

Five months after his father's death, Edward started at Bloxham School at the age of ten. He was clearly a bright boy, and swiftly earnt promotion from Form II to Form III, and then to Form IVa a year after his arrival. He won the Form III Latin prize in July 1907, receiving his prize from Old Bloxhamist Admiral Sir Gerard Noel, KCB. Two years later, at the start of the school year in September 1909, he was promoted to Form V. Following success in the Oxford Locals in July 1910 and carrying off the Classics prize, he achieved his final promotion, to the Sixth Form, at the young age of 14.

Edward's first appearance for a Bloxham sports team came in May 1911, when he travelled with the school's 2nd XI to play cricket against Abingdon School. Unfortunately, the motor vehicle specially hired from Banbury sustained a number of punctures en route, so the start was delayed and the match was left drawn decidedly in Bloxham's favour, with the home side, chasing 85 to win, stumbling at 35 for 6, with Edward having taken all six wickets to fall. The following season he played for the 1st XI and also forced his way into the first team for football. According to *The Bloxhamist*, he had 'a fairly good kick, but is rather slow, and does not get to the ball fast enough. Has played some useful games.' At the end of the season, in which the 1st XI won four of its eight games, he was one of six boys awarded colours.

Edward chose not to join the new OTC, turning out for the Civilians against the Corps at fives in 1911. He was made a prefect in January 1912. In the same year, he received Second Class Honours in the Oxford Locals and won the Sixth Form French prize. At the end of the 1913 cricket season, during which he served as vice-captain and won the fielding prize, he was judged by *The Bloxhamist* to be 'a sound and useful bat, with a good forward stroke. Must learn to back up. A very fair change bowler. A thoroughly reliable field, and a sound catch in the deep.' He also shared the shot put ('putting the weight') cup with Herbert Cain, with a distance of 29 feet and 9 inches. In July 1913 he passed the Oxford Locals, once again with Second Class Honours and exemption from Responsions (an elementary examination at Oxford set to ensure an equal standard between new students). At his final prize giving in the same month he was awarded the Sixth Form Latin and French Prizes.

On leaving Bloxham, Edward went up to Hertford College, Oxford. He revisited the school at the end of May 1914 to play cricket for the Old Bloxhamists against the school, again on All Saints Day 1914 and twice more the following year. Edward's relatively humble service record may be connected to his lack of a background in the OTC. He enlisted into the RFC in 1917 – the photograph of him in uniform is from this period – and was given clerical work. It is likely that the frustration of not being able to fly is what led to him transferring to the Artists' Rifles, still as a private, in 1918. He was killed in action on 22 August 1918 on an attack near the village of Le Barque, south of Bapaume, and is commemorated on the Vis-en-Artois Memorial as well as on a memorial in St John's, Frome. His mother, who donated two pounds to the school's war memorial fund, lived to see the outbreak of the Second World War, dying aged 86 on 8 September 1939.

Lieutenant Arthur Whiting
Royal Naval Volunteer Reserve
Pupil at Bloxham School 1900-1902
Killed in action 22 August 1918, aged 32
Commemorated on the Chatham War Memorial, England
Panel 31

Arthur Whiting was the fifth son of Henry William Whiting, of Caldecote House, Newport Pagnell, and his wife Mary Elizabeth. He was born on 21 March 1886 and attended Bloxham School between May 1900 and December 1902. He was one of eleven children. Three of his brothers also attended Bloxham. Harry (born 1876) and Joseph (born 1877) were both at the school between 1888 and 1890, while Philip (born 1893) was there between 1905 and 1908. Philip served in the Royal Bucks Hussars before transferring to the Machine Gun Corps and being wounded on the Western Front, while Harry was an engineer like Arthur, and like him served in the RNVR.

Arthur's father was one of four brothers who dominated the farming scene in North Buckinghamshire. Following the death of their father, Joseph Evan Whiting, in 1888, Joseph, George and Charles formed the Whiting

Partnership, which had farms at Castlethorpe, Gayhurst, Lathbury, Moulsoe, Newport Pagnell and Hanslope, farming over 3,000 acres and employing 160 labourers. As a sideline, they also started up garages where farm machinery could be worked on (at the time of writing, one of these is still standing on the edge of Newport Pagnell). Four of Arthur's cousins, George's sons (Francis and John) and Charles' sons (Joseph and Benjamin) attended Bloxham shortly after Arthur. Joseph served in the RFA, was wounded in the German spring offensive in March 1918 and was awarded the MC while John served in the Royal Bucks Hussars, was wounded at Gallipoli and awarded the DCM for his role in the cavalry charge at El Mughar in November 1917.

Rather than join the family partnership, Henry Whiting preferred to focus on his successful dairy farm, as well as a motor business which was thriving by the outbreak of war. Whiting Ltd. of Euston Road, London, were the importers of tractors made by the Bull Tractor Company of Minneapolis, and also imported cars from the Grant Motor Company of Ohio, selling them as Whiting-Grant cars, and acted as the agents for the Hupmobile car, made in Detroit by the Hupp Motor Car Company.

Arthur arrived at Bloxham at the start of the Summer Term in May 1900, joining Form III and being promoted to Form IV in September. He was one of 23 boys confirmed in the school chapel by the Bishop of Reading in March 1901. He reached the giddy heights of the school's 2nd XI in June of that year but contributed only 17 runs in five innings to the side's three victories that season. The following season he was promoted to the 1st XI, but as often happens in schoolboy cricket, his contribution was minimal, batting at number 11 and never bowling. While conceding that he had 'some defence and can cut very fairly', *The Bloxhamist* brutally declared that he 'lost his place in the team owing to his bad fielding in games'. Arthur was promoted to Form V for his final term, in September 1902. He appeared in the school's football 1st XI that term and left at Christmas 1902.

After leaving school, Arthur trained as an engineer at Blackstone & Co., which made agricultural machinery, at Stamford in Lincolnshire. At the time of the 1911 census, Arthur was lodging in a boarding house in Osnaburgh Street, Regents Park and was managing the motor engineering department of the family business, Whiting Ltd., which was based in London. The firm was to benefit from a huge increase in orders for vehicles for the war effort, including Whiting-Denby vans for the navy and army canteen and lorries for use as horse ambulances. So lucrative were these orders that the company was forced to open a second office, in Liverpool in 1915.

At the outbreak of war, Arthur enlisted straight away, along with several of his brothers and cousins. He volunteered for the Navy, and on 15 September 1914 he was gazetted a Sub-Lieutenant, RNVR, as second officer on a patrol boat working the Irish coast, where he had several thrilling experiences. In the following spring he joined his brother Lieutenant Harry Whiting, with whom he worked upon anti-submarine devices in home waters. After a further course of training, he was appointed to command a patrol boat in the Eastern Mediterranean, where he remained until 1917, when he received his promotion to Lieutenant, and was appointed to command one of the North Sea transport escorts and subsequently was made Division Leader.

On the afternoon of 21 August 1918, the steamer *Griselda* left the port of Whitby and when she was just out of the harbour, the mate spotted a disturbance in front of the ship. A torpedo, fired by a submerged German U-Boat, missed the front of the ship by a matter of inches and crashed into the rocks on the left-hand side of the bay. Despite the impact the torpedo mounted the rocks and was stranded, undetonated.

The following day, Whiting, in command of HMML 403 was ordered to recover the torpedo. HMML 403 was a patrol boat built by Elco – the Electric Launch Company Inc. of New York – weighing 45 tonnes and measuring 18 metres in length. The boats were known as Tinder Boxes owing to the highly dangerous mix of petrol and paraffin which was used to power the 440 bhp engine.

Whiting left port with a crew of ten and two torpedo experts, watched by a large crowd of onlookers who gathered on the clifftops and beaches. The torpedo was recovered successfully on board, but when one of the experts attempted to remove the detonator, something went wrong and the torpedo exploded. This in turn ignited the fuel tank on the ship and caused the four depth charges she was carrying to detonate. HMML 403 was blown to pieces. The explosion was so severe that houses in the shoreline village of Runswick were damaged, windows were blown in, roofs collapsed and the stern of the ship was launched over 100 metres and landed on the beach.

Miraculously, the first mate was feeling unwell and was resting in the bunks below decks and was blown clear of the ship, becoming the only survivor. In a letter published in *The Bucks Standard* for 31 August 1918, the Senior Base Officer wrote to the mother of Lieutenant Whiting (little knowing that Arthur's mother had passed away in September 1911):

> I need hardly tell you how his loss has affected all the officers and men on the base, and I know they will join with me in offering our very sincere and deep sympathy to you and the family. He was always a favourite among us, and without any empty flattery he was without doubt one of the most popular men on the -------. His cheery dry humour always made him welcome to all our gatherings, and he will be terribly missed by us all.

The Motor of Tuesday 8 October 1918 contained the following:

> The £100 subscription to the Cycle and Motor Trades Benevolent Fund to perpetuate the memory of Lieut. Arthur Whiting, RNVR., has been oversubscribed, and in view of the desire expressed by many friends who have not yet sent in their subscriptions, the organisers of the memorial have decided to keep the list open for a few more weeks, and to hand the total amount over to the London Centre of the Benevolent Fund to augment a list of donations which will be added to the results of the forthcoming annual appeal of the President, Sir Charles Wakefield.

Arthur Whiting is commemorated on the Chatham War Memorial as well as on the memorial in his home village of Willen, and also on the reverse of the gravestone of his parents in the graveyard at St Mary Magdalene, where his father was churchwarden for 29 years. Henry Whiting died at 14 Bulstrode Street, Marylebone on 29 December 1918, four months after his son, and left a sizeable sum (£19,563 6s 3d) in his will.

Second Lieutenant William Arthur Barr
328th Siege Battery, Royal Garrison Artillery
Pupil at Bloxham School 1900-1901
Killed in action 27 August 1918, aged 36
Buried in Croisilles British Cemetery, France
Grave V.B.32

William Arthur Barr was the only son of Robert and Eva Barr; there was also an older sister called Laura. The family lived at 2 Priory Road, Chiswick. Robert Barr had been born in Glasgow in 1849 but emigrated with his parents to Canada when he was four. He became a teacher in Windsor, Ontario before quitting his job to become a journalist with *The Detroit Free Press,* rising to become its news editor before relocating to London in 1881, the intention being to set up a weekly English edition of the paper. As well as being a journalist, Robert Barr was a prolific author, mostly in the then very fashionable genre of crime fiction, and he also founded the monthly magazine *The Idler* in 1892, procuring the services of Jerome K. Jerome as its co-editor. *The Idler* contained short stories, serialised novels and humorous pieces, and employed many of the leading writers of the time, including Rudyard Kipling, H.G. Wells and Mark Twain. Barr's London literary friends included Arnold Bennett, Joseph Conrad and H. Rider Haggard. His

most successful character was the conceited French detective Eugene Valmont. Another friend was Sir Arthur Conan Doyle, and Robert Barr was responsible for the first Holmes parody, a story in *The Idler* entitled 'The Adventures of Sherlaw Kombs'. Conan Doyle does not seem to have held this against Barr, describing him in his memoirs as 'a volcanic Scot-American, with a violent manner, a wealth of strong adjectives, and one of the kindest natures underneath it all.'

William arrived at Bloxham at the age of 17 in January 1900, joining Form V, and swiftly made his mark, becoming one of the managers of *The Bloxhamist* the following term and joining the Camera Club. After winning the Form V Divinity and English prizes he was promoted to the Sixth Form in September of the same year as well as being appointed a Prefect. He also joined the school choir as a tenor, taking the place of Wilfred Bury when he left the school. On All Saints' Day 1900, William took part in the school play, an obscure comedy entitled *Our Lottie,* essaying the role of the hero, Edward Esher. *The Bloxhamist,* while praising his acting, opined that he made 'a decidedly interesting lover, but was perhaps lacking somewhat in the ardour which is supposed to be necessary for success in these matters.'

In March 1901, William was awarded first prize, ahead of numerous competitors, for the paper on Walter Scott's 'Ivanhoe', set to be done over the Christmas holidays and presented by the Founder. At prize-giving in July, he was once again involved, his last action as a Bloxham pupil being to receive the Senior Divinity Prize from the hands of the Bishop of Southampton. He is next heard of in January 1904, attending the Old Bloxhamist dinner at the Trocadero Restaurant in Piccadilly, and he returned to school for All Saints' Day in November 1905.

On leaving Bloxham, William studied journalism at the London School of Newspapers, having graduated from Exeter College, Oxford with a degree in English. A number of journalistic appointments followed, including *The Aeroplane* and his father's magazine *The Idler*, though that ceased after the magazine closed down in March 1911. Robert Barr died from heart disease in October 1912.

William spent some time in Morocco, with a particular interest in the tribes of the Atlas mountains and was in the process of writing a book on the subject when war broke out. He enlisted immediately, as a private in the 4th Battalion, Seaforth Highlanders, going out to France in November, thereby earning the Mons Star. He then served throughout all of the major campaigns and battles the battalion was involved in and rose to be a serjeant. During the war he continued to write regularly for a number of the London papers.

In 1917 he returned to England for training in the Artillery and was commissioned as a 2nd Lieutenant in the Royal Garrison Artillery in November 1917. He then served with the 328th Siege Battery in France. The unit's war diary is extremely detailed in its description of its involvement in the Battle of the Scarpe in August 1918. The battery took up position south-west of Croisilles, facing directly the Heidenkopf (Heathen's Head) system of enemy trenches. On 25 August the guns ranged on the German lines, carrying out a 25-minute High Explosive barrage which was curtailed by heavy fog. The Germans responded with HE, shrapnel and gas and caused heavy casualties, killing two officers and seven other ranks, with another 32 men wounded. The following day the battery was involved in a bombardment in preparation for the forthcoming attack, the battery firing over 800 rounds in the course of a 90-minute bombardment. Another nine officers were killed that day, along with 45 other ranks.

On 27 August, in response to urgent requests for assistance from the 1/8 Manchesters, a heavy shrapnel and gas barrage was dropped on the Heidenkopf system at 10:22 a.m. The ranging was completed quickly and a yellow smoke was seen at 11: 37 a.m. suggesting a satisfactory result. According to the war diary, D battery on the right end of the line suffered most heavily from a 'spiteful' enemy barrage, even though it was some 1100 metres behind the front line, and it was during this engagement that William Barr was killed. One of the Heavy Artillery pieces had jammed with a munition trapped in the breach. Whilst trying to free the munition a German shell landed close by, and the shock wave caused the munition to explode in the breach of the gun. The force of this ejected the casing from the breach with such force that Barr was decapitated. Seven other ranks were killed or wounded.

The following day Barr was buried behind the battery positon. According to the war diary, 'There is much sadness amongst his fellow officers and men'. The other men killed in the incident were also buried but, in a sobering illustration of the grim reality of modern war, it was recorded that 'owing to destruction of bodies, what remains has been placed in one grave and marked by the Chaplaincy recorder'. It was also recorded that 'personal effects were recovered by Captain Thomas'.

William's body was exhumed in 1919 and moved from the small battlefield cemetery where he had been buried into Croisilles Cemetery near Arras, where he now lies. He is listed on the school memorial – one of two names to have been painted rather than carved, suggesting that news of his death reached the school late in the day, which is confirmed by the fact that it was only announced in *The Bloxhamist* in June 1921, nearly three years after the event. The inscription chosen by his mother, now remarried, for William's headstone reads 'Love, Remembrance, Hope'.

Second Lieutenant Roland Rice Powell
1st Battalion, Somerset Light Infantry
Pupil at Bloxham School 1913-1916
Killed in action 29 August 1918, aged 19
Buried in Ligny-St. Flochel Cemetery, France
Grave III.B.25

Roland Rice Powell was the oldest of three sons of Walter and Margaret Powell of 30, Hill Road, in Weston-super-Mare, Somerset. His father was a lawyer by profession. Roland was born on 18 March 1899. He arrived at Bloxham in September 1913 and left at Easter 1916. One of his younger brothers, Ernest, also attended the school between 1914 and 1916, leaving two terms after him.

Roland's greatest contribution in his three years at Bloxham was in hockey, a sport which was a relatively recent innovation – the first match had been played against perennial rivals Magdalen College School, Oxford in February 1910. He made his first appearance in the 1st XI in a match against Banbury Hockey Club in February 1914, and appeared once more that season, at the end of which *The Bloxhamist* commented that 'he can hit well, but is slow, and has as yet but a slight knowledge of the game.' The following season he was a stalwart of the team, providing stability in defence and earning his hockey colours.

By this time, the war was in its first year. When war broke out, Roland was only fifteen years of age, so well short of the age to enlist, but he would have observed the growing list of Bloxhamists joining up, not least his hockey master James Pastfield, the first Bloxhamist to lose his life in the conflict. Roland was an enthusiastic member of the OTC, joining in 1914 and being promoted to Lance Corporal in November 1915, then Corporal the following term. He appeared in the school's 2nd XI for football and was a competent gymnast, but he made slow progress in the classroom, still being in Form V when he left school in April 1916. *The Bloxhamist* reported in July 1917 that he had passed the entrance examination for Sandhurst, following which he was commissioned as a Second Lieutenant in the 1st Battalion of the Somerset Light Infantry. He arrived in France to join the battalion as it was engaged in the series of attacks east of Amiens which would ultimately lead to victory.

On the night of 28 August 1918, the Battalion was moving up into trenches between Arras and Bapaume, where they were due to relieve the 4th Canadian Infantry. They set off at 7:45 p.m. The war diary describes a very dark night, with difficult conditions which made it very hard to see where the men were heading. The Germans were reported as harassing the men with constant machine gun and sniper fire and during the relief Powell was shot and killed. About twenty other ranks were killed and wounded before the battalion reached the front line.

Roland Powell was buried in Ligny-St Flochel Cemetery, fifteen miles west of Arras alongside four men from his battalion killed on the same day. His parents chose a biblical inscription ('I thank my God on every remembrance of you,' Philippians 1) for their eldest son's headstone. This cost them 11s 4d, as families were charged threepence halfpenny per letter, though it seems that these 'debts' were not vigorously chased up. MD has observed that of all the pictures of the 80 Bloxhamists to perish in the war, it is Powell's which saddens him the most – 'little more than a boy, thrown into a man's war'. Along with Leonard Burton, Roland was the last of the 80 to leave school, and he was 19 years old when he died. Roland Powell is commemorated on the Weston-super-Mare war memorial as well as that of his old school; he had contributed five shillings to the fund for the Bloxham memorial a year before his own death.

Private Lawrence Edward Courtney
24th Battalion, Royal Fusiliers (City of London Regiment)
Pupil at Bloxham School 1896-1900
Killed in action 11 September 1918, aged 36
Commemorated on the Vis-en-Artois Memorial, Arras, France
Panel 3

Lawrence Courtney was the son of the Rev. Stanley T. Courtney and his late wife Gertrude and came from Beckenham in Kent. He was born on 25 August 1882 and was a pupil at the school between 1896 and 1900, arriving with his older brothers, Harold and Raymond, at the start of the summer term in April 1896. All three brothers were gifted sportsmen, especially Henry and Lawrence. Henry was a goalkeeper and played for three seasons in the school's 1st XI, captaining the side in his last term. He was in goal when the side was beaten 10-2 by the team from the Britannia Works, though the editor of *The Bloxhamist* had a simple explanation for the scale of the defeat: 'As a matter of fact, the majority of the goals secured on this occasion were "off-side" owing to absolute ignorance of the "off-side" rule or wilful blindness on the part of the referee.' Similar complaints can be heard from losing Bloxham sides to this day.

Lawrence joined his brother in the team at the start of the 1898-99 season, and on 9 November history was made when Raymond was selected for the 1st XI, meaning that all three Courtney brothers played in the same side, against MCS, Oxford. By now Harold had passed on the goal-keeping gloves to Frederick Horner, one of five brothers to represent the school, and Harold and Lawrence formed a formidable defensive partnership as left and right back, while

Raymond was tried in a variety of positions. While *The Bloxhamist* was muted in its praise for Raymond ('he is very erratic') and Harold ('he should learn not to dribble so much and to control his temper better'), it was effusive about Lawrence: 'He kicks cleanly and with judgment. Tackling and heading well, he has proved very reliable.'

After Christmas, with Harold having left the school, Lawrence took over as captain for the remainder of the season, earning praise for his leadership. He also played cricket for the 1st XI, as a lower order batsman and occasional bowler, and earned his colours after the Old Bloxhamist match in July 1899. He then played football for the 1st XI for a second season, forming a powerful mid-field alongside his brother Raymond and Wilfred Bury. Though no longer the captain, he was praised by *The Bloxhamist* as 'a tower of strength'.

The following term Lawrence, now the only Courtney in the school after Raymond had left at Christmas 1899, finally acceded to the Sixth Form and was made one of the school's nine prefects. Lawrence played one final term's football for the school, now as a forward, scoring good goals against Abingdon School and MCS, Brackley, though handicapped by a weak ankle. When he left the school at Christmas 1900, neither he nor those Bloxhamists who would return the following term could have known that they would do so as subjects of a new sovereign, for the long reign of Queen Victoria came to an end with her death on 22 January 1901.

Frustratingly, Lawrence and his brothers did not keep in touch with their old school after leaving – there is no mention at all of any of them in *The Bloxhamist* after 1900, which is surprising. We know from Charles Wilson's records that Harold pursued a career in medicine, becoming a member of the Royal College of Surgeons and a member of the Royal College of Physicians. Harold was employed as the Medical Officer and Public Vaccinator for the Barton District in Lancashire before moving to St George's Hospital in London. Raymond went out to Toronto after leaving school, and served in the war as a private in the Canadian Expeditionary Force, returning to Toronto after the war.

Given their prominence while at school, especially their sporting prowess, one would have expected the brothers to have been active Old Bloxhamists, and both Harold and Raymond did play football in a 2-2 draw between the Old Boys and a School team which included Lawrence in November 1900, but there is nothing after that, not even a report of Lawrence's death. We know that he was a stockbroker by profession. He served in the City of London Regiment, the 24th Battalion of the Royal Fusiliers – also known as the 2nd Sportsmans Battalion – with service number 74978 and was killed in action on 11 September 1918, but there is little additional information about his service. The CWGC lists his death as occurring on 11 September though the school has 13 September. His body was never recovered and he is commemorated on the Vis-en-Artois Memorial, one of 9,847 names listed there of men who have no known grave, having fallen in the period between 8 August and the end of the war in the advance to victory. 2nd Division, which included Lawrence's battalion, was at the forefront of this advance. Lawrence was 36 years of age when he died.

Herbert Courtney is recorded as having contributed £2 1s to the school's war memorial in his brother's memory.

Private Charles Raymond Hammill
1/4 Australian Infantry
Pupil at Bloxham School 1900-1900
Killed in action 18 September 1918, aged 39
Buried in Roisel Communal Cemetery, France
Grave III.H.10

Charles Hammill could not be further from the stereotype of the fresh-faced young subaltern that we tend to think of schools such as Bloxham producing in great numbers in the Great War. He was 38 years of age when he died, he was a private soldier rather than an officer, and he was serving in the Australian forces. Furthermore, he could be said to have led a colourful life before the war, and, if we stretch the euphemism almost to breaking point, seems to have been something of a rogue. And yet, he could have hardly had a more impeccable family background, at least on the surface, as the son of a general and grandson of a baronet.

Charles Raymond Hammill was born on 18 September 1879 and arrived at Bloxham School in September 1891. Charles' mother Maude was the daughter of Sir Henry Piers, and she married Denzil Hammill, a Major in the Gordon Highlanders, in September 1870. They had four children in all, two sons and two daughters. Charles was the youngest of the four children, along with John Eustace, Evelyn Maude and the oldest, Cicely Mary. She would go on to become a leading member of the Suffragette movement and an important writer on women's rights. Cicely provided the lyrics for the Suffragettes' battle hymn, 'The March of the Women', with the music by the noted composer Ethel Smyth. Finding the Pankhursts too autocratic, she joined the rival Women's Freedom League and, changing her surname to Hamilton, became an actress and a prolific author of plays and novels as well as acting as press secretary for the International Suffrage Conference in Geneva in 1919. During the war she served as an administrator with the Scottish women's ambulance unit outside Paris.

Charles seems to have endured a miserable and disjointed childhood. By the time he arrived at Bloxham School in September 1891, his mother had long disappeared, being absent from the family home since 1882 when he was two or three years of age. Though the family chose never to talk about this in later years, it is believed that she had been committed to an asylum. His father was frequently away on active service – the battalion he commanded, the Gordon Highlanders, played a leading role in the victory at Tel-el-Kebir in Egypt in September 1882, and he was then engaged in the Sudan campaign. The children were farmed out to foster parents; at the time of the 1881 census the one-year-old Charles was recorded as being in the care of Octavia Huntington and Amelia Coombes, a Foreign Bond Holder and a children's nurse respectively, living in the house of Isabella Style, widow of Baron Style of Avon, at 102 Sydney Place in Bath. Later on, Charles and the other children were boarded in Clapham, a wretched experience according to Cicely's biographer; she was sent to school in Malvern and then studied in Germany, later teaching in the Midlands before becoming an actress, appearing in a string of successful romantic comedies and melodramas.

When he returned from the Sudan, Hammill, now a Major General, took the younger children to Bournemouth to live with his sisters – on Charles' arrival at Bloxham his address was recorded as being 'c/o Miss Hammill, Fairlight Glen, Bournemouth', Fairlight Glen being a boarding house, while by the time he left it was listed as Cumnor Terrace, Bournemouth. Later still the address of Miss A.J. Hammill had changed to Lyall Rd., still in Bournemouth. The Major General's death at the age of 57 on 2 December 1891, three months after Charles had started at boarding school, left him an orphan.

Charles was placed in Form III on his arrival as an eleven-year-old, at a time when classes were based on ability rather than age, so boys could be studying alongside others considerably older or younger. By January 1893, he had progressed to the Upper II Division. By now he was making his name as a sportsman, playing for the 3rd XI in football as a goalkeeper and in cricket as an opening bowler. At the start of the 1895 season, he forced his way into the 1st XI, taking five for 20 in a convincing win against Trinity College, Stratford. The following month the 1st XI travelled to Dean Close, still one of Bloxham's arch-rivals 120 years later, and particulars of their journey makes interesting reading – nowadays the trip to this fixture takes 45 minutes on a coach. In 1895 the team left the school at seven o'clock after an early breakfast and set off from the station in Bloxham by the 7:20 a.m. train for Cheltenham where they arrived soon after 10:00 a.m. The match began about 11:15 a.m., and Dean Close chose to bat first. Charles took three wickets in each innings but Bloxham lost by 14 runs, the game being decided on the first innings.

In our first clue as to a possible strain of unreliability in Charles' character, *The Bloxhamist* lamented his inconsistency as a bowler: 'A curious feature of the cricket has been the strange inequality displayed in the bowling of Hammill, who at times seemed utterly unplayable by our opponents, whilst at other times he was hit all over the field.' This might seem a harsh judgement, as *The Bloxhamist* also adjudged him 'the best bowler in the team', and he did take six for 22 in the first innings against Heyford Cricket Club and five for 14 in the second while against Lord North's XI, one of several country house games then on the school's fixture list, he had figures of six for 32. At the end of the 1895 season the school magazine reported of him that he 'tried to bowl too fast at the beginning of the season, but afterwards bowled slower, with great effect on occasions.'

Charles was now approaching his sixteenth birthday, and it was to be expected that he would be a leading figure in the school, especially in its sports teams, for the following two years, but instead it was announced in *The Bloxhamist* that he had left hurriedly – 'having found an opening in Canada, (he) has suddenly left us and gone out there.' Many Bloxhamists of the time went out to Canada to farm, and this may have been the case for Charles, but we can only speculate. We know that by 1916 he was in Australia, but we know little of the time between school and war. To add to the confusion, Charles Wilson wrote on his record card below the Canada entry that he had 'gone out to New Zealand'.

When the war broke out Charles was living in Stewart Street in Leichhardt, a suburb of Sydney, and his occupation was listed as 'labourer'. There is some confusion over whether he was married or, as the embarkation roll suggests, single. He enlisted into the Australian Army (4th Australian Infantry Battalion) on 16 April 1916. He had actually tried to enlist previously, but his application had been refused on the grounds of being 'morally unfit' and also due to his extensive and seemingly untreatable collection of sexually transmitted diseases. His medical examination recorded that he was suffering from skin cancer on his right leg and had a substantial tattoo of a decapitated woman on his right arm – one wonders what his suffragette sister Cicely would have made of that.

Charles left Sydney on HMAT *Euripides* on 9 September 1916 and arrived in England in November 1916, where he promptly went absent without leave. He was detained by the Military Police in Swanage and was subsequently punished by the military authorities. Further disciplinary issues followed, mainly involving his frequent and excessive alcohol consumption. He was in and out of hospital before progressing to France, when he was severely wounded in May 1917 at the Battle of Bullecourt. He spent some time in hospital and appears to have developed problems with his right wrist, caused by a gunshot wound. Further surgery followed and he finally rejoined his unit in November 1917.

He was once again in hospital in June 1918 and had surgery to remove his tonsils, before finally rejoining his unit on 3 August, just in time for the great Allied push which would take them to victory. By now the Australians under Monash were regarded as something of a vanguard element in the British army. The 4th Battalion of the AIF played a vital part in the advance on Hargicourt on 18 September 1918. The 6,800 Australian infantry, machine gunners and trench-mortar men engaged that day captured their objective, breached the outer defences of the Hindenburg Line and took 4,300 German prisoners and 76 guns at a cost of 1,260 casualties to themselves. The British commander General Rawlinson reported to Haig that after this attack the Germans would no longer stand to face the Australians.

Sadly, Charles Hammill was killed during the day's fighting near Hargicourt and is buried in nearby Roisel Communal Cemetery. The day he died was his 39th birthday. According to the CWGC, he left behind him a widow, Mary D. Hammill, whose address is listed as Laburnum Cottage, West St., Chickerell, Weymouth in Dorset, but it is not known when they were married. It was she who chose the inscription for his headstone ('I thank my God for every remembrance of thee') and who paid the 10s 6d for its cost.

Private Leonard William Campbell Burton
Royal Air Force
Pupil at Bloxham School 1914-1916
Died 22 October 1918, aged 17
Buried in Hither Green Cemetery, Lewisham, England

Leonard Burton is one of those of the 80 of whom we know the least, even though, uniquely, a family member, Paul Burton, was a pupil at Bloxham (in Crake House) in living memory. Sadly, he and his family were unable to provide any information about their ancestor. The fact that the date underneath his photograph on the original board was wildly inaccurate (27 September 1916, more than two years out) made researching his story even more complicated.

Leonard William Campbell Burton, son of Mrs C.M.C. Burton, was born on 8 December 1900, which makes him the youngest of the 80 when he died. He was a pupil at Bloxham between April 1914 and March 1916 and was a member of Form IV. He joined the school's OTC in May 1914; he was a member of No. 2 Section, which was commanded by Sergeant Kingsley Fradd. We know little about what happened after he left school in March 1916 other than that he applied to become a pilot cadet in the Royal Flying Corps. Private 298895 Leonard Burton 2nd class of the RAF Recruits Training Wing, joined Flying School Number 3 at Blandford Camp in Dorset.

At the Cadet Wing pupils received basic military training during a two-month course which included drill, physical training, military law and map-reading. Once completed they moved on to the School of Military Aeronautics to begin a two-month course of military training and ground instruction. The topics covered included aviation theory, navigation, map reading, wireless signaling using Morse code, photography and artillery and infantry co-operation. The students were also taught the working of aero engines and instruments and basic rigging.

The next phase involved flying at a Training Depot Station (TDS). Cadets were expected to complete a minimum of 25 hours elementary flying training - both dual and solo - on Avro 504 aircraft logged over three months. Thorough ground instruction was also provided. This achieved, student pilots received the grade 'A'. Cadets remained at the same TDS for the second phase of their instruction. This two-month course included a further 35 hours flying time with a minimum of five hours on a modern 'front-line' type of aircraft. Student pilots also had to demonstrate proficiency in cross-country and formation flying, reconnaissance work and gunnery. Successful cadets were graded 'B' and commissioned.

Sadly, Leonard Burton never made it through the training programme. He died of influenza at Blandford Camp on 22 October 1918, one more victim of the pandemic which was now sweeping through the British population. According to the school's Roll of Honour, he died after being nursed by his mother 'who herself died before the letter reached us which she had written concerning her son's death'. His demise was not reported in *The Bloxhamist* but he is on the school's war memorial and on the Roll of Honour, and a photograph was provided to the school. He is buried in the enormous Hither Green Cemetery in Lewisham.

Private Robert Craig Murray Nisbet
A Squadron, 7th (Queen's Own) Hussars
Pupil at Bloxham School 1912-1914
Killed in action 28 October 1918, aged 20
Commemorated on the Basra Memorial, Iraq
Panel 4

Robert Nisbet was the penultimate Bloxhamist to die in action in the Great War, and the last of 12 who died fighting the Turks. He was the son of Robert Craig Nisbet and Joan Murray Nisbet and lived in Lower Haddon, Bampton, about five miles south-west of Witney in Oxfordshire. The family were originally from Lothian in Scotland, where Robert was born on 7 June 1898.

He was a pupil at the school between September 1912 and April 1914. He joined Form IVA and was confirmed in March 1913. He joined the OTC on 14 October 1912 and was a member of No. 1 Section, commanded by Arthur Stevens. He attended the annual camp at Rugeley, Staffordshire from 29 July to 7 August 1913, and at the start of 1914 he was transferred to No. 2 Section, commanded by Kingsley Fradd; both Fradd and Stevens were to perish in the Battle of the Somme in 1916. Other than that, we know little about Robert Nisbet's school career or what he did after leaving Bloxham at the age of 15. We do know that he eventually enlisted into the 7th (Queen's Own) Hussars, which was Douglas Haig's old regiment.

The 7th Hussars landed in Mesopotamia as part of the 11th Indian Cavalry Brigade in November 1917 and took part in the advance along the Euphrates to victory in the final months of the war. By the summer Mesopotamia had become a sideshow, and the British commander in the theatre, General Sir William Marshall, was ordered to release troops for Palestine and Persia. However, the opening of armistice negotiations between the Allies and the Ottoman

Empire in October persuaded the War Office to inform Marshall that 'every effort was to be made to score as heavily as possible on the Tigris before the whistle blew.' The battle of Sharqat, launched against Ismail Hakki Bey's Sixth Army, was to be the final engagement of the Mesopotamian campaign.

At 08:00 a.m. on 28 October the 7th Hussars left the army's main position and crossed the Wadi Muabbah to attack the left of the enemy's infantry. By dismounted action the Hussars drove the Turks back for more than a mile with considerable loss. At that point Turkish cavalry appeared on the Hussars' right flank and it was decided to fall back, during which 30 casualties were sustained. At around 12:30 p.m. the regiment took up a new position covering their guns, and they remained there until dusk, suffering a further 40 casualties, mostly from shrapnel fire, as well as a large number of horses, some of which were hit by shrapnel and others which bolted as shells burst among them. It was at this point that Robert Nisbet was killed, one of 14 fatalities (3 officers and 11 men) in the regiment over the previous two days. Having suffered a total of 70 casualties, the regiment was moved to the rear and remained in reserve for the next two days, while the Turkish resistance collapsed. Ismail Hakkı Bey surrendered on 30 October and an armistice between the Ottoman Empire and the Allies came into force that day.

When the 7th Hussars entered Mosul on 3 November, only 290 men remained of the 514 who had left summer camp a month earlier. Robert was not one of them. He was 20 years old when he died. His squadron commander wrote to Robert's parents, informing them that 'my estimation of your son was of the very highest. He was a most excellent soldier in every way, and always ready to volunteer for anything.' Another officer wrote 'Your son was killed by a shell instantaneously, during an action which was one of the most brilliant cavalry exploits in this country. The endurance and personal courage demanded of each man was very large, and no one came through this test better than your son, who was killed during the afternoon.' He concluded by expressing the hope that 'you will find consolation in the fact that he more than helped us to our great victory'.

Robert's parents were informed that 'We buried him in the evening, below the ridge on which he was killed with others of his comrades', but it would seem that his grave was subsequently lost, unsurprising given the circumstances of the advance to Mosul, and he is remembered on the Basra Memorial and the war memorial in the village of Bampton as well as that of Bloxham School. Robert's parents were present in the school chapel to see the unveiling on All Saints' Day 1921.

Captain Philip Francis Davy MC
13th Battalion, Rifle Brigade
Pupil at Bloxham School 1906-1911
Killed in action 4 November 1918, aged 24
Buried in Ghissignies British Cemetery, France
Grave B.26

Philip Davy was born on 23 February 1894 in Islington, London, the son of William and Ada Davy. William's profession was listed as being a stock jobber. By the time Philip arrived at Bloxham School his mother, a widow, was living at 24 Shelley Road, Hove in Sussex. Five of the eleven new boys who started at Bloxham in January 1906 would perish in the war, making this the most grievously affected cohort. Philip joined Form II, winning a Mathematics prize

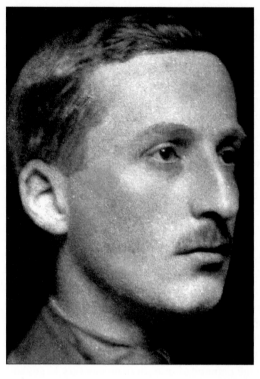

at the end of the school year. *The Bloxhamist* reported of his cricket that 'Davy is distinctly promising and is moreover very keen.' A year later it was reporting of the junior division that 'Davy is by far the best bowler, but he will have to bowl with more care if he wants to last and improve.' He only forced his way into a school team, the 2nd XI, in June 1909, taking a wicket in his third over in a draw against St Edward's, Oxford. Overall, though, *The Bloxhamist* was of the opinion that 'Davy scarcely fulfilled the promise given last season.' He was still in the 2nd XI a year later, taking 5-12 as Abingdon School were dismissed for 40.

Philip's greatest achievement at school was probably in the field of drama. He appeared as a schoolgirl in the three-act play staged by the school in July 1908. *On 'Change*, billed as 'A Farcical Comedy by Herr G. von Moser' was typically undemanding fare, but Philip earned *The Bloxhamist's* praise: 'P. Davy as Iris was distinctly lady-like; he looked well and walked well, and his voice was very good. He had a somewhat difficult part for a boy to play, and he performed it with the greatest credit to himself.' He was then part of a cast of five which presented the play *A Silent System* for charity at Chipping Norton in November of the same year.

The following year he once more played a female role in another long-forgotten comedy, *The Upper Crust* by Henry Byron. The school magazine decided that 'of the female characters, we should most decidedly assign the palm for natural action and good enunciation to P. Davy (Norah Doublechick), who had the advantage of possessing a less masculine voice than the others.'

A Silent System was presented as the school play in November 1910. This was a one-act farce with a cast of only six and had already been presented a year before, and it was recognised that this was a much less ambitious venture than in previous years, thanks to the effort the school had already gone to in July for the school's 50th jubilee. Yet again Philip had a female role, playing Mrs Wideawake, the wife of the character played by Mr Attwood, the energetic member of staff who directed the play. *The Bloxhamist* judged that Philip was once more the most convincing of the female characters, although the comment that 'his voice had rather a masculine ring' shows how the 16-year-old was growing up fast.

He was made a prefect and promoted to Form V at the start of the 1910-11 school year. In his final year he served as a Lance Corporal in the school's newly formed OTC. He left the school in April 1911, and like so many Bloxhamists of his generation, headed to Canada. He arrived in British Columbia, where he worked on a fruit and sheep farm at Metchosin, about 17 miles from Victoria, where, according to *The Bloxhamist* in October 1911, 'he seems to find plenty of work to do.'

He enlisted as a private in the 7th Battalion, Canadian Expeditionary Force at the start of the war and immediately served overseas. He was wounded for the first of three times at the Battle of Festubert in May 1915, where a gunshot wound amputated a finger from his left hand and he also suffered an ankle injury. On recovery, he was deemed fit for continued service and was returned to the front line, being sent to the 30th Reserve Battalion of the CEF. He saw action through the Somme campaign, having been commissioned into the Rifle Brigade. He was wounded for a second time on 29 July 1917 and was then gassed on 6 October 1917. He was awarded the Military Cross in 1917, and on 5 April 1918 received the Croix de Guerre from the French; on the same day, he was made a Chevalier de l'Ordre de la Couronne by the Belgian government. The citation for his Military Cross reads as follows:

> For conspicuous gallantry and devotion to duty while in command of a company. When two of his officers had become casualties he went forward and took charge of the attack. He returned, and four times guided up carrying parties to the front line. He personally visited the advanced posts and gave them the order to withdraw. By his coolness and utter disregard of danger, he set a magnificent example to all ranks.

Philip was promoted to Captain in August 1918, and in November he found himself in action once again, as the Allies made their final push to end the war. On the morning of 4 November, the 13th Rifle Brigade went into action, to drive the Germans out of the small French village of Caudry. As the 13th RB crossed an apple orchard, Philip's luck finally ran out. A burst of machine gun fire rang out and he was shot through the chest, dying where he fell.

Just seven days later the bells rang out to mark the Armistice. It seems terribly sad that a man who served through the whole war should die so cruelly close to the end (the same day that the poet Wilfred Owen died). Like Mrs Owen, Philip's mother, who had by now remarried and was living near Guildford, received the telegram informing her of her son's death on the day that the war ended, when all around her were celebrating the Armistice. He was the final Bloxhamist to die in combat in the Great War, having also been one of the first to enlist. He was 24 years old when he died and is buried in Ghissignies British Cemetery alongside 67 other British soldiers, most of them riflemen, killed that day. Originally he was buried in Louvignies British Cemetery, which was made by the 13th Rifle Brigade in November 1918, but his was one of 26 bodies exhumed and moved to Ghissignies in April 1921 as part of a process of concentrating burials in a reduced number of cemeteries.

The Reverend William David Abbott
Army Chaplain's Department
Master at Bloxham School 1907-1908
Died 3 December 1918, aged 34
Buried in Janval Cemetery, Dieppe
Grave II.A.1

Although the fighting on the Western Front ceased on 11 November, there was no end to the loss of life among troops on both sides. The influenza pandemic which ravaged civilian

and army populations alike from January 1918 onwards, took a heavy toll among troops whose immune systems were already weakened by malnourishment, fatigue and combat stress. The overcrowded and insanitary conditions on the Western Front served to increase the threat. The death of the Rev. William Abbott while conducting the burial of soldiers presents a good opportunity to be reminded of the vital work played by the Army Chaplains' Department.

Chaplains were the only British Army officers who did not carry standard officer ranks, although they did have grades which equated to the standard ranks, and they wore the insignia of the equivalent rank. They were officially designated Chaplain to the Forces (CF) (e.g. 'The Reverend John Smith CF'). Chaplains were always addressed as 'Padre', never by their nominal military rank. The grades went from Chaplain General (Major General) and Deputy Chaplain-General (Brigadier General) to Chaplain to the Forces 1st Class (Colonel), 2nd Class (Lieutenant Colonel), 3rd Class (Major) and 4th Class (Captain). The latter was the Rev. William Abbott's grade.

William David Abbott was born on 22 July 1885 to the Reverend David Wyley Abbott and Mrs Mary Abbott in Kirmington, Lincolnshire. When William was three the family moved to Cherry Wilmington where his father was vicar, and then to Knowbury in Shropshire. William was a pupil at Christ College, Brecon between 1896 and 1901, with a short, unexplained gap between 1898-99. He did well academically, earning the Under 12 John Morgan Exhibition worth £10 a year, a valuable award for a family on a parish priest's income. William was a keen performer at school, appearing in Gilbert and Sullivan's *The Sorcerer* in 1898 and singing the popular and, for William, highly appropriate satirical song *The Vicar of Bray* at a musical evening in the Autumn Term 1900. He played for the 1st XI at hockey and cricket, earning praise for his bowling, 'with a tricky slow ball', according to the *Breconian* magazine. It did, though, note that he was a poor fielder 'owing to shortness of sight', which is confirmed by the spectacles he wears in his photograph in uniform.

On leaving Christ College in July 1901, William Abbott went on to University College, Nottingham, where he played cricket for their 1st XI, as well as playing the kettledrums for the orchestral society. Armed with a degree he entered the teaching profession and arrived at Bloxham in January 1907. *The Bloxhamist* noted that 'he has had some years' experience in teaching, and we are glad to see that he has already taken his place in the football team'. Sure enough, he is listed as playing at half back in the school football, one of several masters who were able to play in 1st XI matches against club sides though not against other schools. In May

1907, he made his debut for the school's cricket 1st XI against Jesus College Oxford, batting at number four (making 0 and 3) and opening the bowling. That season he took 22 wickets, including 4 for 28 in one match and 4 for 13 in another. Abbott continued to play both football and cricket for the school in the following season, and left Bloxham at the end of the summer term in 1908, when *The Bloxhamist* paid tribute to the impact he had made in his five terms at the school:

> Mr. W.D. Abbott has left us; like Mr. Buckwell, he has gone to Lichfield Theological College with a view to being ordained eventually. We are sorry to lose him, and while thanking him for all his work in connection with the School, can assure him that he carries with him our best wishes for his happiness and our prayers for God's blessing on his life and work.

News of his appointment to the curacy of S. John-in-Bedwardine, Worcester followed in 1909 and then his ordination as Priest by the Bishop of Worcester the following year. On 7 October 1909, he married Miss Ruby Williamson, and a year later they had a son, Kenneth David George Abbott, followed two years later by a second, John Williamson Abbott. In 1914 the family moved to St Paul's, Blackheath, and William then became the organising secretary for the Society for Promoting Christian Knowledge in the north-west of England as well as Ireland. This was the oldest Anglican missionary organisation and enabled William to combine his twin vocations of religion and teaching. William and Ruby lived at 75 Mauldeth Road, Withington, Manchester.

William Abbott enlisted in the army on 7 June 1918 as a Chaplain 4th Class and arrived in France on 7 August with the official designation of Clerk Chaplain. In addition to tending to the troops' spiritual needs, one of the most important roles for an Army Chaplain was overseeing the burial of soldiers, and it was while undertaking this grim duty in the unimaginable conditions created by four years of fighting that he caught a chill. He carried on as best he could, but the chill developed into influenza and then bronchopneumonia, from which he died on 3 December 1918. He died at No. 5 British Red Cross Stationary Hospital and was buried in nearby Janval Military Cemetery, Dieppe. The inscription on his headstone reflects his religious faith: Why seek ye the living among the dead?'

His Commanding Officer wrote:

> I have had an exceptional opportunity of learning what he was, what an inspiration he was to all around him; what a tower of strength he was on the side of everything manly and clean. He was one of the bravest men in moral courage I have ever met......he was loved by all ranks, and his influence was unbounded; he was so human and so straight. His loss to us here is a calamity.... the good he did and his inspiring personality will leave their mark till we all get home.

William Abbott's death on 3 December 1918 meant that the first and last Bloxhamists to die on the Western Front were both masters rather than pupils at the school. He is commemorated on the Memorial of the Royal Army Chaplains' Department in the Royal Garrison Church of All Saints', Aldershot. His is the first of 172 names on the memorial there, as it is on the war memorials at Bloxham and his old school, Christ College, Brecon.

1920

Able Seaman Eustace Bishop Cree
Royal Naval Volunteer Reserve
Pupil at Bloxham School 1899-1903
Died 12 March 1920, aged 32
Buried in Bognor Regis Cemetery, England

For the purposes of the Imperial War Graves Commission (now the Commonwealth War Graves Commission), the First World War is considered to have lasted from 4 August 1914 to 31 August 1921, the official end of the war. This date reflects the fact that the fighting did not stop on 11 November 1918 (for example, it continued in Russia as part of their Civil War), and nor did the dying, as shown by the case of Eustace Cree. His name is not included on the CWGC records and his grave does not have a CWGC headstone, but the school took the decision at the time that he should be included on the war memorial in chapel and so he is included as one of the 80, and the last of them.

Eustace Bishop Cree was born on 22 July 1887 at 12 Nevern Square, Kensington. Apparently, he was born in the same four-poster bed as his father had been, and the same one in which his own son would be born in his turn. Eustace's father, Charles Edward Cree, was born on 25 March 1850, the son of Thomas Cree (the younger) and Maria Bishop Walker. Charles was known as Stansfield Charles Edward Cree – the Stansfield came from his aunt Elizabeth Stansfield, wife of his uncle Thomas George Cree. There was a strong family tradition of careers in the law - Charles was a barrister, while both his father and grandfather had been solicitors.

There also seems to have been a strong family connection with the sea, despite the family home being in fashionable and decidedly land-locked Kensington. Charles was a founder member of the Royal Cruising Club, and Eustace's eldest brother Donald later served as its secretary. The family owned the sixty-foot yawl *Gulnare* for more than seventy years – a pleasure sailing vessel, *Gulnare* was named after a rock in western Scotland. When the 1911 census was conducted on 2 April, Charles was living aboard the vessel, moored at Rochester in Kent, along with Donald; they described themselves in the census as 'part owner and crew.' The long family association with the boat only ended when she was sold in 1962. Charles Cree died in May 1920, two months after his youngest son's death.

Before he reached his second birthday, Eustace had to cope with the death of his mother, Clara Zillah Cree (née Holt), who died in May 1889. Eustace had three older brothers, Donald (born 1879, a barrister like his father), Lionel (born 1880) and Wilfred (born 1884, a Commander in the Royal Navy), and one sister, Marjorie.

Eustace arrived at Bloxham as a new boy in September 1899 and was promoted to Form IV after a term. His greatest impact in his four years at the school came in the field of music. *The Bloxhamist* reported of the duet (*O Beautiful Violet*) which he sang in a school concert in March 1900 that 'C. Boissier and E. Cree deserve a word of praise for the way in which they rendered their duet, which was quite a success.' He also sang in the chapel choir, *The Bloxhamist* noting in its report of the Easter Day Service in April 1900 'the solo being sung exceedingly well by E. Cree.' Over the next few years he was ever-present at school concerts, singing *Oh! Oh! Hear the wild wind blow*, and a duet, once again with Boissier, *The Flight of the Swallow*, in August 1900. By now he was also performing solos on the piano, from Gounod's *Marche Romaine* in February 1901 to Schubert's ballet music from *Rosamunde* in July 1903. By now his voice had broken and he was an alto, a fact recorded in the choir report in *The Bloxhamist* for July 1901.

Eustace was also a member of the Camera Club, an extremely active and enthusiastically pursued activity at the school. Class promotions continued – from Form IV to Form V in September 1901, and then to the Sixth Form in his final year.

Eustace's forte was not in the sporting arena, though he seems to have had an unsuspected talent for cross-country running. *The Bloxhamist* reported that 'E. Cree created a surprise by coming in first' in the Junior Steeplechase for 1902. He also played football as a forward for Dormitory V, and his team won the final in December 1902 when they scored the winning goal in extra time. He played for the 2nd XI at football, for example in a 3-1 defeat at Abingdon School in October 1903, but his selection was probably not such an accolade as it might seem at a time when numbers in the school had dropped to barely one hundred.

By now Eustace was showing talent in areas outside the strictly academic. In July 1902, he was awarded the Drawing Prize, and he repeated the performance the following year. He was also a keen member of the school's Debating Society. Though he seems to have been an infrequent speaker, he was elected secretary of the society in November 1903, defeating his rival by seven votes to six. He was caught up in some of the great issues of the day, voting against a motion in April 1903 which held that 'the abolition of the House of Lords would benefit the legislation of this country', and delivered a rare speech in December of that year when he spoke in a debate attended by a 'vast crowd' on the motion 'Woman is Man's Intellectual Equal, and ought to be granted equal privileges with him.' He supported the motion in terms which will appear excruciatingly condescending to modern readers but which were relatively enlightened for their day (sadly, the result of this debate is not recorded):

> The Hon. Sec. (EB Cree) then rose to support the ladies, who may always be sure of finding a chivalrous and zealous upholder in this gallant gentleman. He showed how ladies were distinguishing themselves in science, bringing forward Madame Curie as an example. He also pointed out the magnificent administrative genius of Queens Elizabeth and Victoria. In the field of literature he mentioned the ever famous names of Mesdames de Stael and Ouida. With regard to women enjoying equal privileges with men, he said that up till now, as a general rule, women had been too light-headed and frivolous to support any heavy mental work, but that with higher education they would be brought to an equal intellectual level with men.

Eustace was also a keen thespian, at a time when the school was just starting to put on full-scale plays, where previously the standard fare had been scenes from Shakespeare. He made his dramatic debut in *Our Boys*, a comedy in two acts by Henry Byron which had run for four years in London and was the world's longest-running play until surpassed by *Charley's Aunt* in the 1890s. Two performances were given, a matinee at 3pm and an evening performance at 7:30 p.m., 'both of which were attended by large and appreciative audiences, whose evident enjoyment did much to encourage the actors and make the play the success that it undoubtedly was.' Playing one of the two lead parts in the role of Sir Geoffrey Champneys, it was recorded of Eustace that he 'hit off the character of the proud and important county magnate with great success, and showed considerable resource. His frigid and aristocratic demeanour contrasted well with that of the impulsive and plebeian Middlewick' (played by one of the masters, Mr Attwood). Another master, Walter Heath, who acted as stage manager for the play, was later killed on the Somme in August 1916.

Having passed the Oxford Local Examinations in July 1903, Eustace spent one more term at the school; his ascent to the top ranks of the Sixth Form was confirmed by his election to the prestigious Committee of Games in September as well as his appointment as a prefect.

Eustace left the school at the end of the Michaelmas Term in 1903. Little is known about him after school except that he studied engineering and married Ruby Harrison Ainsworth in Wandsworth in November 1910. He was recorded in the 1911 census as living in the family home in Nevern Square with his wife Ruby, being listed as an engineer and a manufacturer's agent. The couple had two servants living in. Eustace and Ruby went on to have two children, Charles Eustace Audley Cree DSC RN (born 30 August 1911, died 4 July 2009) and Hermione Clara Cree (born 2 September 1914, died 26 December 1947). Charles emulated his uncle Wilfred in pursuing a naval career and reaching the rank of Commander, commanding HMS Birmingham between 1951 and 1953 and serving as Naval Advisor to the British High Commission in Australia between 1953 and 1957. He ultimately emigrated to Australia in 1958 with his wife and two children, and died there in 2009, having served as an intelligence officer with the Australian Defence Department in Sydney between 1958 and 1976.

When war came, Eustace enlisted in the Royal Naval Volunteer Reserve, maintaining his family's nautical connection. Joining up on 8 October 1914, he served with service number AA193 in a Searchlight battery. These units operated anti-aircraft guns from the tops of key buildings in Whitehall and at the Thames docks, as well as near key facilities such as the Woolwich Arsenal. They used acetylene-lit searchlights to light up the Zeppelin airships flying over London. However, he is recorded as having resigned on 25 January 1915 due to 'ill health'.

His cause of discharge from the military was 'severe burns to the respiratory tract following inhalation of smoke and fire - 20th March 1915'. The death certificate from March 1920 states that he had suffered from this condition for almost five years. It also reveals that he died from pulmonary phthisis (or tuberculosis). It is unclear if the effects of smoke and fire were related to an air raid, and there are no records of any air raids on London during this time. There is a tantalising message in his papers relating to his discharge – 'for full details please see attached medical report' – but sadly the report is missing!

After his death on 12 March 1920 at the age of 32, Eustace's name was added to the school's Roll of Honour and, ultimately, to the War Memorial in chapel. He is not included in the CWGC's records and so does not lie in a war grave, and as he did not die on active service it could be argued that he should not be on the school memorial but given his inclusion at the time it would clearly be wrong to remove his name now. His death was recorded in the parish of Westhampnett in West Sussex, and he is buried in Bognor Regis Cemetery close to where the Cree family had their boat *Gulnare* moored. Sadly, as of 2020, Cree's headstone is completely illegible and lies horizontally, broken into two pieces.

4

The 80 – A statistical analysis

It should be stated at the outset that 80 individuals is a very small sample on which to base a statistical analysis, so one should be wary of coming to very definite conclusions based on the following figures. Statistics on their own conceal complex individual stories. Several of the 80 started in the ranks before being commissioned as officers and many changed units as the war went on. Some started in one branch of the services before moving into another. For the purposes of this analysis, the rank and unit are taken as those at the moment of death.

	no.	%
Pupil	75	93.75
Master	4	5.00
School servant	1	1.25

AGE

Unsurprisingly, most of those who died were young men. The youngest, Leonard Burton, was just 17 years old and the oldest, Cyril Jackson, a senior officer with a long career behind him, was 47. Every age between 17 and 40 is represented among the 80 except for 27 and 31. Between them, 20-, 21- and 22- year-olds accounted for a third of all the deaths.

	no.	%
17-19	18	22.5
20-25	28	35.0
26-30	5	6.25
30-35	11	13.75
35-40	12	15.0
41-45	5	6.25
46-50	1	1.25

RANK

The vast majority of former public school pupils served as officers in the Great War; only 3 percent of Etonians and Harrovians served in the ranks. This figure could be considerably higher depending on the school, for example 50 percent of old boys of Monmouth School did not hold commissions. For Bloxham School, the figure was 30 percent (of the names in the Roll of Honour whose rank can be ascertained, 266 (69.8 percent) were officers and 115 (30.2 percent) 'other ranks'.

Of the 80 Bloxhamists who died, just under two thirds (63.75 percent) were officers and slightly more than a third (36.25 percent) served in the ranks. However, if we examine the figures for those Bloxhamists who joined the newly formed OTC between December 1910 and the outbreak of war, the proportion of officers is a great deal higher (80 percent of the total of 95), which would appear to confirm that the OTC was doing precisely the job that it set out to do and that its name implied. It should also be remembered that of the 51 Bloxhamists who were officers when they died, 13 of them had started in the ranks before being commissioned. Once again, this was much less likely to be the case for those who had been members of the OTC.

	no.	%
Private (or equivalent)	26	32.50
Corporal/Lance Corporal	2	2.50
Sergeant/Sergeant Major etc.	1	1.25
Second Lieutenant	22	27.50
Lieutenant	12	15.00
Captain	9	11.25
Major	6	7.50
Lieutenant Colonel/Colonel	1	1.25
Brigadier General	1	1.25

DATE

The 40th Bloxhamist to die, marking the statistical half-way point, was Thomas Thomas, killed on the Somme in November 1916. That year was the most costly of the war for Bloxham School, with 28 deaths. Some schools, those with a military tradition and a strong presence in the pre-war Regular Army, for example Eton, Wellington and Cheltenham, experienced heavy losses in the opening months of the war. Eton had already suffered the majority of its deaths by the end of 1915 and its worst day of the war was 14 September 1914, with 20 OEs lost on the Aisne, where the Guards regiments suffered terrible casualties. For others, the Battle of the Somme, with its heavy toll on men from Kitchener's New Armies, witnessed their heaviest losses of the war, as was the case for Bloxham, with 18 of them lost in a single five-month battle. Another factor which could account for marked variations between schools could be the involvement of a local regiment in a particularly costly engagement, such as 30 June 1916 for the Sussex Regiment or 16 May 1915 for the 2nd Inniskillings. For comparison, Magdalen College

School Oxford, which was a similar size to Bloxham, suffered 18 percent of its deaths in 1915, 24 percent in 1916, 34 percent in 1917 and 18 percent in 1918.

	no.	%
1914	1	1.25
1915	13	16.25
1916	28	35.00
1917	19	23.75
1918	18	22.50
1920	1	1.25

LOCATION

These figures need careful handling, as three (Ayres, Holmes and Harold Robinson) who died of wounds at home (in the United Kingdom) are shown under 'Western Front', where they sustained those wounds. Samson, Cree, Burton and Marshall all died at home from illness. Whiting is shown as having died at sea, having been killed, probably on shore, while commanding a patrol boat in Whitby Bay. Of the Western Front deaths, the greatest number, 20, occurred in the Somme sector, with other sizeable numbers around Ypres and Arras, a pattern which holds true for the British Army as a whole. For other fronts, four were in Mesopotamia, two in Palestine, and one each in the Sinai, Aden and East Africa.

	no.	%
Western Front	56	70.0
Dardanelles	4	5.0
Other fronts	9	11.25
At sea	4	5.0
In the air	3	3.75
At home	4	5.0

FORCES

Reflecting the growth of the aerial arm over the course of the war, two of the three deaths in the air (both in training rather than combat) came in the final months of the war. Two of the four naval deaths happened on the same day, at Jutland. The vast majority were in the Army.

Twelve of the 80 served in armies other than the British (though the distinction is a problematic one given that some of them transferred or were seconded at some point, and all were British subjects). Of the twelve, five served in the Canadian forces, two in the Australian, one in the Indian Army and one each in the South African and New Zealand forces, the Malay States Guides and the King's African Rifles.

	no.	%
Army	73	91.25
Navy	4	5.0
RFC/RAF	3	3.75

COMPARISON

80 Bloxhamists died in the Great War, a small number when compared with the vast losses suffered by the likes of Eton and Wellington but a very comparable scale of loss when taking into account the small size of the school in 1914. The percentage of those who died compared to those who served (19.9 percent) is very close to the figure for most of the public schools, that is, approximately 20 percent. The table below compares Bloxham with 14 other schools, some but not all of them its competitors and some a similar size, but most more prestigious and a great deal larger. The table is revealing for two main features, firstly that as a very rough rule of thumb, the number each school lost was usually very close to the size of the school at the start of the war, and secondly that the rate of loss for all these schools, very different from each other in so many ways, was very similar, i.e. roughly a fifth. This compares with a figure of 12 percent for the general population, a disparity usually explained in terms of the much higher proportion of officers among the old boys of public schools, and the greater rate of loss among officers, especially junior officers. This was an important factor, but the truth is rather more complex and nuanced.

School	Number of pupils killed	Number of pupils in 1914	Number of pupils who served	% killed
Abingdon	68	111	369	18.4
Bloxham	80	84	402	19.9
Cheltenham	675	584	3,540	19.1
Clifton	577	594	3,063	18.8
Eton	1,157	1,028	5,656	20.5
Harrow	644	504	2,917	22.1
Magdalen CS Oxford	50	64	231	21.9
Marlborough	733	590	3,418	21.4
Radley	225	213	1,165	19.3
Rugby	686	555	3,244	21.1
St Edward's, Oxford	114	132	520	21.9
Uppingham	451	450	2,500	18.0
Warwick	88	200	410	21.5
Wellington	707	526	3,500	20.2

Numbers taken from A. Seldon and D. Walsh, *Public Schools and the Great War* (2014)

5

Remembrance

Discussion of the most fitting way in which to commemorate those Bloxhamists to have lost their lives began while the war was still being fought. Bloxham experienced the same debate that took place in schools across the Empire as to how to spend the money raised to commemorate those killed. There was often a divergence of opinion between younger Old Boys, many of whom had served and now wanted to put the war behind them, and older ones who were keen to see memorials to commemorate the fallen. Headmasters, meanwhile, were anxious to have some of the money spent on buildings which would benefit future generations; many schools, Bloxham among them, were in dire need of new facilities and this seemed an ideal opportunity to procure them. Another point of contention centred on the question of whether any memorial should be sacred or secular in nature.

As elsewhere, especially at other Woodard schools, the school chapel was the focus of proposals for commemoration at Bloxham. The idea for a memorial in chapel was first raised in March 1916, with the Chaplain, Hugh Willimott, suggesting that, in addition to any tablet or plaque the school council should decide to erect, 'a really good Processional Cross' would be a suitable memorial, indicating 'victory through suffering'. He proposed a silver cross with a total cost of approximately £75 and hoped that donations would be forthcoming from parents and Old Bloxhamists. As at many schools, for example Winchester and Marlborough, there was a heated argument between proponents of the different proposals, and as with Marlborough, the controversy was played out publicly through the correspondence pages of the school magazine.

By July 1916 an illustration of the proposed cross had been published and the first donations had been made, with the Headmaster leading the way with a donation of £1 10s. By October, when the number of the fallen had grown substantially thanks to the fighting on the Somme, a total of £15 2s 6d had been raised including sizeable contributions from Gordon Peecock's mother and 'In Memoriam K.M.C.F.' (Kingsley Fradd). By December the figure had risen to £28 1s 10d, with donations from the Board, Potter, Long, Smith, Guest and Harris families, and the scheme now included, in addition to the processional cross, an album containing photographs of the fallen.

There was a steady stream of donations throughout 1917, each listed in successive *Bloxhamists*, with a big jump in donations (a further 144) between March and July. The total was now £95 1s 10d. It was at this point that an unseemly and very public row developed, played out in the pages of *The Bloxhamist*. F.B. Palmer, owner of *The Church Times* and the Old Bloxhamist representative on the School Committee (the Council of Governors), wrote to say that excellent though Willimott's proposal was, it had not been considered either by the Committee or by the Old Bloxhamists, and he had reason to know 'that it does not commend itself to some of us as the most suitable memorial for the purpose'. Palmer went on to express the hope that the school would raise enough money to erect 'a memorial that shall be a witness for all time to our gallant dead, and at the same time be of some service to the future of the School of which we have now more reason than ever to be proud'. By this he meant the Governors' plans for development, for example the long-awaited swimming pool. The Chaplain, who was also the editor of *The Bloxhamist*, was clearly angered, responding that the processional cross was not intended to be the only form of memorial and pointing out that 'not one word of disapproval reached me from any quarter and no alternative proposal was made by anyone'. He added that it had originally been suggested that the fund might be sufficiently large to cover the cost of the education at Bloxham of the son of any Old Bloxhamist who had been killed or suffered loss in the war, but that this proposal had met with little support.

The processional cross, made by Keith & Co. and costing £105, was blessed on 23 July 1917, the day the school observed as Founder's Day. The very next issue of *The Bloxhamist*, in December 1917, brought news of the memorial fund reaching £110 3s 4d as well as of the Chaplain's departure from Bloxham. The new editor expressed the hope that 'soon steps will be taken to put in hand a suitable scheme for a memorial to those who have fallen in the war'. Given that he noted that although a memorial had already been given, 'we feel that perhaps another kind would meet with a wider support', it is hard not to see Willimott's departure as being linked to the row over the memorial. He would return in 1926 for a third spell as Chaplain before a disagreement with a new Headmaster brought about his resignation once more the following year.

In July 1918 the Headmaster called an informal meeting of Old Bloxhamists to consider the vexed question of a war memorial. Those present included Palmer as well as Douglas Cain, to represent the younger Old Boys, and the architect Leonard Shuffrey from the older generation. As a result of the meeting it was proposed that the names of those Old Bloxhamists who had fallen in the war should be engraved on oak panels and a place for the processional cross made in the middle. In addition, the idea of a scholarship fund for the sons of Old Bloxhamists who had fallen was resurrected. A committee was convened, with Colonel Henry May of the Artists' Rifles (*28th* County of *London Battalion, London Regiment)* as its chairman, to organise a fresh appeal for funds.

The Bloxhamist for July 1919, the first after the ending of the war, reported that the appeal for the war memorial had not raised as much (£244 14s.) as had been hoped for, though this was 'perhaps as large as could be expected when the great number of these appeals from schools, localities, regiments, professions, and others is taken into account'. It was hoped that the bulk of the money raised would be kept for the education of the children of the fallen: 'This, it is believed would be the wish of the young men themselves if they were able to decide it.' However, although May announced in 1922 that 'one applicant, who was now seven years old, would wait another seven years and then be educated at Bloxham for three years', there is no evidence that this happened or that any children of fallen Old Bloxhamists were ever educated at the school. As elsewhere, many of those who had fallen were simply too young to have had sons who required such assistance. The closest the school came to educating the son of one of its fallen was Tim Boissier Wyles, a pupil at Bloxham between 1925 and 1929 and eldest child of

William Boissier, son of the former Headmaster but the only one of four brothers who was not an Old Bloxhamist.

Eventually, the memorial fund (not including the money donated for the processional cross) reached £400 and this enabled the committee to proceed with the memorial, designed by Shuffrey, a former President of the Institute of British Decorators who also designed war memorials at Ealing and Witney. Shuffrey's son, Lieutenant Gilbert Leonard Shuffrey of the South Lancashire Regiment, was killed at Gallipoli in August 1915 and is commemorated by the extraordinary reredos Leonard created in oak for St Peter's, Ealing.

His war memorial for his old school was less ornate. It was also made of oak and was composed of a central panel, containing the inscription surmounted by the silver crucifix, and two side panels, containing the 76 names of the fallen. It was unveiled by Colonel May and dedicated by the new Headmaster, Frank George, at a service on All Saints' Day in November 1920. A large congregation included the parents of Frank Bolton, Edgar Mitcalfe, Robert Nisbet, Edward Peecock, Frank Riddle and Herbert Standage. This seems a small proportion of the 76, though *The Bloxhamist* assured its readers that 'others expressed their regret at not being able to be present, but they were with us in mind though not in body.'

Of the total raised by the appeal, £100 had been expended on the memorial in the Chapel. Instead of paying for the education of the sons of fallen Old Bloxhamists, the remainder was put towards a scheme which Valentine Armitage, Headmaster from 1925 to 1940, devised for a memorial gateway at the front of the school. A further £346 was raised by subscription and the gateway, designed by Cotswold architect Thomas Falconer, was unveiled by Lord Saye and Sele on 30 June 1933. Remembrance thus presented the opportunity to provide the school with the fitting entrance that the Founder had always wished for, though it is a safe bet that many recent generations of Old Bloxhamists had little idea that the archway was a war memorial at all.

There were other memorials to the fallen. Colonel May arranged for a Roll of Honour, in which each Bloxhamist's war service was meticulously recorded, to be typed and beautifully bound, and he presented it to the School on All Saints' Day, 1923. Photographs of the 76 were mounted in four boards and hung in the Chapel corridor. Finally, the Old Bloxhamist Society decided in 1927 to spend some of the remaining money in the War Memorial Fund on the purchase of bugles, fifes, and drums for the Officer Training Corps.

The archway became the venue for the most regular and still fondly remembered act of remembrance for the next half-century, the playing each night of the Last Post on one of the OTC bugles. The custom of a school bugler sounding Last Post at 8:30 p.m. in the main quadrangle, which had actually started at the beginning of the war, was now transferred to the memorial gateway in the summer, the Inner Quad in the winter. This moving ceremony is recalled by successive generations of Bloxhamists who sat in silence to listen in their houses. One bugler, John Catton, a pupil between 1946 and 1951, remembered that 'at its best one might stretch the duty to fifteen minutes, thereby missing some rather dreary moments of prep. At its worst, having to face the sly grins from one's peers when the last high note had turned out to be more like something being strangled.'

Apart from the nightly Last Post, the main form of remembrance in the post-war years came on Armistice Day, when the OTC contingent would lead the school up to the village's War Memorial to take part in Bloxham's act of remembrance. This has continued up to this day on Remembrance Sunday. Occasionally the OTC would attend the service at one of the surrounding villages – Bodicote (1934-35), Great Tew (1936-37) or Adderbury (1939). By this stage the main commemoration had been transferred from 11 November to Remembrance Sunday (or, as *The Bloxhamist* for 1940 confusingly called it, 'Armistice Sunday'). Pupils from the 1950s and 1960s do not recall any specific commemoration of the dead of the two World Wars except for the nightly Last Post, and this continued to be the case once the Last Post ended, which seems to have been in the early 1970s, though there was a short-lived attempt to revive it soon afterwards. The nightly ceremony now seemed out of step with society's attitudes to commemoration, though a more prosaic reason it ended might be the demise of the CCF band and the resultant loss of competent buglers.

In the 1960s, a decade which brought a challenge to cherished public school rituals and practices such as CCF and compulsory chapel, it became fashionable to question the patriotism and sense of duty which had motivated so many of those who joined up to fight in the Great War. Commemoration at Bloxham had reached its nadir by the 1980s, with the removal from public view of the photographs of the fallen and little done beyond the boarders' attendance at the village war memorial on Remembrance Sunday; according to Old Bloxhamists from this period, Armistice Day was not observed at all, mirroring the state of affairs in society as a whole.

By the time of the school's sesquicentenary in 2010 the first steps had been taken to give remembrance a higher profile. A new chaplain, Michael Price, instituted two minutes' silence on Armistice Day and the reading of the Roll of Honour, and this was augmented in 2011 with the introduction of a Garden of Remembrance, with a poppy for each of the 136 pupils killed in war. The next decade would see a remarkable upsurge in the scale of commemoration, with the whole school gathering around the Headmaster's Lawn on Armistice Day for a service which has grown in complexity with the involvement of choir and CCF, but which retains at its heart the sounding of Last Post and Reveille and the reading of the Roll of Honour. The 2020 ceremony, which took place at the time of the COVID-19 pandemic, played a vital part in bringing the whole school community together on Main Field, and its online broadcast left a profound impression among parents and Old Bloxhamists.

Two further events completed the process. A tree planted on the Chapel lawn in memory of the 80 was unveiled on All Saints' Tide in November 2018, and a plaque to commemorate them was placed in St George's, Ypres and dedicated at a poignant service of dedication in March 2019. Why the last decade should have witnessed such a resurgence in commemoration is a complex question to answer. The school's staging of the drama *79* in November 2014 may be one factor. This remarkable production, devised by the Director of Drama Sam Brassington and his cast and featuring 80 actors and musicians, drew on the stories of some of those who fought in the Great War, with relatives of one, Basil Brooks, among the audience. Another contributing factor might be the introduction of regular History Department trips to the Western Front. Others might be the country's observation of the centenary of the Great War and the prominence of the war on History and even English syllabuses (the latter thanks to the war poets). The most likely reason, however, seems to be society's wish to live out a greater sense of remembrance as the 1914-18 generation disappeared, and its need to take part in ceremonies that express community cohesion. These wider factors are reflected in the current popularity of battlefield tourism and genealogical research and epitomised by the huge increase in the nightly attendance at the Last Post ceremony at the Menin Gate in Ypres, where Bloxham's school choir were privileged to sing in April 2015.

If there is one episode which illustrates the changing nature of remembrance over the years, it is that of the photographs of the fallen. The idea of displaying the images of those who had made 'the ultimate sacrifice' began in 1915 with the presentation to the school of a photograph of Frank Riddle by his father, who expressed the hope that it 'should serve to keep bright the memory of one who was a credit to the British Army'. Other families followed suit, and by March 1917 the first set of photographs, 18 in number, had been put into a large frame and were ready to be displayed. Eventually there were four boards in all, costing £3 3s according to the accounts published at the time. Three of the boards contained 18 photographs and the fourth, mostly covering 1917 deaths, contained 21, making a total of 75 photographs, suggesting that even then one was missing. They were flanked by portraits of Field Marshal Haig and Admiral Beatty painted by Old Bloxhamist Albert Chevallier Tayler, the originals of which are to be found in the National Portrait Gallery. The boards were still on display in the Chapel Hall (where the Games notice boards hung for many years) after the Second World War, but were subsequently taken down and stored, apparently at some point in the 1950s or 1960s when commemoration of the Great War was at a lower ebb.

One of the four boards was destroyed in the vestry fire of March 1985, and the remaining three would also have been lost at this point – they had been placed in a skip for disposal – if not for the intervention of Shaw McCloghry, then the school's Archivist. That they were intended to be thrown away seems unthinkable in today's climate but tells us a great deal about attitudes at the time. As well as ensuring the survival of the photographs, Major McCloghry made a new frame in the school workshop for one of the boards. After twenty years when the boards were stored in the Chapel, only to be brought out on Armistice Day each year, the decision was taken in 2010 to restore the frames and the photographs they contained and to attempt to find pictures to replace the 18 on the board which had been destroyed. Most of these were of Bloxhamists who had died in 1916, in particular in the Battle of the Somme. This project owed a great deal to the initiative of Peter Barwell, an Old Bloxhamist and School Governor, and the support of the Chaplain, Michael Price.

A ten-year search by the authors eventually succeeded in finding images of each of the men, some by trawling through the school's old albums and countless team photographs, others by painstaking research in regimental or newspaper archives along with contact with the families. In addition, images were found of four Bloxhamists (Pullen Burry, Wilson, Ayres and Simons), who were not listed on the original war memorial; their names have been added to a new board since 2014 as a result of our research.

The refurbished boards were unveiled in their new location in the school's Egerton Library in June 2011 alongside James Pastfield's campaign medals. Whereas the original ones had been made as the school received the photographs, the new ones are arranged alphabetically. Thus Private Horace Kruger sits between Lieutenant Colonel Cyril Jackson and 2nd Lieutenant Harold Long. The photographs provide invaluable material for pupils studying the Great War as well as serving as a constant reminder of the scale of loss suffered by one small school.

Bibliography

Archival Sources
Service records in The National Archives (TNA), Kew, London.
Liddle Collection, 1914-1918, Leeds Special Collection, Bretherton Library, University of Leeds.
The War Diaries of the Battalions who fought the Great War on the Western Front (DVD-ROM, Naval & Military Press Ltd. 2014).

Unpublished Sources
Personal papers belonging to families of the following Old Bloxhamists, Harry Ayres, Edward Board, Basil Brooks and Hilary Pullen Burry.
P. Methven, 'Children ardent for some desperate glory: Public schools and First World War volunteering', MPhil Thesis, Cardiff University, 2013.
Bloxham School Archives: *The Bloxhamist* (1875-2020), Bloxham School Roll of Honour (1922). OTC records (1910-1920) all photographs.

Published Sources
S. Batten, *A Shining Light: 150 Years of Bloxham School* (London: James & James, 2010).
D. Bebbington, *Mister Brownrigg's Boys: Magdalen College School and the Great War* (Barnsley: Pen & Sword, 2014).
B. Blades, *Roll of Honour: Schooling and the Great War 1914-1919* (Barnsley: Pen & Sword, 2015).
A. Churchill with A. Holmes, *Somme: 141 Days, 141 Lives* (Stroud: The History Press, 2016).
J. Cooksey, *Barnsley Pals: The 13th & 14th Battalions York & Lancaster Regiment* (Barnsley: Pen & Sword, 2008).
S. Cooper, *The Final Whistle: The Great War in Fifteen Players* (Stroud: The History Press, 2012).
F. Davies & G. Maddocks, *Bloody Red Tabs: General Officer Casualties of the Great War, 1914-1918* (Barnsley: Pen & Sword, 1995).
N. Franks & H. Giblin, *Under the Guns of the Kaiser's Aces* (London: Grub Street, 2003).
A. R. Haig-Brown, *The O.T.C. and the Great War* (London, Country Life, 1915).
T. Halstead, *A School in Arms: Uppingham and the Great War* (Solihull, Helion & Company, 2017).
---------- 'A Ragged Business': Officer Training Corps, Public Schools and the Recruitment of the Junior Officer Corps of 1916' in S. Jones (ed.), *At All Costs: The British Army on the Western Front 1916* (Warwick: Helion & Company, 2018).
---------- 'Public Schools and Great War Memorials – Sacred and Secular' in *Stand To! The Journal of the Western Front Association* No. 120, November 2020.

J.R. De S. Honey, *Tom Brown's Universe: The Development of the English Public School in the Nineteenth Century* (New York: Quadrangle, 1977).

G. Horridge with F. Kilpatrick, *The Toll of War: Christ College, Brecon 1914-1918* (Builth Wells: Abernant Publishing, 2015).

C.F. Kernot, *British Public Schools War Memorials* (London: Roberts & Newton, 1927).

J. Lewis-Stempel, *Six Weeks: The Short and Gallant Life of the British Officer in the First World War* (London: Weidenfeld & Nicolson, 2010).

---------- *The War Behind the Wire: The Life, Death and Glory of British Prisoners of War 1914-1918* (London: Weidenfeld & Nicolson, 2014).

A. Rawson, *The British Army 1914-1918* (Stroud: Spellmount, 2006).

S. Ridley, *Remembering the Fallen of the First World War* (London: Watts Publishing Group, 2015).

A. Seldon & D. Walsh, *Public Schools and the Great War* (Barnsley: Pen & Sword, 2013).

B. Smith, *A History of Bloxham School* (Bloxham: Old Bloxhamist Society, 1978).

M. Stedman, *Salford Pals: A History of the Salford Brigade: 15th, 16th, 19th and 20th Battalions Lancashire Fusiliers,* (Barnsley: Pen & Sword, 2007).

S. Todd & N. Pudney, *St John's School Leatherhead and the Great War 1914-1919* (Exeter: Short Run Press, 2019).

A. W White, *No Easy Hopes or Lies: The World War I Letters of Lt. Arthur Preston White* (London: London Stamp Exchange, 1991).

E. Wyrall, *The Somerset Light Infantry: The History of the Somerset Light Infantry (Prince Albert's) 1914-1919* (London: Methuen & Co., 1927).